Identity and Agency in England, 1500–1800

Edited by

Henry French and Jonathan Barry

palgrave
macmillan

Editorial matter, selection, Introduction © Jonathan Barry and
Henry French 2004
Remaining chapters © Palgrave Macmillan Ltd 2004
Softcover reprint of the hardcover 1st edition 2004 978-1-4039-1764-5

First published 2004 by
PALGRAVE MACMILLAN
Houndmills, Basingstoke, Hampshire RG21 6XS and
175 Fifth Avenue, New York, N.Y. 10010
Companies and representatives throughout the world

PALGRAVE MACMILLAN is the global academic imprint of the Palgrave
Macmillan division of St. Martin's Press, LLC and of Palgrave Macmillan Ltd.
Macmillan® is a registered trademark in the United States, United Kingdom
and other countries. Palgrave is a registered trademark in the European
Union and other countries.

ISBN 978-1-349-51352-9   ISBN 978-0-230-52310-4 (eBook)
DOI 10.1057/9780230523104

This book is printed on paper suitable for recycling and made from fully
managed and sustained forest sources. Logging, pulping and manufacturing
processes are expected to conform to the environmental regulations of the
country of origin.

A catalogue record for this book is available from the British Library.

Library of Congress Cataloging-in-Publication Data

Identity and agency in England, 1500–1800 / edited by Henry French &
Jonathan Barry.
    p. cm.
"Derives from papers given at a colloquium held at the University of
Exeter in September 2002"—Pref.
Includes bibliographical references and index.
    1. Social status – England – History – Congresses. 2. Social
role – England – History – Congresses. 3. Marginality, Social – England –
History – Congresses. 4. Group identity – England – History – Congresses.
5. England – Social conditions – 16th century – Congresses. 6. England –
Social conditions – 17th century – Congresses. 7. England – Social
conditions – 18th century – Congresses. I. French, Henry, 1968– II. Barry,
Jonathan, 1956–

HN 398.E5I34 2004
305'.0942'0903—dc22   2004052089

10 9 8 7 6 5 4 3 2 1
13 12 11 10 09 08 07 06 05 04

Transferred to Digital Printing in 2014

Identity and Agency in England, 1500–1800

Also by Jonathan Barry

RELIGION IN BRISTOL *c*.1640–1775

WITCHCRAFT AND DEMONOLOGY IN SOUTH-WEST ENGLAND (forthcoming)

PALGRAVE ADVANCES IN WITCHCRAFT STUDIES (forthcoming)

Also by Henry French

THE CHARACTER OF ENGLISH RURAL SOCIETY, 1500–1750

Contents

List of Tables and Figure

Tables

Figure

Preface and Acknowledgements

This volume of essays derives from papers given at a Colloquium held at the University of Exeter in September 2002, on the subjects of 'Social Identity, Class and Status in England, 1500–1800'. The idea behind this event was to draw together some of the leading researchers on the subject of social identity, to explore what was left in terms of explanations, after the weakening of Marxist, and other 'structural' accounts of human agency in the past. The aim of the organisers was to focus primarily on empirical research, but to use the colloquium as an opportunity to draw out common themes, and discuss the more abstract methodological implications of these studies.

This discussion, and the degree to which the disparate subjects addressed a set of common themes, inspired the editors to seek publication of these papers, for their own sake, and because they addressed a series of themes of contemporary relevance in historical studies. In particular, these were the extent to which ordinary individuals could shape their own destinies, and the degree to which they were limited by social, moral, gender or other conventions. Identity is an extremely broad subject, and in organising the original colloquium, and collecting these essays, some conscious decisions were made regarding subject matter. Two significant areas of historical interest in identity were not addressed. These are, first, national identity or the creation and meaning of 'British-ness' in the early modern period. The second was sexuality and its relationship to gender identity. In both cases, the reason for this omission is because such themes have been the subject of intense and vibrant existing debates among historians. These themes appeared not to require revisiting, in the same way that questions of social agency did, particularly as they related to poverty, estimations of status and repute, and corporate identity, in the light of recent research developments.

The editors would like to thank the contributors to this volume, first for the stimulating discussions at the Exeter colloquium, and then for their co-operation, speed and efficiency in turning their papers into completed chapters, and their helpful advise in relation to the introduction. Thanks are also due to Tim Hitchcock for his stimulating paper at the event in 2002. The colloquium was organised with the assistance of Mark Overton and Jane Whittle, and benefited greatly from their historical and organisational advice. The colloquium was also a precursor to the much larger biennial Exeter Early Modern England Workshops starting in July 2003, organised by Jane Whittle, as a way of bringing together scholars with an interest in the early modern period of English history, from a wide range of subject areas and from other disciplines.

The editors would also like to thank Luciana O'Flaherty, Publisher for History and Philosophy, and Daniel Bunyard, Editorial Assistant, History at Palgrave Macmillan for their assistance in the preparation of this volume.

Notes on Contributors

Jonathan Barry Head of School of Historical, Sociological & Political Studies, University of Exeter. Publications include (edited with Christopher Brooks) *The Middling Sort of People. Culture, Society and Politics in England, 1550-1800* (Basingstoke, 1994); (edited with Marianne Hester and Gareth Roberts) *Witchcraft in Early Modern Europe*, (Cambridge, 1996); and essays in P. Burke, B. Harrison, P. Slack, eds., *Civil Histories: Essays Presented to Sir Keith Thomas*, (Oxford, 2000); W. De Blecourt and O. Davies eds., *Beyond the Witch Trials: Witchcraft and magic in Enlightenment Europe* (Manchester, 2003); J.C. Crick and A.M. Walsham, eds., *The Uses of Script and Print* (Cambridge, 2003).

Helen Berry Lecturer in History, University of Newcastle Publications include *Gender, Society and Print Culture in Late-Stuart England. The Cultural World of the Athenian Mercury* (Aldershot, 2003); (edited with Jeremy Gregory) *Creating and Consuming Culture in North-East England, 1660–1830* (Aldershot, 2004).

Henry French Lecturer in Early Modern History, University of Exeter. Author of a number of journal articles on the social order of early modern England, and (with Prof. R.W. Hoyle), *The Character of English Rural Society, 1550–1750: Earls Colne Revisited* (Manchester, 2005).

Steve Hindle Professor of History, Department of History, University of Warwick. Publications include *The State and Social Change in Early Modern England, c.1550–1640* (London, 2000); and *On the Parish?: The Micro-Politics of Poor Relief in Rural England, c.1550–1750* (Oxford, 2004).

Peter King Professor of Social History, University College, Northampton Publications include *Crime, Justice and Discretion in England, 1740–1820* (Oxford, 2000); and 'The Poor, The Law & The Poor Law' in S. King and R. Smith (eds), *Poverty and Relief in England, 1500–1800* (Woodbridge, forthcoming).

Craig Muldrew Lecturer in History, Queen's College, Cambridge Publications include *The Economy of Obligation: The Culture of Credit and Social Relations in Early Modern England* (London, 1998).

Alexandra Shepard   Lecturer in History, Christ's College, Cambridge Publications include (edited with Phil Withington) *Communities in Early Modern* England (Manchester, 2000); Meanings *of Manhood in Early Modern England* (Oxford, 2003).

Judith Spicksley   ESRC Research Fellow, Department of History, University of Hull. Publications include 'To Be or Not to Be Married: Single Women, Money-lending and the Question of Choice in Late Tudor and Stuart England', in L. Amtower and D. Kehler, eds., *The Single Woman in Medieval and Early Modern England: Her Life and Representation* (Arizona, 2003); she is preparing an edition of the Diary of Joyce Jeffreys for the *British Academy: Records of Social and Economic History* series.

Phil Withington   Lecturer in History, School of History and History of Art, University of Aberdeen. Publications include (edited with Alexandra Shepard) *Communities in Early Modern* England (Manchester, 2000); *The Politics of Commonwealth. Citizens and freemen in early modern England* (Cambridge, forthcoming).

'Identity and Agency in English Society, 1500–1800' – Introduction

Henry French with Jonathan Barry

It has never been easy for historians to explain the activities of groups of people in the past. The problem has always been to establish a *collective* motive for their behaviour, particularly in the absence of direct evidence about such a motive, or when contradictory explanations exist of why people acted as they did. In theory, if we could reconstruct the shared understandings that people in the past had about themselves in relation to society, we might then be able to explain why they acted as they did – even when their actions appear to have been at odds with their professed visions of themselves.

In practice, two sets of problems have emerged, both stemming from a lack of clear evidence. First, historians have argued furiously about *which* vision of the self was the most important influence in forming groups in society. Was the most important determining element of identity the individual's self-image, or his or her consciousness of wider 'belonging'? What was the most significant force in determining this identity? Was it economic position or social power or cultural knowledge or religious opinion or regional origin or gender role or sexual orientation or ethnic character? If more than one element was at work, which ones were significant and how did they combine? Second, historians have generally found it difficult to agree *how* these expressed identities provided the strongest or most sufficient explanation of an individual or collective action. Why should one way of viewing oneself, or one notion of 'belonging' have been more potent as a rallying cry than a number of other, equally convincing forms of identity? Historians have also delighted in pursuing detailed case studies so as to discover exceptions to each other's hypotheses about the relationship between social perceptions and types of behaviour.[1]

These questions emphasise the importance of 'identity' in historical explanations of group behaviour, but how should we understand the term? The history of the word illustrates an inherent tension in its meaning that complicates its function in analysing 'agency'. As Jonathan Barry has observed, in the eighteenth century 'identity' implied the membership of *groups*, because it meant 'the sameness or agreement of two or more things with one another'.[2] Today, while identity still retains this meaning, we tend to associate the term with *individual* (self) identity – how we, as individuals, understand our position in society, and how we describe and present ourselves to others. Within this apparently small definitional difference lie not only a large conceptual gap, but also two entire sociological theories about behaviour in society.[3] These are called, confusingly, 'identity theory', and 'social identity theory'. The former focuses on how the individual acquires *self*-identity, exploring how far he or she understands and acts in accordance with socially defined roles – as parent, worker, neighbour, relative or friend. The latter concentrates more on the eighteenth-century definition of 'identity' – how individuals *identify* with others, how they generate a sense of belonging together, and to what extent they separate themselves from other, different, collections of people.

Historians have long been familiar with these two approaches, even if they have understood them primarily through the Marxist distinction between classes 'in themselves' (self-identity) and classes 'for themselves' (identification with others).[4] When exploring the 'identity' of people in the past they have often analysed both these elements, looking both for signs of their self-image or their chosen roles, and for indications of the groups with whom they identified, or from which they differentiated themselves. In the last 30 years, frenetic scholarly research has uncovered many different types of identity in early modern England. Their sheer number has complicated explanations of historical agency – if a group was composed of individuals, and these individuals possessed a variety of self-images, which of these supplied the most widely applicable identity, and the most imperative motive for the action of the group as a whole? As a consequence, identifying, understanding and describing 'identity' and its links to historical agency is now much more problematic than it was for earlier generations of social, economic and cultural historians. The 'grand meta-narratives' of historical identity, agency and change – most notably that provided by Marx – have withered, if not to extinction, then certainly to shadows of their former selves. The eclipse of these unifying stories has deprived us of coherent, comprehensive definitions of historical groups, based (in the case of Marx) on 'classes' generated by unequal relations to the means of production, and the forms of action engendered by these positions. Conversely, this process has also broken open the constrictive, deterministic methodologies of these 'meta-narratives', and removed the distortions that these imposed on the definitions of identity and their imagined relationship to agency.

In the social history of early modern England, as in other subject areas, there has been a shift from consideration of the influence on individual behaviour of impersonal, involuntary collective identities ('classes' or social groups, regions and localities), to the influence of those that were personal and, to some extent, voluntary (gender, individual power relations and cultural knowledge). Evidence of this shift came with two parallel challenges to notions of identity based primarily on social division. The first of these questioned the bases and the causal power of these social divisions – particularly 'class' divisions – in early modern society. The second demanded the insertion of gender into the framework of identity creation, and argued that existing 'gender-neutral' considerations of society ignored this fundamental building block of understandings of the self and the social order.

These changes in historical understandings are discussed in Sections I–V below. The literature on such changes in causal explanations is huge, spanning both detailed debate about methodologies (in history, sociology, anthropology, cultural studies and linguistics), and a wide array of particular subject debates. Since the potential for omission and confusion is immense in any general literature survey, this introduction bases discussion of important methodological issues on a few specific historical debates. In particular, three areas of debate about identity and historical causation have been selected. These are: first, the debate among social historians about whether the law in the eighteenth century acted as an instrument of ruling class 'hegemony', and whether this implies both the existence of social classes, and their direct connection to historical agency; second, the debate initiated by feminist historians about the place of 'gender identity' in general discussions of identity in society, and whether it was the *most* important means by which people understood themselves; and third, through a further exploration of recent trends in gender history, the degree to which all understandings of identity are predicated on systems of language, and whether 'identity' can be separated from, or regarded as existing before, the terms that give it meaning. By outlining the current lines of argument in these three restricted fields of study, this introduction sketches out the 'state of play' in the relationship between identity and agency in social history, after the decline of Marxist 'class' hypotheses. In the absence of such a 'determinist' methodology linking 'class' directly to action, historians have tried to reconcile two apparently contradictory elements. First, historians are aware that people are born into existing societies, and values, institutions and cultures, over which they have extremely limited influence. Second, they also understand the deficiencies of all previous 'meta-narratives' that claimed, but failed, to explain and determine the actions of individuals and groups. While we continue to see patterns in behaviour, association, expression or values, painful experience has made us reluctant to weave these into generally applicable hypotheses. Section V asks how far should we attempt this, and how might we realise it? The final sections of the Introduction (VI–VIII) explore the patterns that emerge out of the chapters in this volume. They illustrate how this research casts new light on the formation of identity across society, and between the sexes, in early modern England. This discussion also examines how far identity and action were constrained in this society, and the extent to which these constraints point to new ways of reconciling the intrusions of 'structures' with the initiative or choices of individuals in the past.

(I)

In the last thirty years, debates about the influence of social position on the actions of individuals and groups in the past have diverged far from the stereotypical economic determinism of 'vulgar Marxism'. Some of the most subtle and effective of these have been studies of the social profiles of criminal offenders and the social biases at work in the administration of justice. The examination of this subject area provides a concrete example of how detailed research has disputed the causal power of social (or 'class') divisions, and how a comprehensive explanatory framework based on them has been dismembered, and replaced by more complex understandings of power relations and agency.

   The social history of crime, particularly research into the social 'meaning' of crime, has been influenced heavily by the later historical work of E.P. Thompson, and the associated 'Warwick School' of studies. Thompson eschewed the notion that the law was simply a crude instrument of 'ruling class' power in eighteenth-century society, a means just to protect private property and punish any who threatened the elite's hold on property and power. Instead, he depicted the law as a more sophisticated mechanism of elite ('patrician' in Thompson's lexicon) power. It was not enough for the ruling elite merely to use the law to defend their interests. Rather, for their rule to be accepted, 'their' law had also to be accepted by the wider society as broadly just and fair. As a consequence, Thompson saw the law as the heart of 'the gentry's overarching hegemony'.[5] It had to overpower competing, alternative popular 'customs' of legality, justice, fairness and criminality. 'The conservative culture of the plebs as often as not resists, in the name of custom, those economic rationalizations and innovations ... which rulers, dealers, or employers seek to impose ... Hence the plebeian culture is rebellious, but rebellious in defence of custom.'[6] While such displays of power, and negotiations about the meaning of justice could take place in all areas of society (in home, workplace, common field, village green or in the street), Thompson gave particular attention to the legal arena.

The competing plebeian and patrician ceremonies that encrusted the law in the eighteenth century formed a microcosm for Thompson's understanding of early modern society in general. It provided the auditorium in which Thompson's 'theatre of power' was played out.[7] For Thompson legal administration became the monopoly of the gentry,[8] through which they exercised 'the prerogative of mercy ... the powers of life and death [which] greatly increased their hegemonic charisma'.[9] If the 'patricians' performed the role of solemn dispensers of justice, cloaked in the studied formality, and awful majesty of the Quarter Sessions or the Assizes, the 'plebeians' also enacted their role. They performed outside, as the quixotic crowd, who were supposed to learn from the last dying speeches, and the moment of exemplary punishment, but who often transformed the process into a time of popular festivity, satirical comment or anonymous sedition. In Thompson's reading of the theatre of law, many on both sides performed their parts with a knowing wink – patricians saw the weakness of their claims to impartiality, probity and power, plebeians understood the hollowness of the judicial rituals, which dignified a process in which they participated primarily as victims. However, both were (to varying degrees) 'prisoners of their own rhetoric', and although the elite could manipulate the rules of these power games, if they violated them 'the whole game would be thrown away'.[10]

For Thompson, power, social relations and social conflict were performed and experienced.[11] This produced his belief that 'class' was generated by the conscious experience of such processes, that the subjects of 'class' (people) had to understand what was happening to them before they could perceive common interests and engage in common responses. This reversal of the Marxist orthodoxy that the conditions that create 'classes' have to exist *before* the consciousness of these 'classes' earned Thompson numerous rebukes from other commentators.[12]

Thompson's ideas about the patrician 'hegemony' of the law derived from his researches into the highly inequitable game laws, and from Douglas Hay.[13] Hay argued that the value system beneath concepts of justice supported rule by 'no more than 3 per cent of the population'.[14] He highlighted two contradictory movements. On the one hand, an increasing number of crimes in the eighteenth century were deemed capital offences. On the other, the proportion of convictions ending in execution declined, yet government, judiciary and the ruling elite generally opposed legal reform. Hay suggested that the disparity between severe statutes and lenient practice allowed the social elite to act as arbiters of law, primarily through the discretionary dispensation of pardons, which gave them power, but cloaked it in the form of dispassionate judicial administration. The law 'allowed the rulers of England to make the courts a selective instrument of class justice', but also functioned as an ideology by which a minority exercised power over the rest, in the name of justice for all. Hay asserted that 'the ideology of the law was crucial in sustaining the hegemony of the ruling class'.[15]

Hay was in no doubt either that this *was* hegemony, or that there *was* a coherent 'ruling class' in eighteenth-century society. The fact that legal decisions might sometimes favour the poor or convict the rich helped secure 'consent and submission' by demonstrating the apparent autonomy of the law from the social hierarchy. Decisions that favoured the 'class interests' of the elite were so well disguised by the impression of flexibility and discretion, that they were accepted among other sections of society as 'the product of their own minds and their experiences'.[16] This theory of the insidious effect of ideology derived from the works of Antonio Gramsci (via those of Thompson), in which ordinary people's daily experience, and 'common sense' knowledge of the world was bound up in ways of thinking, language, and understandings of reality sanctioned by, and supportive of, the powerful.[17]

While this interpretation was based on an explicitly Marxist reading of the social order, it offered a subtle illustration of the relationship between social identity and historical agency. Hay emphasised that although a group – the elite – had acted together to attain a common objective – to rule – they had done so via 'the product of countless short-term decisions' by 'living men', not through the workings of the impersonal forces of an inescapable, all-embracing social 'system'.[18] The law was a structure in society, which Hay believed operated in the interests of the social elite, partly by conscious design, but partly also by the unconscious, unintended collective assumptions and actions of this elite in solving the practical problems of legal administration and the necessity of upholding the existing social order. It was this necessity that linked directly, but in ways that were largely unsuspected, to the 'hidden hand' of the 'class system'. This meant that although most people subscribed to the concepts of 'justice', 'order' and 'property', they did not all benefit equally from their implementation. The logic of the 'class system' ensured that although the elite defended them in the name of all, the elite themselves derived most material benefit from these values.

This causal process complicates the template of simple determinist thought about the relationship between social identity and agency, in sociology and history. This can be depicted of using Ray Pahl's formulation of:

Structure $\rightarrow$ Consciousness $\rightarrow$ Action[19]

In this model, 'structure' – whether an orthodox Marxist 'relationship to the means of production', or the social order as it engages with an institution such as the law – produces the relationships and conflicts that inform and shape 'consciousness' – that is, the perception of the group interest in relation to the social order. In turn this perception conditions the type of action taken by the group. The problem with all such causal chains is the relationship between the three elements – *how* does 'structure' affect 'consciousness', and *how* does the perception of identity actually affect the actions taken?

The formulations of Thompson and Hay posit complex relationships between these elements. As noted above, Thompson was criticised by more orthodox Marxists for arguing that 'structure' (the emergent 'working class') was formed and was articulated by, 'consciousness' (the struggle to defend 'plebeian' customary rights). He defended himself succinctly, by arguing that 'classes do not exist as separate entities, look around, find an enemy class, and then start to struggle', but rather were formed by that struggle.[20] This was directly contrary to one strand of Marx's thought, which emphasised that the dictates of 'structure', determined by relations to means of production, compelled 'historical action', whatever the implicit or explicit 'consciousness' of the group.[21] The law-like quality of the theory demanded that certain structural relations produced consequent actions, irrespective of the thoughts of the actors. Contrary to this, for Thompson as the 'working class' *saw* their true interests, so they described them, so they formed into a social group to defend them, so the sham 'theatre' of paternal society during 'Old Corruption' was exposed. People could fashion themselves into active groups in society as these became evident, but *only* as they became evident, and in a long, messy and uncertain historical process.

These interpretations attempt to strike a balance between an insistence on an ultimate determining power of 'class', and the belief that history is made by the decisions of individuals, rather than those of 'classes' – so that historical explanations of action or inaction depend, in part, on understanding contemporaries' ideas and reasoning. As a consequence both eschewed simple economic determinism – that 'class positions' compelled people to act in particular ways, like electric charges motivating an automaton. At the same time though, both rejected the notion that either 'patricians' or 'plebs' were entirely free to choose how to behave. Both groups were constrained by inherited circumstances and roles, which gave them immediate interests that they sought to defend, and more shadowy perceptions of wider common loyalties. This raises important questions about whether these were sufficient to weld the groups into 'classes' that could act with the coherence and effectiveness suggested by Thompson and Hay, and whether their characterisation of these 'true' interest groups in early modern society is sufficient to account for such activity.

As noted above, the tendency of recent detailed research has been to complicate and challenge such encompassing, coherent explanations of social agency. Research into the social history of criminal law enforcement has followed this trend.[22] In particular, the concept of the law as the mechanism by which elite hegemony was enacted has been subject to substantial empirical revision. The work of Peter King, a contributor to this volume (Chapter 2), poses two fundamental challenges to the assumptions of Thompson and Hay. The first of these is about the nature and composition of the legally dominant 'social elite'. The second questions the degree to which instances of discretion illustrate the 'class hegemony' suggested by Thompson and Hay. King explodes Hay's unquantified assumption that legal administration was in the hands of the aristocracy and major gentry. He finds that most indictments for serious property or violent crime were 'initiated by middling men, while about a quarter of property crime indictments were brought by labouring families'.[23] The administration of the criminal law at the stages when the maximum amount of discretion was possible (*before* matters went to trial), was largely in the hands of groups below the gentry, and even decided by the perpetrator's immediate neighbours. As King observes 'the decisions that pulled the levers for fear and mercy were not taken by propertied men alone'.[24]

Even when cases reached the courts, he suggests that formal instances of the exercise of judicial discretion were not designed primarily to project or reiterate the power of the elite. Instead they were the result of a complex of values, claims and presentations of the self, and the outcome of a process of negotiation between judicial elite, lower rungs of the legal enforcement system, opinions of patrons, neighbours, and religious, moral and gender norms. Those who were favoured were those who matched 'a set of broadly held social ideals about how justice should work'.[25] In contrast to Thompson and Hay, King demonstrates that a shared 'ideology' of justice was not necessarily merely a cloak beneath which elite concepts were imposed. Rather, he suggests that it was a shared resource, a collection of values and meanings that were disputed, compared and reordered by a variety of interest groups. Although he is careful to emphasise that the implementation of law took place in a highly unequal society, this very stratification, and the variety of social groups involved in the justice process offered opportunities for the property-less to exploit 'a complex triangle of forces involving three broad groups – the labouring poor, the middling sort, and an increasingly distanced magistracy'.[26] For example, the poor sought to overturn decisions about relief made by the 'middling sort' among the parish officers, by appealing over their heads to the magistracy (and the gentry). Such appeals also exposed the divisions of interest within the supposedly homogenous group of the 'propertied'.

King questions whether the labouring poor's use of the law demonstrates that they subscribed to the social and cultural hegemony of the elite. He argues that the poor used the law, but were rarely fooled into believing that social equality was inherent in abstract notions of justice. Although their use of the law displays awareness that it 'could protect their property as well as that of the elite' it does not mean that they 'felt any real deference towards the law and those who administered it'.[27] This 'instrumental' attitude to law, and deference, means that we cannot infer belief or consent directly or simply from public behaviour.[28] In Hay's terms, therefore, the 'conspiracy' operates on both sides, rather than merely being effected by the rich against the poor.

King's study further complicates the relationship between 'structure', 'consciousness' and 'action'. It suggests that there were multiple social structures in eighteenth-century English society, which cannot be boiled down to Thompson's bi-polar 'social fields of force' – the 'patricians' versus the 'plebs'. More than this, the exercise of legal discretion was not just the projection of 'class power' by the elite, but rather the outcome of unequal negotiations between a variety of social groups, using a series of shared concepts about 'guilt', 'innocence' and 'premeditation'. There were no single straight lines running between simple social structures, consequent 'class consciousness', and resultant actions. Second, by questioning the concept of elite 'hegemony', and emphasising the 'instrumentality' of labouring groups' use of the law, King demonstrates explanatory flaws in Thompson and Hay's interpretation. They argue that the elite could conspire to exploit shared notions for their own, well-defined 'class' ends, while to some degree the poor are painted as the dupes of such a process, albeit, spirited, satirical and insubordinate dupes. King's study recognises both the conscious choices of the poor in their attitudes to law, and the extent to which these were channelled into particular forms because of their lack of institutional power.

His study also has a further implication. If the constraining or enabling 'structures' in society were multiple, and if the actions of the labouring poor were the result of conscious (but often unappealing) decisions made in relation to this variety of structures, these features disrupt our efforts to reduce historical agency to the workings of a single, ultimate 'cause' – such as 'class'. Instead, we are presented with a series of 'power relationships', where parties have a variety of positions, and conflicting, competing or complementary loyalties. A litigant might be, variously, male, a father, aged, disabled, economically dependent but formerly prosperous, highly religious, and in dispute with parish authorities. His 'action' might have been precipitated by his immediate need to sue to the Justices for poor relief, but the way that his case was presented invoked a series of judgements about his position within a number of overlapping 'power structures' – as a 'pious', 'respectable', 'ancient', 'resident', 'householder', who was now unfortunately also an 'aged', 'impotent', 'deserving' 'object of charity'. This was a conscious effort at self-presentation to establish belonging and responsibility, negotiated by reference to a set of social definitions shared with the judicial elite and the parish authorities, and through the invocation of moral norms to which they subscribed publicly. It was the result of traversing several hierarchies of power and meaning, rather than the operation of a single 'hegemonic' ideology.

As noted at the start of this chapter, the main consequence of this subdivision of 'structures' is that it becomes more difficult to explain action in terms of the causal power of large 'collectivities' (as *the* result of 'class', 'regional' or 'gender' identity), because these tend to dissolve under close scrutiny. Instead, the individual becomes the site in which these structural 'identities' are enacted. While this diminishes the determining power of overbearing structures on the individual, it also suggests that although the choice is free, the options from which to choose are limited and rarely determined by the individual. Such individuals can choose how to represent themselves, but only in a limited number of ways. These ways change over time, but slowly, cumulatively and unpredictably, and rarely because of personal initiative alone.

(II)

This understanding of the individual as the key site in which structural constraints operate, consciousness is generated and action produced offers a link to the influential hypothesis of anthropologist James C. Scott about the 'official' and 'hidden transcripts of power'.[29] In some respects, this idea may be viewed as an extension of those of Hay and Thompson. Scott suggests that the history of power relations is not merely, for example, the elite 'conspiracy' of the official record of the law and the elite's interpretation of this record, but also contains within it the understandings, interpretations and manipulations of the poor – their 'conspiracy' in the face of power. However, he disputes the all-embracing Gramscian idea of 'hegemony' as employed by Hay and Thompson. Although elites *attempt* to project their values as the 'routine', 'normal' or 'natural' order of things in society, he argues that this has never produced 'the quiescence of subordinate classes'.[30] For Scott, theories of hegemony offer too tidy an explanation of elite power, and deprive the subordinate of any belief in the possibility of change.[31]

Instead, he demonstrates that even in the most repressive totalitarian regimes of the twentieth-century elite 'hegemony' was never total.[32] Scott emphasises that although resistance was not usually overt, articulated clearly or concerted, that does not mean it was either inconceivable or impossible among subordinates. Such hidden resistance allows 'the poor to appropriate, as it were, the ideological resources of the well-off and turn them to good advantage ...' without the need for overt revolt, and the risks that might entail.[33] Many other forms of resistance were available that did not require the subordinate to risk all by putting their heads above the parapet.[34] These included studied differences of dialect, dress, manners,[35] anonymous protests,[36] dissent disguised in euphemistic or allegoric terms,[37] grumbling, foot-dragging or systematic pilfering,[38] and the popular subversion of official festivals – notably the reversals and subversions of carnival before the disciplines of Lent.[39] These forms were founded upon alternative readings of the 'official transcript' – of slaves refusing to believe passages in the Bible about the obedience of servants, for example[40] – or on 'customary' interpretations of law, evidence of which Scott finds in E.P. Thompson's study of poaching.[41] They occurred in social sites that were public, but largely obscured from the view of the authorities.[42] Only at exceptional, cathartic moments, did this resistance break cover, but when it did the effects could be electric, particularly when they took the form of a mass *public* demonstration of the invalidity or impotence of the power of the elite.[43]

This means that acts of deference or obedience to elites cannot be taken at face value, either. Deference invoked a reciprocal relationship between elite and subordinate, but at the cost of the repression of the true feelings of those offering deference.[44]

Scott's ideas have influenced social historians, because they provide a method for recovering the 'consciousness' (and even the 'class consciousness') of subordinate groups in the past, whose beliefs and ideas are rarely recorded overtly in the sources. The main problem of Scott's model of power relations is the same as Thompson's – he depicts a bipolar distribution of power, between the 'powerful' and the 'powerless'. As King's Essex study showed, in practice in early modern England power was distributed quite widely, even within a society containing highly unequal hierarchies of wealth and status. In Scott's model, power tends to be absolute (individuals either have power, or are subject to it), whereas in most complex societies, power is relative and the network of power relations is dense.

As a result, it is difficult to apply Scott's model of such relations at a macro-level except in societies where there is, or was, a clear bi-polar power division. It is notable that many of Scott's historical examples tend to be drawn from slave societies (whether the Antebellum United States, or nineteenth-century Russia), or early modern 'peasant' cultures, which conform more closely to such a power structure.[45] It is also difficult to translate Scott's subtle and penetrating methodology from the sphere of personal, face-to-face relations, into an explanation of the power relations between wider, more impersonal social groups. Scott suggests that 'hidden transcripts' are shared by groups that belong to what some sociologists term 'communities of fate' – particularly occupational groups (such as merchant seamen, miners, or lumberjacks) that face shared dangers, as well as shared working and living conditions, and few opportunities for alternative employment. Such groups are 'nearly a race apart', so it is unsurprising that they are the most likely to 'create a distinctive and unified subculture', which can form 'a powerful force for social unity'.[46] Scott admits that this produces a social identity different from that of the bulk of the population.[47]

This implies that among *most* social groups in complex societies, sites of resistance will be dispersed, power relationships will be diverse, and forms of resistance will depend on context. As a result, they may not accumulate sufficiently to resolve themselves clearly into the struggle between two defined and general groups – the 'powerful' and the 'powerless'. Despite this, Scott's ideas about power relations and the resistance of subordinates have considerable value at the micro-level, particularly within individual or small-scale relationships. Everyone within a society lives within a series of relationships with others in which they are more or less powerful. These relations reflect the multiple 'structures' of society (based on 'class', 'status', 'gender', sexuality, age, ethnicity and so on), and Scott's distinction between 'official' and 'hidden transcripts' allows historians to explore these for individuals or groups within a particular historical setting or event, without the need to reduce this social complexity to the two blanket labels of 'powerful' and 'powerless'.

(III)

To the contemporary reader, one of the most noticeable characteristics of the work of an earlier generation of historians such as Hay or Thompson is their unabashed elision of the words 'men' and 'people' – the subjects of history.[48] The consequence of this assumption was that the study of class – the prime mover in history for Thompson and Hay – would consist primarily of the study of the historical actions of males, rather than females, and that the 'class position' of men could simply be applied to the women to whom they were related. Thus, the actions of the male half of the population produced the history and the structures that constrained the lives and aspirations of women as well.

Such assumptions were the target of the first generation of women's history in the 1970s. As Gerda Lerner noted, until that time conventional history had been the history of elite politics, 'a small elite group of upper-class white males', whose activities had been called 'the history of all humankind'.[49] Therefore, the immediate research imperative for this first generation of scholars was to reinstate the experience of women into history, particularly into the history of defining periods, such as the 'Industrial Revolution' – to chronicle the experiences of the female 'working class' along side Thompson's (largely) male study.[50] Other women's historians focused their attention on identifying a distinct female culture in the past, the product of the inequalities, disadvantages and restrictions imposed by 'patriarchal' societies.[51] Joan Wallach Scott noted that 'as a result, the category "women" took on an existence as a social entity apart from its historically situated relationship to the category "men" '.[52] This produced what Scott has called a 'tension' in women's history, between, 'an essentializing tendency' which assumed that there were 'fixed characteristics belonging to women', and 'an historicising approach', which emphasised 'differences among women and even within the concept of "women" '.[53]

Does the experience of inequality, stereotyping and the consequent social restrictions imposed by past societies mean that all women experienced life differently from all men, whatever their social position, and so this experience must be understood separately from that of men? Or, are differences of status, culture, religion, race, age and sexuality sufficient to fracture the unified categories of 'women' and 'men'? The central question is, therefore, whether gender identity is separate from, and perhaps more fundamental than, all other societal identities, or whether it is merely another division between people who are already divided in a number of other ways.

There have been several attempts to resolve this interpretative 'tension'. One was to extend Marxist concepts of oppression and class domination into the sphere of gender relations, positing men as the exploiters of women's economic labour and sexual or reproductive services. The problem with this attempt to link social and gender differences was, as Joan Kelly noted, that 'it is one thing to extend the tools of class analysis to women and quite another to maintain that women *are* a class'.[54] Kelly and Gerda Lerner have argued for more subtle, multifaceted approaches in relating gender to other forms of social difference. Both highlight what Scott calls the ' "sameness versus difference" conundrum'.[55] Kelly insisted 'that women do form a distinctive social group', because they 'are excluded from the benefits of the economic, political, and cultural advances ... which gives women a different historical experience from men'.[56] This undermines other forms of social identity, so that 'although women may adopt the interests and ideology of men of their class, women as a group cut through male class systems'.[57]

The problem was to establish the nature of the relationship between the socially constructed categories of 'gender', 'class' or 'race'. Kelly did this by linking changes in the sexual division of labour to a broadly Marxist schema of economic development.[58] She developed Marx's idea that alienation from the means of production produced social alienation. Where Marx thought that this alienation manifested itself in greater individualism, Kelly argues that it also resulted in greater alienation in 'sex-roles', with women being reduced to 'the property of men', concerned primarily with social and biological reproduction in the family, and excluded from public roles and economic activity not associated with the 'private' realm of the household and family life.[59]

Kelly believed that while female inequality was likely in most historical societies, the precise form taken by patriarchy was historically variable, and dependent on 'the society's mode of production'. Where family and society were closely associated (where society was organised around families as in 'clan' societies or in feudal households within a weak state), women could transfer their importance in the household to a wider social role. Where family and society were distinct and separate (such as 'middle-class' society in the nineteenth century), women were restricted to the domestic sphere, excluded from economic or political power, marginalised socially and forced to perpetuate existing sexual inequalities. In this way, Kelly argued that although 'sex-roles' provided a fundamental vertical split in all societies, how they differed depended on the nature of a given society. The investigation of these variations could reveal something about the underlying 'structures' of that society and its other forms of difference.

Gerda Lerner engaged in a similar attempt to integrate gender difference into the wider analysis of identity within society. Lerner stressed that ' "women" cannot be treated as a unified category any more than "men-as-a-group" can. Women differ by class, race, ethnic and regional affiliation, religion, and any number of other categories.'[60] However, simply identifying and describing differences risked ignoring 'the power relations built on differences' – black women were different from white women in antebellum America, but the mere description of their divergent experiences of womanhood would not explain the unequal power relationship between them based on race.[61] Lerner suggests that the social construction of 'differences' is essential to the creation of such unequal power relations. Her researches into Bronze Age civilisations led her to assert that the first 'institutional' difference created and enforced through society was female subordination.[62] Women had to enter a Faustian 'patriarchal bargain' whereby 'in exchange for their sexual and reproductive services to one man, they will be guaranteed protection and resources for themselves and their children'.[63] This pact laid the foundations of subsequent social orders, trapping women into an unequal, exploitative relationship with men.

However, Lerner does not restrict her 'difference into dominance' hypothesis to gender. It is equally applicable to the creation and institutionalisation of social and racial hierarchies, as those with less power are defined as 'other', and ideologies are created that justify the 'naturalness' of their inferiority and the necessity of their subordination. Implicitly, Lerner employs a Gramscian concept of 'hegemony', as she suggests that 'dominance is only possible if it can be justified and accepted both by the dominant and the dominated and by the larger majority who are neither'.[64]

For Lerner, the problem with applying such a notion of power relations across history is to produce an explanatory template in which gender is enshrined as a socially constructed point of difference, alongside the more familiar categories of 'class' and 'race'. She suggests that it is not possible to subsume gender within either of these two existing categories. The experience of 'class' is *always different* for men and women', because women experience social difference *through* their relationships with men.[65] The problem with racial categories is that these tend to mask the different experiences of men and women, where the latter are exploited not just through unpaid labour, but also through coerced provision of sexual and reproductive services. In the same way as Kelly, Lerner identifies the main explanatory issue as the method by which we integrate all these forms of social difference into a single system that will explain the relationships between gender difference, social distance and racial domination in particular historical contexts, instead of dealing with them as compartmentalised hierarchies of 'vertical boxes into which to sort people in history'.[66]

Lerner illustrates how these power relations could interact within a single system of inequality and exploitation through the example of the antebellum South. Here, class, gender and race provided three systems of exploitation, but within them individuals could occupy very different relative positions, with some elements being mutually reinforcing. For example, gender reinforced racism, through the racial 'double-standard' whereby white men were allowed to exploit black women sexually without legal or social penalty, but black men suffered increasingly severe punishments for sexual contact with white women. In this instance, racism ameliorated 'class', by providing a group of 'others' to whom all whites were superior, whatever their internal differences. Lerner posits a re-conception of social difference in which 'race, class, and gender oppression are inseparable; they construct, reinforce, and support one another'.[67]

Such an approach embeds the implications of this research into the wider historical methodology, by treating male as well as female roles in society as 'constructed', rather than innate. In 1976 Natalie Zemon Davis had urged that the history of women could only be understood through women's dialectical relationship to men and their history, because 'we should not be working only on the subjected sex any more than an historian of class can focus exclusively on peasants'.[68] However it was not until the 1990s that historians began to research masculinity in detail. These researches highlighted that 'men' were no more a homogeneous category than were 'women' in the past, and that masculinity was constructed out of a series of roles, which varied with age and social status, and whose exercise was policed by both men and women.[69]

'Men's history' was seen to consist of something other than the residue of gender-neutral 'history' after 'women's history' had been subtracted from it.

(IV)

These developments linked gender to other power structures, but they could not stretch to incorporate a further methodological twist – the 'linguistic turn' or 'post-structuralism'. Sexual, racial or social difference may all be 'facts' in the operation of society, now and in the past, but we understand these through the medium of language and the constructs of culture. The problem lies in the unstable relationship between the experience and the concepts by which we understand it. As Joan Wallach Scott has observed, 'those who would codify the meanings of words fight a losing battle, for words, like ideas and things they are meant to signify, have a history'.[70]

Therefore, categories and concepts such as 'class', 'race' and 'gender' are constructed both socially *and* historically – they can mean different things at different times in different contexts. Obviously, this impinges on our use of such terms and the study of history. In one sense, women's historians had long recognised this. Scott's essay 'Gender: A Useful Category of Historical Analysis', first published in 1986, illustrated how the grammatical concept of 'gender' – designating objects as masculine, feminine or neuter, according to linguistic rules that were agreed socially – could be transferred to understandings of sexual difference. This allowed the possibility that sex roles were determined socially, rather than being biologically innate to women and men. Therefore, language became 'the appropriate place for analysis' in the study of concepts of gender, because meanings of masculinity and femininity were located here, rather than in the biological differences between males and females.[71]

The same was true of other categories of identity, such as 'class' or 'race'. This integration of historical variability into these analytical concepts helped to undermine faith in them as the building blocks of 'meta-narratives'. If there was no single, stable definition of the 'working class' or of 'women' as a concept, then theories of historical change constructed upon unproblematic connections between 'term' and 'group' might simply fall apart. The danger was that *our* linguistic understandings, of 'class' or 'gender', had created the illusion of unitary categories of 'workers' or 'women', by selecting one definition out of many, and applying it as the only possible one. If this was the case, because language mediated and transmitted our understandings of the past, there might be no past beyond language, and no historical identity 'out there' to be discovered after all.[72]

Scott tried to avoid this philosophical cul-de-sac by suggesting that we could recover the particular historical understandings of such concepts in past societies, and so explain historical agency by reference to them. This required first, the identification of the range of cultural symbols by which, for example, femininity could be represented in a society; second, the identification of the legal, religious, scientific, educational and political ideas that regulated understandings of these symbols; third, analysis of the process by which one interpretation became dominant, and transformed into a 'hegemony' – that is, became uncontroversial 'common sense'; and fourth, how individuals and groups actually constructed their gender identities in relation to these socially determined norms.[73] Instead of taking certain identities as given, such as masculine or feminine, and instead of subsuming others within contemporary understandings of social difference, such as 'class' or 'race', historians had first to understand *why* individuals and groups chose to represent themselves, or were represented, through a particular identity. This required understanding the symbolic selections and power struggles inherent in the construction of these identities.

The problem with this approach is, once again, reductionism. 'Class'-based analyses have fallen out of favour because it has become evident that economic forces are not the only or ultimate determinants of the actions of individuals or groups. Post-structuralist analyses posit that language is the ultimate driver – individuals or groups act only because of the meanings that they give to particular situations, and language is depicted as the *only* medium for the transmission and understanding of those meanings. Therefore, the 'discourse' about events is given priority in motivating and explaining action, and the historical subject is depicted as the prisoner of language. As a result, historical explanation is transformed into the deconstruction of symbolic language, which is sufficient to explain the subject's actions, because all actions are mediated and motivated by linguistic understandings. The relationship to cultural or symbolic concepts displaces the relationship to the means of production as the key driving force for historical action, and in neither case do inhabitants of the past have much say in the matter.

In attempting to escape the python-like coils of language, historians have identified at least two alternative containers and mediators of meaning – the body, and the subconscious mind. In the face of the all-embracing determining power of language, Kathleen Canning has asked where and how the actions of historical subjects can be inserted.[74] 'How can discourses figure as anything but fixed hegemonic systems without the interventions of agents who render them contingent and permeable?'[75]

In this sense, 'discourse' cannot function in the historical manner posited by Scott or other post-structuralists without people to replicate, resist and reformulate its concepts, in the same way that for Thompson people configured 'class' in response to their social circumstances, rather than being mere creatures of this 'structure'.[76] However, where else, other than in language, could alternative understandings of discourses and 'discursive systems' be generated? Canning suggests that the site for the production of such social and conceptual knowledge was the body, specifically women's bodies and the way that discourses and historical processes were 'inscribed' onto them, and the means by which these experiences were turned into subjective understandings of the world.[77] She suggests that the 'insurmountable' biological limits of the body, of the limits of physical and medical endurance, formed a tangible measure of, and site of resistance to, discourses and cultural norms. The body was a site of mediation, where linguistic understandings of the world were placed alongside physical experiences. Individual agency followed in 'the way in which female activists mobilized and recast their embodied experiences' within the wider discourse of the particular historical period.

Lyndal Roper has developed similar ideas about the body as a limit to ever-shifting discourse, although her conclusions are more far reaching than Canning's. She questions the axiom of recent feminist thought that 'if gender was created through discourse, or through social behaviour and interaction, the substance of sexual difference was historical – and therefore, it was something we could change'.[78] Consequently, she asserted that ' "Gender" as a sociological category is an illusion created by the terms of its own delimitation'.[79] While she agreed that language was inherently important in providing the concepts, categories and orders by which people understood the world in the past, she suggested that the body confronts 'discursive creationism' with 'a reality that is only partly a matter of words'.[80]

While this interpretation was similar to Canning's – that the body provided the site of a further experience of the world different, and perhaps in opposition, to the meanings of 'discourse' – Roper went further. She questioned the assumptions of 'discourse' theories that 'language, by means of its social character, simply impressed a social construction of gender upon the wax of the individual psyche'. Similarly, those who favoured the formative power of wider social experiences also assumed that 'collective rituals, performances, habits of work or sociability' imprinted themselves automatically on the individual. In arguing that 'bodies are not merely the creations of discourse', Roper suggested that psychoanalysis provided the bridge between understanding the relationship between structures of meaning and the body.[81] It would allow us to interpret experiences of the body that were inarticulate, such as pain or pleasure, and the resultant understandings of the body and sexual difference, 'which lie below the surface of language'.[82] This focus on the individual body, and the ways in which physical and conceptual understandings were assimilated by the individual psyche, disrupts the deterministic power of 'discourse', and gives greater agency to these individuals.

This is an approach highly suited to the interpretation of Roper's subject matter, the individual testimonies of women (and men) accused of witchcraft in early modern Germany, where depositions provide an unparalleled 'window into the soul' of the accused, or into the preoccupations of her accusers. However, in other historical situations, when such sources are absent, it is difficult to see how Roper's approach could be pursued. Historians are also wary of the a-historical aspects of psychoanalytical approaches, which tend to relate individual identity and behaviour in the past to a range personality models derived from modern society. This begs difficult questions about how far the 'individual', and aspects of the conscious and unconscious mind, can remain unchanged when there has been so much radical alteration in family relations, value systems, sexual mores and social organisation between the sixteenth and twenty-first centuries.[83] Roper applies some of these 'essentialist' assumptions of psychoanalysis to overcome the 'relativism' of linguistic analyses that stress the historically changing nature of concepts such as 'gender'. The danger lies in replacing one problematic interpretation that assumes the infinitely variable meanings of words with another premised on static psychological categories.

Nevertheless, Canning and Roper's arguments highlight the relationship between 'discourse' and the social structures and concepts that historians have until recently depicted in largely unproblematic ways. They suggest that while language may provide the concepts through which we understand the world, it may not *determine* that understanding directly, any more than 'class position' did. This implies that it will be difficult to complete the fourth step of Joan Wallach Scott's methodology, of establishing the relationship between concepts of gender (or of social power more generally) as defined by a society, and the ways in which individuals or groups used those concepts as motives or justifications for their actions. Even where individuals *do* appear to identify themselves through common concepts, we cannot be sure that they share common understandings of this 'shared discourse'. A study of the cultural understandings of modern Cumbrian villagers provides a salutary warning about such assumptions. In social interactions, Nigel Rappaport found that individuals in the village adopted 'a number of different personae', so that 'even close neighbours in a small village' came to occupy 'a miscellany of highly diverse social worlds'.[84] These 'social worlds' helped to condition both their self-expression and their understandings of others, causing them to 'realise and reaffirm prior definitions in the social landscapes around them'. The net result was that individuals developed their own, personal definitions of common words and concepts, which did not always intersect with those of their neighbours. There were endless possibilities for misunderstandings (often unconscious), even among people who had known each other all their lives. This meant that despite describing the world to each other using shared symbols and language, they often talked 'past one another unknowingly, misconstruing intended meanings to a possibly farcical extent'.[85]

This implies that the role of the individual in using, modifying, comprehending and misunderstanding language may be greater than allowed for in 'discourse' analysis. It complicates *both* the ways in which we might seek to understand past concepts, and their effects on the understandings of historical subjects. In fact, these subjects might be not so much the prisoners of language as jugglers with it – however, while this might make them freer as historical agents, it does not necessarily make their activities easier for us to understand or explain.

(V)

These recent research impulses have highlighted the individual as the site within which these competing social forces contend. As this research has multiplied the numbers of these forces, and complicated the nature of the links between them and 'consciousness' and 'agency', it has become more difficult to maintain that universally applicable, monolithic 'structures' such as 'class' determine the circumstances in which people live, and the ways that they react. It is no longer possible to assert that 'consciousness' generated by these circumstances simply provokes actions in fulfilment of such a monocular perception of the world. Such simple causal chains have been chopped to pieces by research into social relationships, power structures, understandings of gender and the role of language. There appears not to have been a single site of power (such as the relationship to the means of production, or 'the market'). Evidently there was no single hierarchy of power either, whether based exclusively on 'class', 'race', 'gender', 'ethnicity', 'status' or 'culture'. Instead, each of these forms of distinction between people contained power relations within them, because they implied that these people were divided inequitably in relation to these 'differences'. Through their lives individuals had to navigate a variety of these power structures, in which they might be ranked differently, and in which their power might vary as a consequence. In addition, the very categories of 'difference' formed by these definitions were not rigid – 'men' were distinguished from 'women', but both groups contained anomalies such as 'effeminate' men, and 'masculine' women. In addition, these categories changed over time, containing meanings that were potentially unstable in a single context, and between historical periods.

Does this leave us merely with entirely autonomous historical individuals, moving as freely and randomly as atoms? The evidence of the research cited in this introduction suggests that the answer is 'no'. While these studies have disputed the efficacy of monolithic causal 'structures', they do not deny that historical individuals were born into a dense web of social and behavioural constraints, to which they could subscribe, but which they could not generally determine. These constraints included the conceptual constrictions of language; moral, normative or legal restrictions; cultural or customary understandings; the social 'differences' of class, race and gender; distinctions in authority based on status (age, organisational rank, education, patterns of association and residence). All of these imply the existence of unequal distributions of power. While we could simply argue that each individual might reach his or her own accommodation with these power structures, and consequently attain a slightly different position in each, this does not allow us to explain the agency of groups, or work without direct personal source materials.

The research on historical understandings of gender provides one solution. While individuals were able to achieve their own personalised positions within the multiple social structures of 'race', 'class' and 'gender', they also did so by reference to socially validated pathways across these structures, such as the gender 'roles' determined by notions of 'masculinity' and 'femininity'. These inserted social constraints on sexuality, personal behaviour, modes of dress and speech, projections of authority, the exercise of power or deference, and about the expression of emotion. At the same time, they provided socially approved 'roles' for individuals to inhabit – of 'wife', 'husband', 'bride', 'groom', 'maid servant', 'apprentice', or 'bachelor' and 'spinster'. These carried defined assumptions about social position and power, but in their personal performances individuals could interpret these in a number of different (if related) ways. The existence within early modern societies of violent shaming rituals against scolds, effeminate men and other forms of 'deviant' behaviour demonstrates that these roles had limits that were determined socially. We might suggest that the existence of other structural 'roles' is illustrated in the ways that their boundaries were also policed, by the shaming of social upstarts, the evolution of racial barriers or the privileging of age over youth.[86] Such social boundaries also help delimit the apparently endless possibilities for deconstructing meaning in 'structural' concepts like 'male, 'female', 'white' or 'middleclass', by denoting recognised patterns of 'belonging' and exclusion. James C. Scott's research suggests that the social elite were not the sole guardians of the boundaries or producers of meaning. Subordinate groups patrolled social, gender and behavioural boundaries and enforced their own definitions, often by force. Such boundaries indicate that these roles were situated within social and linguistic *stereotypes*, in which meanings were restricted and caricatured. Those who inhabited these roles could hide behind such stereotypes, or exploit them – as did King's Essex paupers when they petitioned humbly to the Magistracy, in opposition to the decisions of the parish officers. They could also be constrained severely by them – particularly those that posited 'innate' inferiority, such as stereotypes of gender and race. Such roles restricted the possible courses of action open to their performers, but they did not dictate them, because of the uneven distribution of power between individuals, the dispersed sites of power in society, and the subtle personalised variations in the meanings of such 'shared' linguistic concepts highlighted in the work of Rappaport.

These elements imply that the autonomy of the individual within society was heavily circumscribed by pre-existing value-systems, and that independent agency tended to be mediated through and restrained by socially accepted pathways. These pathways *were* multiple, and so it is not easy to reduce them to single causal routes in order to re-create simple connections between 'structure', 'consciousness' and 'action'. This blocks any attempts to return to the predictive certainties and interpretative rigidities of the old 'meta-narratives'. At the same time, though, these pathways appear not to have been purely single-track, and this requires us to continue the search for patterns of behaviour, shared definitions, and group activities in order to reach for *collective* identities and agency. A historical landscape littered with multiple structures and fractured identities is much more difficult to traverse, map and reduce into regular patterns, than the 'flat earth' of a more deterministic age. However, it is also methodologically and intellectually more demanding to comprehend and understand, and a more interesting and illuminating context in which to work.

(VI)

The Chapters in this volume depict the relationships between identities and the social norms that shaped the possibilities for self-presentation, or acted to constrain those possibilities. They consider a variety of circumstances in which social identity was produced, and a number of different forms of identity. Chapters by Steve Hindle and Peter King examine the role of the Poor Laws in shaping identity. Hindle (Chapter 1) charts how the administrative exigencies and assumptions of the elite provided the value system by which the 'deserving poor' were defined. King (Chapter 2) examines the obverse of this identity production – the struggles by the poor to attain some social autonomy and agency in the face of such constraining moral norms, illustrated notably by the early nineteenth-century autobiography of the labourer Joseph Mayett. Chapters 3 and 4 by Alexandra Shepard and Judith Spicksley explore the relationship between gender and other forms of identity and estimation. Shepard's research seeks to question existing interpretations that impose simple distinctions between male and female constructions of honour, reputation and worth. By analysing witnesses' professions of good character she demonstrates that the sexes shared forms of moral estimation, such as personal self-reliance, diligence in work and probity in behaviour. This allows her to contextualise areas of difference, which were concentrated on the public social and economic roles attributed to men – the patriarchal standing associated with being a householder, and the economic goodwill connected to a reputation for 'honest dealing'. These were social attributes to which women had access primarily *through* their relationship with men. Judith Spicksley considers the disjunction between the literary opprobrium heaped on spinsters, as social misfits and anomalous examples of their sex, and the social experience of such women, which often integrated them tightly into community networks. She suggests that the functional significance of single women never overcame the social stereotype, and that spinsters never accrued an autonomy and respect in society equivalent to their contribution to it in the localities. The Chapters by Craig Muldrew and Helen Berry consider the mutable nature of status identity, and the ways in which individuals attempted to shape their identity in relation to volatile circumstances, and concealed social boundaries. Muldrew emphasises the uncertainty of status within early modern society, as individuals were exposed to economic and demographic vagaries, without the cushion of status-giving institutions or occupational hierarchies, or the safety nets of banking, insurance or social security. Through the diary of the excise officer John Cannon, he explores how these insecurities permeated understandings of status mobility, and success or failure in life. Berry also examines personal records, to highlight how identity was formed through experiences of social change and transgression – of encountering different estimations and criteria of status, and entering new social arenas, not all of which were receptive or comfortable environments for newcomers. Finally, Phil Withington illustrates the instabilities in another form of identity in the early modern period. This is the corporate, collective and 'customary' identity associated with the borough 'body politic'. He explains how this was shaped by legal and constitutional forms constructed through different 'ways of remembering' the past, and civic precedents. Such identities were influenced by Aristotelian ideal types of polity, as well as having to accommodate the less exalted realities of borough politics, but they moulded the structures and the agency of these corporate bodies through the period.

A number of common themes emerge from these chapters about the process of identity formation, and its relationship to action in society. Repeatedly, this research emphasises how far moral judgements were implicit within social evaluations, or within claims of status. This is seen most distinctly in the studies of Hindle, King, Shepard and Muldrew. Hindle demonstrates that parish authorities and the magistracy constructed the identity of the 'deserving poor' by reference to a series of behavioural and normative characteristics. The deserving were to distinguish themselves and qualify for relief by manifesting a fear of God (through regular and well-behaved church attendance), industry and thrift, sobriety, deference to social superiors and general 'painfulness' in minimising the burden they placed on the parish (by turning away inmates, and apprenticing suitable children). By adhering to these constraints on behaviour, morality and identity production, they transformed their 'eligibility' for relief into 'entitlement' – a distinction that depended on the decisions of the overseers and magistracy. In this sense, parish authorities sought both to reform the poor and to *re-form* them, to reshape their identity, by reconstructing their lives and behaviour.

They faced opposition from those among the poor who resented the accompanying loss of their social autonomy, and who came to regard pensions as an entitlement rather than as a favour.

Peter King's research emphasises the inextricable connection between social autonomy and notions of moral worth in the formation of identity among the labouring poor at the turn of the nineteenth century. The autobiography of the Buckinghamshire labourer, Joseph Mayett, is a record of his constant struggle to assert and maintain his social 'independence' (behavioural autonomy, public voice and personal rights) in the face of ever-greater constraints, brought on by ever narrowing material 'circumstances'. Poverty was the formative experience of Mayett's adult, married life. Apart from exposing him to stark experiences of want, it eroded his economic options by forcing him into poorly paid, exhausting jobs, and undermined his social credit among his 'superiors'. The more he attempted to assert his rights, and advance his claims as a moral equal among them, the more he lost out and was discriminated against. Mayett never submitted meekly to the normative restraints in which the 'deserving poor' were expected to bind themselves. In seeking to preserve independence as he slid further towards dependence, he transgressed the hidden value judgements that policed the boundary between eligibility and entitlement.

These values, and the extent to which they were internalised by individuals and groups, form an important strand of Alexandra Shepard's chapter. She highlights the recurring patterns in the values that witnesses associated with their claims to 'honesty'. Honesty depended both on personal behaviour, and the ability to meet more general behavioural criteria. These included the ability to 'live of one's own' (to maintain economic independence), to preserve good social and business 'credit', and thus to insure the value of one's word by refuting any charges of dependence or undue influence. In many respects, these were the *same* values as those employed by the parish elite to distinguish between the 'idle' and the 'industrious poor'. It is possible that such witnesses were bound up in the linguistic or conceptual hegemony of this elite, forced to claim status by reference to the language of the powerful, thus reaffirming the 'official transcript' in the process. Yet, Shepard also demonstrates that these claims contained hidden social assumptions that point to deeper struggles over moral worth. There was a greater onus on the 'poorer sort', particularly those in receipt of poor relief, to establish their honesty, or their social and moral autonomy. It was assumed that wealth conferred independence. Gentlemen were not required to prove the truth of their word in court, and were offended when this was impugned by an interrogatory.[87] For those dependent on wages, social and moral autonomy was much more difficult to demonstrate. They referred to their 'painful labour', the repute in which they stood with their neighbours, or their household self-sufficiency. Yet, they were forced to swim against the current of social perceptions, to prove they were honest *despite* being poor. As Craig Muldrew observes in his essay, 'there is an element of what I think we could term class formation occurring here with group generalisations being made in moral terms, based on wealth, between the better and poorer in society'. However, as he also notes, the insecurities of the early modern economy, and the mutability inherent in these moral judgements (that were *both* personal, and general), meant that social positions were 'a process of continual achievement' rather than firm, unchanging destinations. The fact that sources of wealth were highly vulnerable and that individuals lacked ways to secure their social and economic status meant that personal fate and moral repute loomed large in contemporaries' understanding of identity formation. Muldrew examines this relationship by focusing on the social and moral value system of John Cannon, a sometime excise officer in Somerset and (in many respects) a material failure in late seventeenth and early eighteenth-century England. Cannon lauded the values of industry, thrift, abstinence and virtue, and saw these as the basis of well-founded (and thus deserving) prosperity. In his later years, he judged some of his own misfortunes by the degree to which he had failed to adhere to these moral qualities. At the same time he excoriated the rich, and his more prosperous neighbours, whose fortunes appeared far to exceed their personal or social merits. He also lamented that although the needy included those 'well born, honest, wise, learned and well deserving' poverty undermined the respect given to them, and the autonomy that they could exercise. He attributed such unwarranted success or failure to the fickle distribution of fortune, but trusted in the long term that providence would ensure that ill-gotten superiority or ill-deserved inferiority would be redressed. For Cannon, moral worth was the true foundation of social repute, even if temporary disjunctions had elevated some of the ill-deserving, and had also obscured the proper appreciation of his talents for much of his life. As Muldrew has noted elsewhere, the main mechanism by which personal repute and economic worth were equated was through the contemporary idea of 'credit'.[88]

(VII)

A second, related, theme running through these essays is the degree to which identity formation and agency in society was influenced by the experience of constraint. Repeatedly, the qualitative accounts cited in this research emphasise that forms of self-presentation or action were limited by the social roles available to individuals, and by a strong awareness of the unequal distribution of power in this hierarchical society. This is evident in the struggles (and, in general, the failure) of Mayett, Cannon and Marsh to achieve acceptance without conforming to the recognised roles of deferential pauper, respectful and obedient clerk, and sporting country gentleman, respectively. They, like Shepard's poor but honest witnesses or Berry's 'singular' subjects, were attempting to withstand the gravitational pull of social expectations.

These constraints are highlighted most strongly in Judith Spicksley's consideration of the identity and social position of spinsters. The gap between their social functions and literary representations of the single woman illustrates the impermeable nature of gender stereotypes in early modern society. Despite evidence of the growing numbers of never-marrying women in seventeenth-century England, their importance as suppliers of credit, carers, surrogate parents and 'brokers' between women, linguistic concepts seem to have hardened against them. The term 'spinster' changed from a term describing what the single women *did*, to one describing what she *was*. Such a concept embodied the idea that unmarried, mature women were socially unproductive because they could not, legitimately, accomplish the woman's 'natural' role of reproduction. Their existence was, therefore, anomalous and 'unnatural', and commentators assumed that such women were sexually frustrated, and socially unfulfilled because 'legal procedures, inheritance practice, religious belief, medical knowledge, occupational training and social custom were all geared to the understanding that adult women would be married'. To remain a 'spinster' was to become an 'old maid', that is, a perpetually immature woman. Spicksley argues that it was not coincidental that male authors attached pejorative connotations to the term 'spinster' at a time when the number of single women was greatest, and when they seemed to pose the strongest threat to the notion of patriarchal household order. This meant that there was a dichotomy, between the effective social role and personal repute that such women could achieve in their localities, and the wider identity that they could claim within society. Local significance appears not to have translated into social autonomy or a public role equivalent to that enjoyed by married women in the period.

Constraints existed, often in cultural form, even among those endowed with the greatest potential for social freedom and re-fashioning. Helen Berry's depiction of the frustrations of the Kent gentleman John Marsh illustrates the burden of formative social norms at this time.

Marsh was educated as a lawyer, but inherited a modest country estate after his marriage in the 1780s. This inheritance projected him from the 'pseudo-gentility' of the urban professions – based around indoor recreations, socialising and display – to the very different norms, status indicators and forms of identity current among the county gentry. Marsh's great passion was music, in which to him the quality of the performance was more important than the social standing of the player, or the setting in which he played. Among the county elite, music was valued as merely another female accomplishment, not to be taken too seriously, and not to be given precedence over the social gathering for which it provided accompaniment. Marsh soon came to feel that he was a fish out of water among county families whose main interests were 'expensive dinners, Fox-Hunting & Cards', and he retreated to urban life, and the more familiar, more intellectually stimulating social rituals of the urban elite. Even here, Marsh's desire to promote music excellence above rank caused him to overstep normative boundaries and social assumptions. Despite his wealth, and his autonomy, Marsh felt unable to carve out a role in among the county gentry, and his meritocratic attitudes to musical performance offended the social proprieties of urban gentility, and broke through the borders that defined its shape. As Berry and Peter King emphasise, it seems that individuals in early modern England possessed only limited ability to reshape their identity, or present themselves in ways that deviated from or ignored embedded social assumptions about status or gender. While these assumptions did not always resolve themselves into consistent patterns, because they were often based on personal, moral evaluations, they do appear to have delineated socially accepted boundaries, within which the roles of woman, wife, mother, spinster, gentleman, householder, craftsman or pauper were to be enacted. Joseph Mayett was more constrained by these than John Marsh, but it is clear that neither had an entirely free choice.

The differing degree to which these social roles allowed individuals to shape their identity reflected the variable relationship between social experience and conceptual frameworks. In some respects, a greater overlap between personal experience and the particular language of status or identity produced social roles that were defined more clearly, but also ones that were more difficult to evade. A divergence between circumstances and role might allow greater freedom for self-definition, but might also expose the individual or the group as socially anomalous or 'singular', lacking the protection and approval offered by a commonly understood identity in society.

The chapters in this volume illustrate both of these variants. As noted above, research by Hindle, King, Shepard and Muldrew emphasises widespread evidence of the equation of status and moral worth – the higher an individual's status, the greater the presumption of moral worth. Here, Muldrew's double-edged concept of 'credit' provides an important link between individual attainments (moral character, personal repute, prosperity, credit-worthiness and consumption ability) and the evaluation of status by reference to more general 'moral' criteria. As Shepard's witnesses, Hindle's parish authorities, and (most poignantly) Joseph Mayett's memories attest, this conceptual framework of status intruded directly and powerfully into daily personal experience. The moral judgements inherent in these status evaluations defined social roles, but also imposed highly inequitable constraints on the social autonomy of poorer groups. The struggles of Mayett and John Cannon also provide evidence of further overlap between concepts and experience, through their idealisation of the notion of 'independence'. Cannon defined this (for male householders) as 'the Art of governing himself and his affairs', which once attained, would never be relinquished voluntarily. Mayett's repeated attempts to retain self-government in the face of encroaching economic dependence, suggest that he regarded it as an essential component of human dignity – the ability to demand treatment as a discerning, autonomous adult. To be defined as a 'pauper' was, in effect, to be judged to have failed in the exercise of these societal liberties, with financial assistance coming at the expense of personal freedom. As has been suggested, other identities contained a greater disjunction between experience and reality, notably between the personal autonomy and societal inferiority of 'spinsters' – who experienced economic and social freedoms that exceeded that of their married contemporaries, but who were condemned to an inferior status identity.

In other contexts, identities could be selected and refashioned more freely, in order to allow greater agency. Phil Withington's Chapter 7 shows that this was most possible at the level of the group, but that it contained the risk inherent in all joint enterprises – that participants might not agree on a single mode of representing themselves. Among corporations, two different forms of structural principles shaped forms of collective agency. On the one hand, corporate forms were sanctioned by reference to 'custom', which conveyed the authority of ancient usage, but also the flexibility necessary for responsive government, through the selective remembering of some customs and not others. On the other hand, corporate polities were also categorised, assessed and shaped by ideas of political thought notably Aristotle's taxonomy of governmental forms (with the Tudor state favouring the 'aristocratic' mode). These intersecting conceptual frameworks offered multiple means of justifying the actual distribution of power in any corporation. They also provided a large amount of ammunition for opponents to attack both the form and the practice of urban government. They could criticise structural and procedural violations of custom, and characterise both the principles and the practice of civic rule in terms of perverted Aristotelian forms – as 'tyrannical', 'oligarchic' or 'popular'. Such distinctions provided the intellectual basis for the governmental wrangles in the Shropshire borough of Ludlow in the late sixteenth century. Withington shows that while civic government in this period was characterised by the 'growth of oligarchy', this was merely one form of rule, and one answer to the question of the distribution of authority, rather than an inevitable consequence of social division or urban decline.

(VIII)

These studies produce a complex picture of the relationship between forms of identity and types of agency. While none of these chapters hark back to determining and all-embracing 'classes', all emphasise the *restrictions* on the choice and expressions of identity imposed by the economic inequalities, and the moral inequities of English society at this time. People like Joseph Mayett might fight against inclusion among the 'deserving poor', and the constraints on freedom that this implied, but it was very difficult for them to escape the confines of such definitions. We may also agree with Muldrew that the consistent social bias against the claims of truthfulness and honesty by individuals such as Mayett could amount to something like the workings of 'class' assumptions.

At the same time, though, the assessment of morality as part of identity was *individuating* as well as generalising. It meant judging individuals by reference to their personal behaviour, as well as by reference to generalised social 'facts', like the assumption that gentlemen were more inherently trustworthy than paupers. Thus it was possible for individuals to be regarded as poor but honest, even if 'the poor' themselves were seen as morally more fallible than the rich. Similarly, a single woman could be regarded, in person, as a highly respected, well connected and socially significant member of the community, while 'spinsters' in general were the object of ridicule. In this sense, individuals *were* able to establish personal reputations and identities that were distinct from (and which occasionally contradicted) public gender, age or status roles. The problem was that these identities were personal, tied to the behaviour of the individual and subject to the constant scrutiny of the neighbourhood. This link may explain why contemporaries chose to use the broadly understood criteria of Christian morality to evaluate normative and social worth in more general terms. However, it also means that individual attainments, failings, revivals and reforms might disrupt a neat reconstruction of the 'morality of class' – for as John Cannon observed, fickle fortune ensured that there were gentlemanly paupers and beggarly gentleman. As a consequence, even though personal 'credit' could change, it usually existed within accepted social roles, where individual agency was subject to normative, economic and cultural constraints.

In this sense, then, although individual and local examples of identity and agency controvert and subvert the concepts articulated by contemporary commentators (particularly about the social and gender orders), they existed within more deeply embedded and often less obvious systems of social judgement. These evaluated behaviour, gender identity and social 'credit' according to amalgams of custom, Christianity and context. They were too varied and inconsistent to be codified easily into a single 'moral framework' or a single 'epistemology' of status. John Marsh's experience of at least two opposing forms of 'gentility' within a single county illustrates this. Nevertheless, such ideas policed and demarcated the social roles available to people. In a highly unequal and hierarchical society it should not be surprising that those at the top of the social order possessed more ways of representing themselves than those lower down the social scale who paced the confines of increasingly 'narrow circumstances'. Even at the top, though, there existed the constraints of 'gentility', and the occasional frustrations of having to put breeding before ability. As the following chapters also indicate, it may be that different social groups often drew from the same pool of symbolic concepts and criteria in making estimations of identity and justifying activity. Like Nigel Rappaport's Cumbrian villagers, we need to be sure that they were employing these concepts in the same way, for the same purpose, and with the same implied meaning, before we can assess the significance of such apparently common usage. We may need to attune ourselves to looking for nuances within shared languages of identity and 'credit', rather than expecting to find social groups delineated by the possession of dialectically opposed definitions of worth, repute and status.

So, although there were a number of different formative elements for social identity and agency in early modern England, their number was finite. They might be summarised in terms of gender roles, economic credit, moral estimation, lifecycle stage, religious sensibility, status preservation, familial or patronage links, perceived regional, ethnic or racial characteristics, and the capacity to achieve social self-reliance. This is a sufficient number of variables to ensure the importance of context explaining particular forms of representation and specific behaviour, but it is not so many as to suggest that identity was endlessly re-fashioned, or permanently unstable. As we re-map identity in early modern England we may find that the terrain is not quite so limitless or quite so fractured as we suspected after we first tore up the railroads of 'class'. However, this may not mean that an understanding of identity formation and its effect on human action necessarily resolves itself into a journey to a single point on the horizon, or is to be reduced to a single method of explanation.

Notes

1. Such disputes are, of course, perennial among historians, but for evidence of one such debate about social identity and agency, with which the editors are particularly familiar, see: J. Barry, 'Introduction', in J. Barry and C. Brooks (eds), *The Middling Sort of People. Culture, Society and Politics in England, 1550–1800* (Basingstoke, 1994); J. Barry, 'Bourgeois Collectivism? Urban Association and the Middling Sort', in Barry and Brooks, *Middling Sort*; J. Barry, 'Consumers' Passions: The Middle Class in Eighteenth-Century England', *Historical Journal*, 34 (1991); D. Wahrman, *Imagining the Middle Class. The Political Representation of Class in Britain, c.1780–1840* (Cambridge, 1995), ch. 1; H.R. French, 'The Search for the "Middle Sort of People" in England, 1600–1800', *Historical Journal*, 43, 1 (2000).
2. J. Barry, 'Identité Urbaine et Classes Moyennes Dans L'Angleterre Moderne', *Annales ESC*, 48, 4 (1993), p. 854.
3. A clear summary of these two approaches can be found in M.A. Hogg, D.J. Terry and K.M. White, 'A Tale of Two Theories: A Critical Comparison of Identity Theory with Social Identity Theory', *Social Psychology Quarterly*, 58, 4 (1995), pp. 255–69; see also, R. Jenkins, *Social Identity* (London, 1996), chs 5 and 6.
4. The best introduction to Marx's historical ideas is S.H. Rigby, *Marxism and History: A Critical Introduction* (Manchester, 1987). For class 'in itself' and 'for itself', see pp. 214–6.
5. E.P. Thompson, *Customs in Common* (Harmondsworth, 1993), p. 9.
6. Thompson, *Customs*, p. 9.
7. *Ibid.*, p. 46.
8. *Idem*, p. 47.
9. *Id.*, pp. 47–8.
10. E.P. Thompson, *Whigs and Hunters: The Origins of the Black Act* (Harmondsworth, 1975), pp. 263–4.
11. Thompson, *Whigs and Hunters*, p. 57.

12. R.S. Neale, *Class in English Society 1680–1850* (Oxford, 1981), pp. 109–11; P. Anderson, *Arguments Within English Marxism* (London, 1980); R. Johnson, 'Thompson, Genovese and Socialist Humanism', *History Workshop Journal*, 6 (1978), pp. 79–100.

13. D. Hay, 'Property, Authority and the Criminal Law', in D. Hay, P. Linebaugh, J.G. Rule, E.P. Thompson and C. Winslow (eds), *Albion's Fatal Tree. Crime and Society in Eighteenth-Century England* (London, 1975), pp. 17–64.

14. Hay, 'Property', p. 61.

15. *Ibid.*, p. 49.

16. *Idem*, p. 55.

17. See Thompson, *Customs*, pp. 10–1.

18. Hay, 'Property', p. 55.

19. R. Pahl, 'Is the Emperor Naked? Some Questions on the Adequacy of Sociological Theory', in D.J. Lee and B.S. Turner (eds), *Conflicts about Class: Debating Inequality in late Industrialism* (Harlow, 1996), p. 89. The nature of 'structural' relationships and causation, and the fate of 'class' as a structure has been the subject of intense debate by sociologists over the last 20 years. The consensus is that 'class' is increasingly insufficient as a means of characterising complex, modern post-industrial society. See (among others), R. Crompton, F. Devine and M. Savage (eds), *Renewing Class Analysis* (Oxford, 2000); J. Pakulski and M. Waters, *The Death of Class* (London, 1996); D. Reid, 'Reflections on Labor History and Language', in L.R. Berlanstein (ed.), *Rethinking Labor History: Essays on Discourse and Class Analysis* (Urbana and Chicago, 1993), pp. 39–54; R. Pahl, 'Is the Emperor Naked?' pp. 89–109; R. Holton, 'Has Class Analysis a Future? Max Weber and the Challenge of Liberalism to *Gemeinschaftlich* Accounts of Class', in Lee and Turner, *Conflicts about Class*, pp. 26–41; J.K. Gibson-Graham, S.A. Resnick and R.D. Wolff, 'Class in a Poststructuralist Frame', in J.K. Gibson-Graham, S.A. Resnick and R.D. Wolff (eds), *Class and Its Others* (Minneapolis, 2000), pp. 1–22; G. Stedman Jones, *Languages of Class: Studies in English Working Class history 1832–1982* (London, 1983).

20. E.P. Thompson, 'Eighteenth-Century Society: Class Struggle without Class?', *Social History*, 3 (1978), pp. 149–50.

21. K. Marx, 'The Holy Family', in *Idem, Collected Works*, 4 (1975), p. 37. As ever, it is possible to find a contrary view within Marx's works, see K. Marx, *The Eighteenth Brumaire of Louis Bonaparte* (1852), pp. 333–4.

22. J. Brewer and J. Styles, 'Introduction', in *Idem* (eds), *An Ungovernable People: the English and their Law in the Seventeenth and Eighteenth Centuries* (London, 1980), p. 20; J.H. Langbein, '*Albion's* Fatal Flaws', *Past & Present*, 98 (1983), pp. 96–120; P. King, 'Decision-makers and decision-making in the English criminal law 1750–1800', *Historical Journal*, 27 (1984), pp. 25–58; P. Linebaugh, '(Marxist) Social History and (Conservative) Legal History. A Reply to Professor Langbein', *New York University Law Review*, 60 (1985), pp. 212–43; J. Innes and J. Styles, 'The Crime Wave: Recent Writing on Crime and Criminal Justice in Eighteenth-century England', in A. Wilson (ed.), *Rethinking Social History. English Society 1570–1920 and its Interpretation* (Manchester, 1993), pp. 201–65.

23. P. King, *Crime, Justice and Discretion in England 1740–1820* (Oxford, 2000), p. 357.

24. King, *Crime*, p. 358.
25. *Ibid.*, p. 332.
26. *Idem.*, p. 360.
27. *Id.*, p. 362.
28. *Id.*, p. 367.
29. J.C. Scott, *Domination and the Arts of Resistance: Hidden Transcripts* (New Haven, 1990).
30. Scott, *Domination*, p. 78. In fact, Thompson emphasised that he did *not* believe that hegemony meant 'any acceptance by the poor of the gentry's paternalism upon the gentry's own terms or in their approved self-image'. Deference by the poor was always conditional, 'the calculated extraction of whatever could be extracted'. Thompson, 'Eighteenth-century society', p. 163.
31. Scott, *Domination*, p. 78.
32. *Ibid.*, pp. 139–40.
33. *Idem*, p. 340.
34. *Id.*, p. 205.
35. *Id.*, p. 129.
36. *Id.*, pp. 140–52.
37. *Id.*, pp. 152–4, 156–72.
38. *Id.*, pp. 154–6, 187–92.
39. *Id.*, pp. 172–82.
40. *Id.*, p. 116.
41. *Id.*, pp. 190–1, 193–5.
42. *Id.*, pp. 120–4.
43. *Id.*, pp. 204, 210–12.
44. *Id.*, p. 34.
45. For example, antebellum slavery features in historical examples on *Id.*, pp. 3, 5–6, 24, 25–8, 33–4, 57, 63–4, 79, 114, 115–7, 188–9 and 208–9; pre-Revolutionary Russia features on pp. 96–101, 168 and 181.
46. *Id.*, p. 135.
47. *Id.*, p. 135.
48. Hay, 'Property', p. 61.
49. G. Lerner, *Why History Matters. Life and Thought* (New York and Oxford, 1997), p. 132.
50. J. Scott, 'Women's History', in P. Burke (ed.), *New Perspectives on Historical Writing* (Cambridge, 1991), p. 53.
51. M. Hartman and L. Banner (eds), *Clio's Consciousness Raised: New Perspectives on the History of Women* (New York, 1974); A. Oakley and J. Mitchell (eds), *The Rights and Wrongs of Women* (London, 1976); S. Rowbotham, *Hidden from History* (London, 1973); B. Carroll (ed.), *Liberating Women's History* (Chicago, 1976).
52. Scott, 'Women's History', p. 53.
53. J. Wallach Scott, 'Introduction', in *Ibid.* (ed.), *Feminism and History* (Oxford, 1996), p. 1.
54. J. Kelly, *Women, History & Theory. The Essays of Joan Kelly* (Chicago and London, 1984), p. 5.
55. Scott, 'Introduction', p. 3.
56. Kelly, *Women*, p. 4.
57. *Ibid.*, p. 5.

58. *Idem*, p. 11.
59. *Id.*, p. 12.
60. Lerner, *Why History Matters*, p. 132.
61. *Ibid.*, p. 133.
62. *Idem*, p. 134.
63. *Id.*, p. 134.
64. *Id.*, p. 135.
65. *Id.*, p. 136.
66. *Id.*, p. 137.
67. *Id.*, p. 143.
68. N.Z. Davis, '"Women's History" in Transition: the European Case', *Feminist Studies*, 3 (1976), p. 88.
69. Recent studies dealing with masculinity in early modern England have included: A. Bray, 'To be a Man in Early Modern Society: The Curious Case of Michael Wigglesworth', *History Workshop Journal*, 41 (1996); M. Breitenberg, *Anxious Masculinity in Early Modern* England (Cambridge, 1996); T. Hitchcock, *English Sexualities, 1700–1800* (Basingstoke, 1997); E.A. Foyster, *Manhood in Early Modern England: Honour, Sex and Marriage* (Harlow, 1999); P. Carter, *Men and the Emergence of Polite Society, Britain 1660–1800* (Harlow, 1999); A. Shepard, *Meanings of Manhood in Early Modern England* (Oxford, 2003).
70. J. Wallach Scott, *Gender and the Politics of History* (New York and Oxford, 1988), p. 28.
71. Scott, *Gender*, p. 39.
72. K. Canning, 'Feminist History after the Linguistic Turn: Historicizing Discourse and Experience', *Signs*, 19, 2 (1994), p. 370.
73. Scott, *Gender*, pp. 42–4.
74. Canning, 'Feminist History', p. 376, quoting J. Wallach Scott, 'The Evidence of Experience', *Critical Inquiry*, 17, 3 (1991), p. 779.
75. *Ibid.*, p. 377.
76. *Idem*, p. 384.
77. *Id.*, p. 386.
78. L. Roper, *Oedipus and the Devil. Witchcraft, Sexuality and Religion in Early Modern Europe* (London and New York, 1994), p. 14.
79. Roper, *Oedipus and the Devil*, p. 4.
80. *Ibid.*, p. 15.
81. *Idem*, p. 17.
82. *Id.*, p. 21.
83. This has been the subject of much debate. Alan Macfarlane has argued for the precocious development of legal, economic and social 'individualism' in England from the late Middle Ages. A. Macfarlane, *The Origins of English Individualism The Family, Property and Social Transition* (Oxford, 1978). Other historians have linked the growth of 'capitalist' economic relations with the growth of individual, rather than 'corporate' forms of identity and self-expression in this period. See M. Mascuch, *Origins of the Individualist Self. Autobiography and Self-Identity in England, 1591–1791* (Oxford, 1997); J. Sawday 'Self and Selfhood in the Seventeenth Century', in R. Porter, (ed.), *Rewriting the Self Histories from the Renaissance to the Present* (London, 1997). Such ideas have been challenged by J. Barry, 'Bourgeois Collectivism? Urban Association and the Middling Sort', in Barry and Brooks, *The Middling Sort of People*, pp. 84–112.

Literary scholars have depicted the sixteenth century as the period in which 'self-fashioning' of individual identity and behaviour became possible. S. Greenblatt, *Renaissance Self-Fashioning From More to Shakespeare* (Chicago, 1980), E. Hanson, *Discovering the Subject in Renaissance England* (Cambridge, 1998).

84. N. Rappaport, *Diverse World Views in an English Village* (Edinburgh, 1993), p. 157.

85. Rappaport, *Diverse World Views*, p. 158.

86. Roles are discussed in relation to the historical application of James C. Scott's work in M.J. Braddick and J. Walter, 'Introduction. Grids of power: Order, Hierarchy and Subordination in Early Modern Society', in *Ibid.* (eds), *Negotiating Power in Early Modern Society. Order, Hierarchy and Subordination in Britain and Ireland* (Cambridge, 2001), pp. 1–42.

87. On the relationship between concepts of truthfulness and gentility see S. Shapin, *A Social History of Truth* (Chicago and London, 1994), pp. 42–125.

88. C. Muldrew, *The Economy of Obligation: The Culture of Credit and Social Relations in Early Modern England* (London, 1998).

1
Civility, Honesty and the Identification of the Deserving Poor in Seventeenth-century England

Steve Hindle

The Elizabethan poor laws, codified in 1598 and 1601, institutionalised the ancient moral distinction between the *deserving* and the *undeserving* poor.[1] The idea that the idle or the shiftless were unsuitable 'objects of charity' had scriptural roots in St Paul's letter to the Thessalonians: 'if a man shall not work, then neither shall he eat'.[2] Discrimination against the wilfully idle, especially those rogues and vagabonds whose lives of itinerant theft by definition threatened the stability of a social order which was anchored in notions of private property, had accordingly been practised long before the Tudor regime began its long series of legislative experiments in social welfare.[3] Just as the sixteenth-century statutes sharpened perceptions of, and punishments for, vagrancy, however, they also articulated a more coherent vision of those who were deemed fit for parish relief in cash or kind. By 1598, policy-makers felt able to distinguish vagrants not only from the *labouring* poor (the under-employed or unemployed who were prevented from adequately maintaining their families either by prevailing levels of wages or structural problems in the economy) but also from the *impotent* poor (who were simply unable through either physical or mental incapacity to maintain themselves through their labour).[4] The deserving poor were, therefore, identified primarily by their *inability to labour*: they were the 'lame ympotent olde blynde and such other amonge them being poore and not able to worke'.[5]

The identification of impotence and (in turn) of deservingness should therefore have been unproblematic: failing eyesight, arthritic limbs and chronic diseases were not only symptoms of incapacity but also symbols of eligibility for relief. In 1618, when the most influential judicial commentator on the Elizabethan poor laws, the Cambridgeshire JP and Sergeant-at-Law Michael Dalton, glossed the tertiary distinction enshrined in the Elizabethan legislation, the issue of who might be legitimately relieved seemed relatively straightforward.[6] He immediately ruled out the 'thriftlesse poore' for whom, he argued, the house of correction was 'fittest'. This category included not only 'the vagabond that will abide in no service or place' but also a very much wider range of delinquents: 'the riotous and prodigall person, that consumeth all with play or drinking'; 'the dissolute person, [such] as the strumpet, pilferer, &c, 'the slothfull person, that refuseth to work'; and 'all such as wilfully spoile or imbesill their work'. The 'poore by casualtie', however, were to be treated more sympathetically. Victims of injury, accident or the lifecycle (especially those overburdened with children) were, he insisted, to be set on work. This left only the 'poore by impotency and defect', amongst whom Dalton included the aged, the orphaned, the disabled and the sick, who were to be relieved by parish officers in cash and kind in their own homes according to their need.[7]

Within a very few years, however, the experience of administering parish relief had made it clear to overseers, magistrates and judges alike that the distinctions enshrined in the legislation were far more easily applied in theory than in practice. By the time Dalton came to revise his passage on eligibility for relief for the 1635 edition of *The Country Justice*, he conceded that parish officers across thousands of communities had found it difficult to discriminate against those whom the statutes had defined as undeserving. He accordingly launched a venomous attack on the granting of parish relief to the thriftless poor. Misguided generosity, he argued, not only nourished these parasites 'in their lewdnesse or idlenesse' and robbed the deserving poor of much-needed relief, it also wronged the ratepayers who underwrote the parish fund and condemned the overseers who had betrayed them. From the 1630s onwards, then, successive editions of Dalton's guidebook actively recommended the denial of relief to drunkards, whores, pilferers and idlers. Even so, he recognised, there was inevitably some slippage between his categories. What, he asked, should become of those delinquents who happened 'to prove impotent' or to experience 'manifest extremity'? Here he was less sure of himself: 'it seemeth', he argued, 'that they are to be releeved by the towne'.[8] By the 1643 edition, Dalton had begun to cite the authority of a statute of 1495 as interpreted in an unspecified Cambridge assize charge, to the effect that the thriftless impotent were merely to be provided with 'bread and water without other sustenance'. He nonetheless insisted that 'charity wills us in cases of manifest extremity' that even the delinquent should not be left to starve.[9] He nonetheless added a caveat, which empowered magistrates and parish officers to make discretionary judgements in such cases: 'I leave that to better consideration'.[10]

It is with the exercise of Dalton's 'better consideration' that this chapter is concerned. The following discussion artificially ignores the wider matrix of social discipline within which the granting of outdoor relief to the deserving was located. Liability for those considered undeserving might, of course, be shifted either onto other parishes (under the terms of indemnity bonds and removal orders) or even onto specific individuals within the parish (putative fathers, for instance, under the terms of those paternity bonds designed to disburden ratepayers of the high costs of their bastard children).[11] This is to say nothing of the whipstocks, manacles and hemp laid up in houses of correction where the self-evidently delinquent were to be punished with hard labour.[12] This analysis focuses rather on the relief of the settled poor of the parish, those for whom the granting of pensions *should* have been unambiguous. By investigating the circumstances in which relief was withheld, suspended or even cancelled altogether as a result of the demeanour or conduct of the recipient, this chapter investigates the methods by which the parish authorities and the magistracy constructed the threshold of eligibility for poor relief, and in turn reveals the process through which definitions of deservingness were created, resisted and enforced. Among the canons of social respectability to which parish pensioners were expected to conform were church attendance; industriousness; sobriety; childrearing and deference. These moral criteria came to function as 'structural' constraints on the individual agency of the poor, and set the parameters according to which the deserving might shape their identity. The poor were sorted, and ultimately came to see the advantages of sorting themselves, into the moral categories approved by the overseers, which were in turn policed by the financial sanctions of the civil parish. One of the most fundamental consequences of going 'on the parish', therefore, was a diminution of the range of personal choice that paupers might make about their personal conduct and ethical behaviour. In administering the Elizabethan statutes, parish officers set the standards of civility and honesty against which the poor would be judged, and publicised the ethics according to which the deserving poor identified themselves.[13]

(I)

Church attendance

The poor were most obviously expected to demonstrate their deservingness by regular attendance at church services. In doing so, they not only participated in communal rituals of worship, but also proved that they recognised their place in the social order and that they feared God. As early as the 1590s, for instance, applicants for relief at St Bartholomew-by-the-Exchange (London) were expected not only to attend church every Sunday morning but also to satisfy parish officers of their knowledge of the creed. In Salisbury (Wiltshire) from 1623, and again in 1626, no persons were to have relief unless they 'usually frequent his or her parish church at morning and evening prayer and at sermons on the sabbath days'. Attendance was initially to be monitored by the provision of 'forms or seats for all [the poor] to sit together'; and subsequently of a bench with '*For the Poore* in great red letters' painted upon it. Surveillance of this kind was probably practised elsewhere, as at Croft (North Yorkshire), where similar inscriptions are still to be found.[14]

The allocation of specific spaces for the poor within the parish church was widely practised. In providing a 'social map' of the local community, the parish officers who drew up church seating plans seem to have institutionalised latent notions of marginality. New seats had specifically been set aside for 'poor folks' in London parishes as early as the 1570s, and 'for the poor and such as took alms' at Bardeswell (Norfolk), for example, in 1608. The poor of Oswestry (Shropshire) were made to sit on rough boards rather than pews from the first decade of the seventeenth century.[15] If any of the poor were conspicuous by their absence from church services, their collection was likely to be withheld. In 1633, for example, the vestrymen of Braintree (Essex) ordered the parish officers to 'do their best indeavour to fynde out such persons as absent themselves from churche', to 'take a course to force them to come', and to ensure that 'the poorer sorte that take collection shalbe abated in their collection until such time as they be reformed in it'. The parish officers of Layston (Hertfordshire) from 1613, Trull (Somerset) from 1677, Stansted Abbots (Hertfordshire) from 1678 and Linton (Cambridgeshire) from 1710 similarly insisted that 'alms people & pensioners' receive their pensions on Sunday only after first hearing the sermon.[16] Distribution in these cases almost certainly took place in the church porch, as it did at Prees (Shropshire) from 1672 and Weedon (Northamptonshire) in the 1690s, a policy that not only encouraged pensioners to attend sermons, but also ensured transparency and publicity in the allocation of parish resources. This was a policy practised in some parishes, such as Colyton (Devon), into the eighteenth century. The vestries at Seaborough and Charmouth (Dorset) even ordered the withholding of pensions for those who failed to attend Sunday services as late as 1726 and 1784 respectively.[17]

These general injunctions to participate in communal worship were inevitably followed by the punishment of those who failed either to attend altogether or to conduct themselves with appropriate decorum when they did so. In 1641 the Warwickshire bench ordered that Roger Hodgkins of Shrewley-in-Hatton was to have his pension paid 'in the parish church there and to receive nothing if he fails to attend'. William Amarys of Salford (Warwickshire) actually had his pension halved in 1641 because the parish officers described him as a 'very disorderly fellow' who had 'behaved himself very rudely and irreligiously in the church there'. If he continued to 'demean and behave himself uncivilly and unreverently', the magistrates agreed, he was to 'have no contribution at all'.[18] Just because the poor were made to attend church that should not lead us to believe that they necessarily communicated with their betters on an equal footing or even at the same time. Poor labourers and servants were often made to attend earlier services than their masters and mistresses, as was the case throughout the diocese of Peterborough in the late sixteenth century. They often received inferior communion wine, cheaper claret being substituted for more expensive malmsey at Oswestry in 1608, for example, in a distinction that, however odious to modern egalitarian instincts, accorded perfectly well with the contemporary obsession with order, hierarchy and degree.[19]

(II)

Industriousness

Perhaps the next most obvious characteristic expected of the deserving poor was industriousness, or at least a willingness to work. Indeed, the provision of poor relief seems in practice to have been less a matter of meeting need than of preserving the incentive to wage labour. Quarter sessions records are littered with examples of pensioners forcibly being reminded of their duty to find work wherever possible. A petitioner from Salthowse (Norfolk) was denied relief by the overseers there in 1603, for example, because 'she may have work if she will'. William Harris of Polesworth (Warwickshire) was awarded a pension in 1632 only on the condition that he shall 'willingly do such work as he shall be able to perform being reasonably satisfied for the same'. If he refused, the bench insisted, his pension was to be cancelled. Two widows of the Warwickshire parish of Southam were similarly threatened with suspension of their collection in 1641 unless they undertook to 'labour at such work as they are able and according to their power'. The complex arrangements for the maintenance of the Archer family of Fillongley (Warwickshire) were confirmed in 1650 only on the condition that Archer 'do diligently follow his work'. In 1675, Mary Harper of Long Itchington (Warwickshire) had her pension reduced from 22*d*. to 12*d*. weekly on the grounds that she was 'a person able in some measure to work for her living'. Alice Parker of Bidford (Warwickshire) had her pension halved in 1676 because the overseers alleged that she was 'able with her labour for the greatest part to maintain herself without any allowance'. Thomas Tilkes of West Wycombe (Buckinghamshire) actually had his pension cancelled altogether in 1680 because the overseers managed to convince the justices that 'he is a man of very able body and well able to work for his own livelihood'.[20] The magistrates of North Yorkshire ordered in 1679 that the overseers of Northallerton (North Yorkshire) cancel a widow's pension and 'be no further chargeable with her than with providing her a stock' with which she might spin or weave. That even this was no guarantee of success is demonstrated by the experience of the parish officers of Westward who pleaded with the Cumberland bench in 1698 that William and Jane Langrigg be denied further relief. Not only was William a competent shoemaker, but his wife had refused to be set on work, complaining that 'she could not live upon spinning hemp' at 5*d*. a hank. Both had allegedly boasted that they could maintain themselves better than at least twenty other families of the parish, and yet they were content to receive relief.[21]

Pensions were never, of course, intended in and of themselves to provide an adequate maintenance, especially in the early seventeenth century. They were frequently combined with the meagre incomes that paupers might scrape together from other sources as part of the 'economy of makeshifts'. As the Norfolk magistrate Robert Doughty put it in one relief order issued in 1664, a weekly allowance to a poor family should amount only to 'what *with their work* will maintain them'.[22] It is nonetheless striking that justices and parish officers should seek to adjust the value of pensions according to the seasonality of the labour market. In 1682, the overseers of Stewkely (Buckinghamshire) granted Joan Daniell only 1*s*. 6*d*. every week 'until harvest be over' but noted that the pension should 'afterwards' be doubled. Similarly, when the Warwickshire bench allowed Elizabeth Edden of Barford, widowed with three small children, a weekly pension of 12*d.* in 1684, it insisted that the sum be halved 'in harvest time' when she might supplement her income with hay raking, straw-plaiting or gleaning.[23]

The fear that entry into the pension lists might actually *encourage* idleness was evident in the complaint of the inhabitants of Radnage (Buckinghamshire) in 1692 that although Thomas Quainton's wife was 'well able to maintain herself', she had 'wholly given herself to an idle life' ever since she had been granted an allowance. The parish officers of Lorton (Cumberland) not only cancelled the relief of John Threlkeld in 1692 on the grounds that he was 'an idle and dissolute young man' who enjoyed 'living at their expense', but also pleaded that the bench punish his 'temerity'.[24] The overseers of Aston Abbots (Buckinghamshire) similarly justified their substantial reduction of Lucy Stratford's pension on the grounds that she 'was able to work, but so indulgent to herself as to refuse work when offered her'. The pension was restored only on the condition that she 'take such work as she was offered to her and endeavour by her honest labour and industry to provide for herself'. When the overseers of Embleton (Cumberland) sought the cancellation of one relief order in 1697, they justified their application on the grounds that 'old widows and orphans' rather than those who had 'gotten a habbit of idelness' were the only legitimate 'objects of charity'.[25]

Concerns that paupers and their dependants would supplement their pensions not through paid work but by begging are evident in the hostility to William Charter of Seaton (Devon) who had been granted 8*d.* a week in 1619 but had nonetheless 'gonne about begginge'. An order of the Buckinghamshire justices in 1680 stipulated that any resident of Aylesbury found begging at 'any inn gate or otherwise' was not only to be incarcerated in the town's house of correction but also 'expunged out of the pension roll for the relief of the poor'. Pensioners were similarly prevented from begging from door-to-door in Linton (Cambridgeshire) under pain of losing their regular allowance in 1697.[26] It was precisely this line of thinking that led the Devon clergyman Richard Dunning to argue in 1685 that those who were relieved by the parish could be compelled to follow their labour by forcing them bring the parish officers certificates of 'how they have been employed and what they have done since last pay-day' and 'to receive no relief' until 'they give a good account of their diligence'.[27]

(III)

Sobriety

Those paupers who spent their meagre pensions on ale were also vulnerable to the sanctions of the civil parish. The case of Richard Jenner, a lame cooper of Havant (Sussex) is instructive. Although Jenner had been allowed a weekly pension of 2s. by a local magistrate in 1638, the overseers thought him well enough to offer him work at 3s. a week. Jenner, they alleged, not only refused employment but wasted his 'time and means in alehouses'. Outright drunkenness probably lay behind the rather vague stipulation in 1652 that unless Sara Woodfall of Napton-on-the-Hill (Warwickshire), a 'woman most malicious against honest people' who 'misspends that which is given to her', conducted herself 'temperately', she too was to lose her pension. William Johnson of Balsall (Warwickshire), who had been awarded a weekly pension of 6d. in 1673, was deprived of it by the county bench the following year when the 'substantial inhabitants' of the parish informed the justices that he was a 'person of very ill behaviour and whatsoever money he gets doth spend the same in rioting and drunkenness through which ill vices he hath spent a good estate' and further that he was 'a great disturber of the whole neighbourhood there'. John Fawcett of Embleton (Cumberland) had his pension cancelled in 1697 because he continually drank away his maintenance money in Cockermouth. Pensions were also withheld from those whom the vestry regarded as 'drunken' or 'disorderly' at Hanwell (Middlesex) in the very late eighteenth century.[28]

The disorder associated with overindulgence in drink might be very wide-ranging, resulting in the pollution of personal morality in all its forms. The vestrymen of Braintree (Essex) were, for example, relatively unspecific in their insistence in February 1620 that one Browne 'being growne very filthy and troublesome shall have his collection denied him until he reform himselfe', though whether it was Brown's speech or his appearance that aroused their indignation is unclear. The suspicion that sexual incontinence might be sufficient grounds for the exemplary suspension of relief is borne out by the experience of the Warwickshire widow Anne Eales who, pregnant by a 'young fellow who would marry her', refused his offer and continued in her 'dissolute life', thereby forfeiting the 6d. a week pension she had been receiving for almost three years.[29]

(IV)

Childrearing

The deserving might equally be distinguished by their attitude towards their offspring. Parish officers very frequently condemned the conduct of those parents who actively encouraged habits of idleness amongst their children, contrasting such fecklessness with the careful childrearing practices of those who took pains to inculcate values of diligence and thrift in the young. The litmus test of good parenthood among parish pensioners was a willingness to have their children bound out by the overseers as pauper apprentices to husbandry and huswifery, often across the parish boundary. Those who refused the apprenticeship of their children were accused of keeping more children at home than was necessary, a tendency which was all the more dubious since the likelihood was that these boys and girls would be sent out begging on behalf of their parents. Parish officers accordingly withheld relief from those who resisted the campaign for pauper apprenticeship. The parish officers of Eaton Socon (Bedfordshire), for example, insisted in 1596 that 'such pore as doe not send their children' to work bone lace, were to 'receive no relief from the collection'. In 1621, Richard Frye of Street (Somerset), 'a very poor man with a great charge of six small children', could 'get no relief of the parish' because those of his children 'which are fit to be bound apprentice' were 'still remaining on his hands'. The justices were prepared to award him a pension only after he had agreed 'to settle and bind them forth'. At Braintree (Essex) in 1635, the overseers allowed Old Father Cleeves 10s. 'to relieve him in his necessity' only 'upon condicion he shall remove his son Dennis out of the towne and not receive him any more into his house'. Two residents of the Hertfordshire parish of Northaw were presented in 1637 for 'keeping their children at home without employment'. Robert Savile, a West Riding butcher, was threatened with committal to the house of correction at Wakefield in 1641 if he continued to refuse the apprenticeship of his 10-year-old son. Francis Sharpe of Bolton (Cumberland) had his pension halved in 1688 because his children were 'now grown' and might be apprenticed. The parish officers of Ireby (Cumberland) countered the 'surprise' relief order granted to Thomas and Janet Lowther in 1700 on the grounds that the couple were 'young people' and their children were fit for apprenticeship.[30]

These sanctions were deployed into the eighteenth century. In 1701 the vestry of Aldenham (Hertfordshire) ordered that if Widow Dickenson 'doth not forthwith put her daughter to service', she was to be 'stricken out of the monthly collection and be wholly excluded from any further relief'. In Brill (Buckinghamshire) in 1703, parents whose children continued to 'live and cohabit' despite their inability to maintain them, and whose presence ensured that 'the collection is likely to be increased to the great prejudice' of the ratepayers, were 'to have no relief or collection' unless the children were 'swiftly bound out'. The parish officers of Hayton-in-Gilsland waged a running battle with the Cumberland bench over a relief order granted in 1705 to John Schollocke, whose children were fit for apprenticeship, and did not get their way until 1711 by which time his youngest child was aged twelve and in service. Another Cumberland pensioner, Anne Hallefax of Torpenhow, refused outright to let her three children be bound and had her pension reduced in consequence. At Colyton in 1747, Widow Hannah Pitfield had her poor relief cut to a third of its original level when she refused to have her children bound out despite being destitute. The threat of the overseers of Gnossal that William Botts' 'pay be taken of[f] he refusing to let his son go out as apprentice' in 1754 certainly seems to have had an effect, for within two months his son was bound out to a Wolverhampton locksmith and his pension was restored.[31] The requirement made at the time of the parish apprenticeship of Humphrey Bernard, another poor child of Gnossal, in 1718 that his mother 'behave herself quietly and peaceably in the parish' is also suggestive of parental resistance. The desperate lengths to which reluctant parents might be driven is demonstrated by the case of Margaret Agar of Brewham (Somerset) whose curses against the parish overseer who 'made her children go to service' allegedly led to his death by witchcraft in 1665. The beggar's curse against the uncharitable, which so often gave rise to witchcraft accusations, might equally, it seems, be applied to parish officers who 'tyrannised' over their poor neighbours by sending their children away.[32] But in verbally abusing overseers in this way, poor householders only emphasised that they lacked the civility expected of the deserving.

(V)

Deference

The deserving should finally, therefore, demonstrate their gratitude for relief and their respect for the ratepayers and parish officers who bestowed it on them. The parish officers of Great Easton (Essex) stated the matter very bluntly in 1603 when they argued that any poor pensioners who 'unreverently' abused any ratepayer were 'to be put from

their pensions for that week'. Here are echoes of the deferential imperative so clearly stated by the vestrymen of Swallowfield in 1596 that
'suche as be poore & will malepertlye compare w[i]th their betters & sett
them at nought, shalbe warned to lyve & behave them selves as
becomethe them, yf suche amend not, then no man to make any other
accompte of theme [but] of comon disturbers of peace & quyetnes'.[33]
The poor then should fear not only God but also their betters, and know
their place with respect to both.

A reputation for ingratitude or truculence could be earned either by
taking the alms of the parish for granted or by pleading the case for relief
too aggressively. The abuses allegedly committed by Elinor Hatchett, a
widow of Barton Stacey (Hampshire), were ill defined, perhaps amount-
ing to grumbling about the relief she was allocated. When she
complained in 1641 that her house was in disrepair and that she was 'in
great want and misery', the overseers were ordered to relieve her only
'so long as she behaved herself orderly as she ought to do' and to commit her to bridewell if she misbehaved further. John Puxty of Buxsted
(Sussex) seems to have had a track record of antagonism to employers
and magistrates stretching back at least six years, which culminated in
the suspension of his 'weekly allowance' in January 1650. Edward
Titmarsh of Harbury (Warwickshire) had his pension halved in 1658
because he 'carrieth himself insolently towards the inhabitants there'.
Insolence also seems to lie behind the case of John Hansell to whom the
overseers of Hillington (Norfolk) were ordered in 1657 to pay 1s. 6d. a
week until they set him to work. If he refused employment, he was to
be committed to Swaffham House of Correction for a month, and his
weekly pay was to be stopped altogether unless he offered a personal
apology to Lady Hovell 'in the presence of the overseers and constables'
to 'acknowledge that he hath done her wrong'. Although Humphrey
Jones of Deriten was granted a pension of a shilling a week in 1692, the
justices threatened him with a whipping and a spell in bridewell 'if he
troubles the court any more for further collection without just cause'.
Goodwife Clapson was finally relieved by the vestry of Maidstone (Kent)
in 1728 'she promising not to be troublesome to us any more'. Due
deference and subordination, was also, moreover, expected of paupers'
families. A pension of 8d. weekly together with arrears of 5s. awarded to
Richard Taylor of Aston-near-Birmingham in 1660 was allowed him
only so long as his wife 'shall be of good behaviour to the officers there'.
Occasionally, it seems that the provision of a pension was itself a
strategem of containment for those who might *otherwise* prove troublesome. In 1690, the overseers of Coleshill (Hertfordshire) were ordered to

provide for Sarah Harwell, 'a person of very evill and bad behaviour' who was regularly abusive of her neighbours and destructive of their property, 'soe that she doth not for the future misbehave herself'. Well into the eighteenth century, the vestry of Wisbech (Cambridgeshire) regularly subscribed its habitation orders with the caveat that a beneficiary was to be given houseroom only 'during his good behaviour'.[34]

The protracted case of Widow Margaret Doughty of Salford (Warwickshire), which attracted the attention of the Warwickshire Bench on at least ten occasions between 1619 and 1652, is particularly instructive of the abhorrence of parish officers and magistrates alike for those who behaved as if a parish pension was theirs by right. By 1633, Doughty had enjoyed a parish pension for 14 years, during which time she had apparently 'grown clamorous', behaving herself 'in a very peremptory manner as if she were careless of the benefit of the said collection or at least altogether unthankful' for it. The bench accordingly instructed the overseers to withdraw her pension until she began to 'behave and demean herself peaceably and orderly' and to 'show herself thankful for the same'.[35] Mary Franklin of Great Horwood (Buckinghamshire) seems to have grown similarly reckless after being awarded a pension of 5s. a week. The overseers complained in 1693 that she 'hath taken the liberty to use very insolent language and threatening speeches towards the parish officers'. The justices accordingly halved her pension and ordered her to keep herself and her four children 'at hard worke and behave respectively and modestly towards her neighbours'. Franklin's dispute with the parish officers of Great Horwood dragged on for 17 years, during which time her pension was repeatedly reduced, withdrawn and reinstated, she even being committed to bridewell in 1700 for having 'passionately uttered divers approbrious and threatening speeches' against the 'inhabitants'.[36] The parish officers of Crosthwaite persuaded the Cumberland bench in 1712 that the shilling weekly paid to Elizabeth Birkett of Keswick should be 'reduced to a more moderate allowance' not only because she had income from casual labour but also because she was 'a proud abusive woman'. The award for the least deferential conduct by a parish pensioner must arguably go to John Baldwin of whom the parish officers of Bocking (Essex) complained in 1665: 'a very refractory fellow, abusing his superiors, and coming for his allowance in so masterly manner which encourageth others in the same'. These were, they argued, sufficient grounds for withholding his relief.[37] The deferential imperative might, therefore, reach 'beyond the relatively small numbers of the poor actually in receipt of pensions and affect the much larger groups immediately above them in the social hierarchy who were potentially dependent on poor relief'.[38] The 'deserving poor' were, to this extent, culturally constructed through the values of civility and honesty propagated by the discretionary administration of the civil parish.

(VI)

Identifying the poor of the parish

From the late seventeenth century, the deservingness of the poor of the parish was symbolised in the cloth badges they were made to wear as a condition of receiving a pension, a requirement stipulated by the statute of 1697.[39] Some paupers may have seen the strategic advantages of wearing the badge, for it publicly advertised the official recognition of their respectability. The badged pauper had satisfied the overseers, and the ratepayers they represented, that they were deserving of the alms of the parish and that they had passed the stringent tests of eligibility on which magistrates and parish officers generally insisted. To be sure, badges symbolised paupers' inability to work, but they also publicised their sobriety, their fear of God, and their past careers of thrift and industry on behalf of themselves and their families. They were, furthermore, evidence that the poor accepted their lot with equanimity, that they deferred to, and accepted the charity of, their betters. In this sense, badges were marks of inclusion, indicative both of a pauper's conformity to the standards of conduct on which the moral community of the neighbourhood insisted and of his or her right to settled residence. Although notions of deservingness were becoming far more begrudging, badging served an invaluable function in helping separate the deserving from the undeserving. It is, indeed, arguable that the authorities were less interested in the meaning of badges, than in the responses of those who were made to wear them. Despite the rhetoric of some contemporary polemicists, it seems unlikely that, even by the late seventeenth century, the more positive implications of earlier experiments with badges or signs – as marks of identification, of patronage and of belonging – had been entirely eclipsed. While there is plentiful evidence that badges were scorned, and that paupers paid the price of forfeiting their pensions for not wearing them, it is nonetheless clear that some, at least, wore their badges with pride. Those who wore them with equanimity, perhaps even with enthusiasm, therefore subscribed to a world-view in which they were expected to be grateful for the charity of the ratepayers and eager for the sponsorship of the overseers. The parish badge was, therefore, a form of *livery* (of the kind worn by male household servants into the eighteenth century and beyond) that functioned as a symbol not only of subordination but also of patronage.

In some respects, therefore, the parish badge was a testimonial of good behaviour and many paupers evidently thought it worthwhile pleading for a pension, even though (possibly even because) it meant wearing one. That so many petitions (and, indeed, appeals), even in the years after the 1697 statute, were sent to magistrates by poor householders claiming that overseers had denied them relief is striking testimony to popular acceptance of the inevitability, possibly in some cases of the desirability, of badging, for without the badge there would be no collection. To this extent badging was one aspect of a welfare process in which, as recent commentators have suggested, the poor had at least some degree of agency.[40]

There are, of course, very great dangers involved in taking these petitions at face value. They were, after all, designed to make a case. Even though they might deploy a subtle blend of deference, exaggeration and distortion, the effectiveness of the petitions depended on the credibility of the claims they made, claims that might more easily have been checked by contemporaries at the time than by historians at a distance of over three hundred years.[41] Indeed, only the most painstaking record linkage with the parish registers and overseers' accounts would now verify the applicants' claims made about age, about the burden of children, about disease or about their previous independence of support.[42] More interesting for our purpose here is the rhetorical mode of these claims on charity. For the most part, the petitions were personalised. They were not usually written in the applicants' own hand and almost invariably went unsigned and unmarked. Applicants for relief doubtless relied upon 'epistolatory advocates'.[43] Petitions were, however, far from standardised, and the scrivener or clerk who drew them up seems to have done so with the claimant at his elbow, perhaps inflecting his or her language to bolster the case where appropriate. Although it is possible that the influence of sermons and prayers was reflected in the idiom deployed in the petitions, a more plausible source of inspiration for their sophisticated charitable rhetoric are the charity briefs that were so frequently read in parish churches by the late seventeenth century, and especially in the early 1660s.[44]

As might be expected, most applicants for poor relief justified their claim in terms of their impotence. The archive of petitions most often discloses tales of creeping old age and chronic illness. With age came the arthritic limbs and failing sight, which rendered poor householders 'decrepit' or 'unable to work'. In addition to these material or physical factors, petitioners placed great emphasis on their character and their familiarity to their neighbours, frequently referring in various ways to their good reputation in local community. It was not uncommon for them to append certificates from groups of 'chief inhabitants' testifying to their honest conduct and conversation. The idiom of these petitions corresponds strikingly with the values on which parish officers and magistrates insisted. Applicants might claim that they had long supported themselves by their 'honest endeavours', that they had lived 'in honesty and neighbourly love' with the parishioners, or that that they were well known to be 'civil, sober, industrious and dutiful'.[45] In all these respects, petitioners struck the postures of deservingness, which overseers had doubtless come to expect.

Those ratepayers, parish officers and magistrates who enforced the Elizabethan poor laws were, whether they knew it or not, echoing the intentions that lay behind the most famous of the sixteenth-century censuses of the poor. The city fathers of Norwich had argued in 1570 that the poor must be enumerated and their characteristics catalogued in order that beggars could be driven off the streets and habits of 'work, learning and the feare of God' could be inculcated amongst poor householders.[46] The logic of discretionary disbursement was that applicants for relief were judged deserving by the extent to which they exhibited these characteristics of civility and honesty. Those occasions when pensions were abated, suspended or cancelled therefore served as exemplary warnings to all the poor of the parish that they enjoyed no right to relief. Nor, it should be emphasised, was the discriminatory administration of relief peculiar to those godly cities and parishes where local office holding was monopolised by cliques of hotter Protestants. Late into the seventeenth century, some zealous overseers seem to have regarded it as their social duty to launch parochial campaigns for the reformation of manners through the management of poor relief. The new overseer of the Devon parish of Awliscombe wrote in 1662, for instance, that 'many shameful offences have been committed in this parish which have made it become odious and contemptible' and blamed those 'remyse officers' who had tolerated 'drunkenesse, fornication [and] unlicensed alehouses' among the poor. The parish, he complained was ridden with 'masterless persons, monsters of schism and deceivers of the relief', all of whom should be punished for their idleness.[47] To be sure, the reformation of manners as carried through the structures of ecclesiastical justice seems to have been particularly intense in rural communities like Terling (Essex) or municipal boroughs like Dorchester (Dorset) where the godly activism of an oligarchy of local officeholders raised the moral tone of governance one more notch.[48] Even so, all parish officers were under an obligation to see that resources were targeted appropriately and that the interests of ratepayers were not prejudiced. The duties of the overseers of the poor, however active their individual moral consciences, accordingly required them to distinguish the deserving from the undeserving in each of the 9000 parishes of England.

The administration of social welfare presupposed the practice of vigilance among overseers and surveillance among ratepayers. The instructions issued to the overseers of all the parishes in North Norfolk in 1623 make explicit the discretionary power of overseers to allocate relief according to the moral and economic conduct of the poor. Parish officers were required to report idle labourers to magistrates who would commit them to bridewell; to ascertain every weekend which of the poor had work for the next week, and supply materials on which they could be employed; to ensure that pauper children be taught knitting and spinning; and to make twice-weekly search for suspected nightwalkers and stolen goods. Most significantly, however, overseers were instructed not only to punish, but also to withhold poor relief from, pilferers and idlers. The money thus saved would be used to reward those inhabitants, some of them perhaps receiving poor relief themselves, who informed on the delinquency of their neighbours, at the rate of sixpence a time.[49] The networks of surveillance and information envisaged here might reap substantial financial rewards for the ratepayers. In the three years 1630–32, for example, the parish officers of St Giles Cripplegate (Middlesex) paid out £8 3s., about half the sum that was annually disbursed in pensions, as 'rewardes' to those that discovered forfeitures amongst the poor.[50]

Such practices of surveillance were to be encouraged, argued Richard Dunning in 1685, for they might in themselves deter applicants from seeking relief. If the poor were forced 'once in a week or fortnight publicly to give an account of their demeanor' to the overseer, 'to whom they will soon give the title of bridewell keeper', he suggested, 'few or none will be willing to accept of relief from the parish on such terms'.[51] Such is 'the impudency of this age', feared the author of *An Ease for Overseers*, 'that many will dissemble their estates to have relief', perhaps even pleading 'to be recorded in the booke for the poore when they are better able to contribute to the poore'. If their households were readily inspected, however, their claims to indigence could easily be tested. Many 'whose maintenance otherwise would lie on the parish', argued Dunning, would strive to 'maintain a decrepit husband, wife or child rather than come under such weekly examination'.[52]

The suspension of relief could only, of course, be a temporary measure. If a pauper died for want of relief in late seventeenth-century England, the sense of shock was palpable: on 22 November 1674, the parish clerk of Wednesbury (Staffordshire) recorded that 'John Russel being famished through want of food (Josiah Freeman being overseer), was buried with the solemnity of many tears'.[53] Indeed, overseers had long been warned that 'if the poore be barred of the benefit of begging' and 'you supplie not their necesseties at home you are guiltie of their deaths if they perish for want of provision'. John Locke argued in 1697 'that if any person die for want of due relief in any parish in which he ought to be relieved, the said parish be fined according to the circumstances of the fact and the heinousness of the crime'. By 1795, Arthur Young could even argue that it was actually against the law to starve in England.[54] The penal administration of the poor laws was therefore designed not as a death sentence but as an exemplary sanction. As Robert Reyce argued in 1618, the poor laws were intended not only to diminish the numbers of the poor but also to 'reform' their 'quality'.[55]

The parish pension was therefore a product of a culture of dependency. Of course, the poor were always *expected* to be content with their lot, to demonstrate forbearance, honesty and civility, in their everyday encounters with their betters. The Essex clergyman John Rogers urged the poor to 'keep a good tongue though men deale not very well with you'. 'Carry yourselves dutifully and humbly towards the rich and all your superiors', he insisted, 'not saucy, surly, ill-tongued: [be] patient and meeke when you receive a reproofe and [do] not swell or give ill words'.[56] But Rogers recognised the extent to which these habits of deference and subordination might usefully be reinforced by the sanctions of the civil parish.[57] Those parish pensioners who idled or pilfered could, he argued, be 'well punisht, either by the whip, *or else their collection that week kept back*'. Only the institutionalised discretion of the overseer could ensure that the poor were disciplined. 'If they be not as well looked to' by parish officers, he argued, 'a greate many' of the poor would 'begge or steale rather than get [their living] by working'.[58] Other polemicists went further in their discursive construction of eligibility. In 1597, Henry Arthington condemned the poor 'misspending of former times in idleness when they might have wrought'; their 'wilful wasting of goods when they had them in bibbing and belly-cheare'; their 'impatient bearing of their present want, complaining often without cause'; 'their dayly repining at others prosperity to have so much and they so little'; 'their banning and cursing when they are not served as themselves desire'; and 'their seldom repairing to their parish churches to heare and learne their duties better'. All these faults, he argued, 'must be amended if they would have their wants supplyed'. Until then, it was entirely reasonable that overseers keep their purses closed.[59] The archives of magistracy and vestry alike suggest that Arthington's advice was taken very seriously not only by those who administered the Elizabethan poor laws, but also by those applicants for relief who identified themselves as deserving on the grounds of their civility and honesty.

Notes

1. The late Elizabethan relief statutes are 39 Elizabeth c. 3 (1598) and 43 Elizabeth c. 2 (1601). The best account of their origins and nature remains P. Slack, *Poverty and Policy in Tudor and Stuart England* (London and New York, 1988), pp. 122–9.
2. 2 Thessalonians 3:10.
3. For attitudes to vagrants, see C.S.L. Davies, 'Slavery and Protector Somerset: The Vagrancy Act of 1547', *Economic History Review*, 2nd ser., 19 (1966), pp. 533–49; and A.L. Beier, *Masterless Men: The Vagrancy Problem in England, 1580–1640* (London, 1985). For discrimination between the deserving and undeserving in late medieval England, see, for example, N.S. Rushton, 'Monastic Charitable Provision in Tudor England: Quantifying and Qualifying Poor Relief in the Early Sixteenth Century', *Continuity and Change*, 16 (2001), pp. 9–44.
4. For the distinctiveness of the 1598 legislation in this respect, see Slack, *Poverty and Policy*, p. 126.
5. Citing clause I of the 1598 statute 'for the reliefe of the poore'.
6. M. Dalton, *The Country Justice* (numerous edns: London, 1618, 1635, 1655, 1661, 1677, 1682, 1697, 1727).
7. Dalton, *The Country Justice* (1618), pp. 76–7.
8. Dalton, *The Country Justice* (1635), p. 101.
9. Dalton, *The Country Justice* (1643), p. 122, citing 11 Henry VII, c.2 (1495). This passage remained unchanged in all the subsequent editions down to 1727.
10. Dalton, *The Country Justice* (1618), p. 77; *Ibid.*, (1635), p. 101.
11. Cf. S. Hindle, *On the Parish?: The Micro-Politics of Poor Relief in Rural England, c.1550–1750* (Oxford, 2004), ch. 5; W.J. King, 'Punishment for Bastardy in Early Seventeenth-Century England', *Albion*, 10 (1978), pp. 130–51; A.J. Fletcher, *Reform in the Provinces: The Government of Stuart England* (New Haven, 1986), pp. 252–62.
12. J. Innes, 'Prisons for the Poor: English Bridewells, 1555–1800', in F. Snyder and D. Hay (eds), *Labour, Law and Crime: An Historical Perspective* (London, 1987), pp. 42–122.
13. On differing constructions of 'civility' at this time see, P. Burke, 'A Civil Tongue: Language and Politeness in Early Modern Europe', and B. Capp, 'Arson, Threats of Arson, and Incivility in Early Modern England', in P. Burke, B. Harrison and P. Slack (eds), *Civil Histories: Essays Presented to Sir Keith Thomas* (Oxford, 2000), pp. 31–48, 197–214, respectively.
14. M. Berlin, 'Reordering Rituals: Ceremony and the Parish, 1520–1640', in P. Griffiths and M. Jenner (eds), *Londinopolis: Essays in the Cultural and Social History of Early Modern London* (Manchester, 2000), pp. 59–60; P. Slack (ed.),

'Poverty in Early Stuart Salisbury', *Wiltshire Record Society*, 31 (1975), p. 88; P. Slack, 'Poverty and Politics in Salisbury, 1597–1666', in P. Clark and P. Slack (eds) *Crisis and Order in English Towns, 1500–1700: Essays in Urban History* (London, 1972), p. 185; J.C. Cox, *Bench-Ends in English Churches* (Oxford, 1916), p. 36.

15. C.S. Schen, *Charity and Lay Piety in Reformation London, 1500–1620* (Aldershot, 2002), p. 121; S. Amussen, 'Gender, Family and the Social Order, 1560–1725', in A.J. Fletcher and J. Stevenson (eds), *Order and Disorder in Early Modern England* (Cambridge, 1985), p. 213; J. Hill, 'Poverty and Poor Relief in Shropshire, 1550–1685' (Liverpool University Unpubl. MA Thesis, 1973), p. 142.

16. F.G. Emmison (ed.), *Early Essex Town Meetings: Braintree, 1619–1636, Finchingfield, 1626–1634* (Chichester, 1970), p.86; Harold Smith, *The Ecclesiastical History of Essex Under the Long Parliament and Commonwealth* (Colchester, 1933), pp. 142–3; Hertfordshire Archives and Local Services (HALS), D/P 65/3/3, pp. 27–8, 30, 32–40; D/P 102/5/1 (19 Sept. 1678); E.M. Hampson, *The Treatment of Poverty in Cambridgeshire, 1597–1834* (Cambridge, 1934), pp. 180, 240, n. 3; I.F. Jones, 'Aspects of Poor Law Administration, Seventeenth to Nineteenth Centuries, From Trull Overseers' Accounts', *Somerset Archaeological and Natural History Society Proceedings*, 95 (1951), p. 91.

17. Hill, 'Poverty and Poor Relief in Shropshire', p. 125; Northamptonshire Record Office, Northampton, QSR 1/176/2; P. Sharpe, *Population and Society in an East Devon Parish: Reproducing Colyton, 1540–1840* (Exeter, 2002), p. 234; S. Ottaway, 'The "Decline of Life": Aspects of Ageing in Eighteenth-Century England' (Brown University Unpubl. PhD Thesis, 1998), p. 176; B. Kerr, *Bound to the Soil: A Social History of Dorset, 1750–1918* (London, 1968), p. 93.

18. S.C. Ratcliff, H.C. Johnson and N.J. Williams (eds), *Warwick County Records* II (Warwick, 1935–64), pp. 85, 106. The sanctions were enforced in Seaborough (Dorset) as late as 1732. Ottaway, 'The "Decline of Life" ', p. 176, n. 64.

19. Hill, 'Poverty and Poor Relief in Shropshire', p. 142. For numerous other examples of, and general comments on, this practice, see C. Hill, *Society and Puritanism in Pre-Revolutionary England* (Harmondsworth, 1964), pp. 413–4; K. Wrightson, 'The Politics of the Parish in Early Modern England', in P. Griffiths, A. Fox and S. Hindle (eds), *The Experience of Authority in Early Modern England* (London, 1996), p. 19; J. Craig, *Reformation, Politics and Polemics: The Growth of Protestantism in East Anglian Market Towns, 1500–1610* (Aldershot, 2001), pp. 59–60.

20. Fletcher, *Reform in the Provinces*, p. 151; *Warwick County Records*, I, p. 141; II, p. 95; III, pp. 24–5; VII, pp. 30, 56; *Buckinghamshire Sessions Records*, I, p. 64. For a Cumberland order using similar language in 1708 see Cumbria Record Office, Carlisle, Q/11//88/11.

21. J.C. Atkinson (ed.), 'North Riding Quarter Sessions Records', *North Riding Record Society*, 1–9 (1884–92), VII, p. 24; CRO, Q/11/1/47/15. A hank was the measure of yarn, which varied according to the material from which it was spun.

22. J.M. Rosenheim (ed.), 'The Notebook of Robert Doughty, 1662–65', *Norfolk Record Society*, 54 (1989), p. 42 (emphasis added). Cf. T. Wales, 'Poverty, Poor Relief and the Life-Cycle: Some Evidence From Seventeenth-Century Norfolk', in R.M. Smith (ed.), *Land, Kinship and Life-Cycle* (Cambridge, 1984), p. 354.

23. *Buckinghamshire Sessions Records*, I, p. 99; *Warwick County Records*, VIII, p. 102. For the medieval view that alms should not be given in harvest time when work was plentiful, see C. Dyer, *Standards of Living in the Later Middle Ages: Social Change in England, c.1200–1520* (Cambridge, 1989), p. 237.

24. *Buckinghamshire Sessions Records*, I, p. 424; CRO, Q/11/1/20/11.

25. *Buckinghamshire Sessions Records*, I, p. 345; CRO, Q/11/1/42/12

26. Sharpe, *Population and Society*, p. 218; *Buckinghamshire Sessions Records*, I, p. 43; Hampson, *Treatment of Poverty in Cambridgeshire*, p. 181.

27. R. Dunning, *A Plain and Easie Method Shewing How the Office of Overseer of the Poor May be Managed* (London, 1685), p. 9.

28. J.S. Cockburn (ed.), 'Western Circuit Assize Orders, 1629–48: A Calendar', *Camden Society*, 4th ser., 17, (1976), nos 347, 388, 695, 705; *Warwick County Records*, III, pp. 124–5; V, pp. 220, 228; CRO, Q/11/1/42/1; P. Carter, 'Poor Relief Strategies: Women, Children and Enclosure in Hanwell, Middlesex, 1780–1816', *The Local Historian*, 25 (1995), pp. 169, 171.

29. *Early Essex Town Meetings*, p. 5; *Warwick County Records*, II, pp. 119, 200.

30. F.G. Emmison, 'Poor Relief Accounts of Two Rural Parishes in Bedfordshire, 1563–98', *Economic History Review*, 3 (1931–32), p. 111; E.H. Bates-Harbin (ed.), 'Quarter Sessions Records of the County of Somerset', *Somerset Record Society*, 23–4 (Taunton, 1907), p. 283; *Early Essex Town Meetings*, p. 101; NA, SP16/344/30/3; J. Lister (ed.), 'West Riding Sessions Records, 1597–1642', *Yorkshire Archaeological Society Record Series*, 3, 54 (1888–1915), II, pp. 26–7; CRO, Q/11/1/5/20, 57/23.

31. W. Newman-Brown, 'The Receipt of Poor Relief and Family Situation: Aldenham, Hertfordshire 1630–90', in Smith (ed.), *Land, Kinship and Life-Cycle*, p. 418; J. Broad, 'The Smallholder and Cottager After Disafforestation: A Legacy of Poverty?', in J. Broad and R. Hoyle (eds), *Bernwood: The Life and Afterlife of a Forest* (Preston, 1997), p. 103; CRO, Q/11/1/76/19, 99/3; 96/13, 102/11, 107/15, 115/4; P. Sharpe, 'Poor Children as Apprentices in Colyton, 1598–1830', *Continuity and Change*, 6 (1991), pp. 256–7; S.A. Cutlack, 'The Gnosall Records, 1679 to 1837: Poor Law Administration', *Collections for A History of Staffordshire, Part I* (1936), pp. 59–60.

32. Cutlack, 'Gnosall Records', p. 58; C.L. Ewen, *Witchcraft And Demonianism: A Concise Account Derived From Sworn Depositions And Confessions Obtained In The Courts Of England And Wales* (London, 1933), p. 33; A. Macfarlane, *Witchcraft in Tudor and Stuart England: A Regional and Comparative Study* (London, 1970), pp.172–6, 195–7, 205–6; K. Thomas, *Religion and the Decline of Magic: Studies in Popular Beliefs in Sixteenth and Seventeenth Century England* (London, 1971), pp. 505, 506–7, 509.

33. F.G. Emmison, 'The Care of the Poor in Elizabethan Essex: Recently Discovered Records', *Essex Review*, 62 (1953), p. 21; S. Hindle, 'Hierarchy and Community: The Swallowfield Articles of 1596', *Historical Journal*, 42 (1999), p. 850 (article 15).

34. *Western Circuit Assize Orders*, nos 455, 914; B.C. Redwood (ed.), 'Quarter Sessions Order Book, 1642–49', *Sussex Record Society*, 54, (1954), p. 201 (and cf. pp. 55, 72, 92, 146, 193); *Warwick County Records*, IV, pp. 46, 122; IX, p. 47; D.E. Howell James (ed.), 'Norfolk Quarter Sessions Order Book, 1650–57', *Norfolk Record Society*, 26 (1955), no. 1008 (and cf. no. 839); M. Barker-Read,

'The Treatment of the Aged Poor in Five Selected West Kent Parishes From Settlement to Speenhamland, 1662–1797' (Open University Unpubl. PhD Thesis, 1988), p. 75; W. Le Hardy (ed.), *Hertford County Records* 9 vols (Hertford, 1905–39), VI, p. 447; Ottaway, 'The "Decline of Life" ', p. 176.

35. *Warwick County Records*, I, p. 172. Doughty's case can be traced in *Warwick County Records*, I, pp. 19, 25, 60, 162; II, pp. 139, 141, 199, 251; III, p. 106.
36. *Buckinghamshire Sessions Records*, I, pp. 462, 472; II, 29, 259, 278; III, pp. 59, 62, 136, 214.
37. CRO, Q/11/1/102/27; Slack, *Poverty and Policy*, p. 107.
38. M.J. Braddick and J. Walter, 'Introduction: Grids of Power: Order, Hierarchy and Subordination in Early Modern Society', in *Ibid.* (eds), *Negotiating Power in Early Modern Society: Order, Hierarchy and Subordination in Britain and Ireland* (Cambridge, 2001), p. 33.
39. For what follows, see S. Hindle, 'Dependency, Shame and Belonging: Badging the Deserving Poor, *c.*1550–1750', *Cultural and Social History*, 1, 1 (January 2004), pp. 6–35.
40. This is the conclusion of the essays collected in T. Hitchcock. P. King and P. Sharpe (eds), *Chronicling Poverty: The Voices and Strategies of the English Poor, 1640–1840* (London and New York, 1997). For the agency of subordinate groups in general, see the essays in Braddick and Walter, *Negotiating Power*.
41. For useful discussions of the interpretative problems surrounding petitions of this kind, see J.S. Taylor, 'Voices in the Crowd: The Kirkby Lonsdale Township Letters, 1809–36', in Hitchcock *et al.*, *Chronicling Poverty*, pp. 112–14; D. Andrew, 'To the Charitable and Humane: Appeals for Assistance in the Eighteenth-Century London Press', in H. Cunningham and J. Innes (eds), *Charity, Philanthropy and Reform* (London and New York, 1998), pp. 91–3.
42. Cf. the correlation of overseers' accounts and parish registers in Hedenham (Norfolk) in the period 1662–1709 in Wales, 'Poverty, Poor Relief and the Life-Cycle', pp. 360–7.
43. T. Sokoll, 'Old Age in Poverty: The Record of Essex Pauper Letters, 1780–1834', in Hitchcock *et al.*, *Chronicling Poverty*, p. 135.
44. T.L. Auffenberg, 'Organised English Benevolence: Charity Briefs, 1625–1705' (Vanderbilt University Unpubl. PhD thesis, 1973), pp. 387–8 notes the comparatively large number of briefs issued in the early 1660s. For the suggestion that the rhetoric of sermons was quoted back to the authorities, especially at times of dearth, see Walter, 'Public Transcripts, Popular Agency and the Politics of Subsistence in Early Modern England', in Braddick and Walter, *Negotiating Power*, p. 276, n. 65.
45. For these examples, see Lancashire Record Office, Preston, QSP/830/2; CRO, Q/11/1/6/6, 74/2. For petitions for relief more generally, see Hindle, *On the Parish?*, chs 6, 4.
46. This was the explicit intention behind the Norwich census of the poor of 1570: W. Hudson and J.C. Tingey (eds), *The Records of the City of Norwich*, II (Norwich and London, 1910), p. 344. Cf. J. Pound, 'An Elizabethan Census of the Poor: The Treatment of Vagrancy in Norwich, 1570–1580', *University of Birmingham Historical Journal*, 8 (1962), p. 143; and J.F. Pound (ed.), 'The Norwich Census of the Poor 1570', *Norfolk Record Society*, 40 (1971).
47. Sharpe, *Population and Society*, pp. 219–20.

48. K. Wrightson and D. Levine, *Poverty and Piety in an English Village: Terling, 1525–1700* (2nd edn, Oxford, 1995), chs 5–7; D. Underdown, *Fire From Heaven: Life in an English Town in the Seventeenth Century* (London, 1992), ch. 3. Cf. M. Spufford, 'Puritanism and Social Control?', in A.J. Fletcher and J. Stevenson (eds), *Order and Disorder in Early Modern England* (Cambridge, 1985), pp. 41–58. For a judicious summary of this debate P. Slack, *From Reformation to Improvement: Public Welfare in Early Modern England* (Oxford, 1998), pp. 53–76.

49. Bodleian Library, Oxford, MS Tanner, 73, f. 390.

50. NA, SP16/226/78.

51. Dunning, *A Plain and Easie Method*, p. 13.

52. Anon., *An Ease for Overseers of the Poore: Abstracted from the Statutes* (Cambridge 1601), p. 29; Dunning, *A Plain and Easie Method*, p. 13.

53. P. Laslett, *The World We Have Lost Further Explored* (London, 1983), p. 133.

54. *An Ease for Overseers of the Poore*, p. 30; J. Locke, 'An Essay on the Poor Law', in M. Goldie (ed.), *John Locke, Political Writings* (Cambridge, 1997), p. 198. Cf. T.A. Horne, *Property Rights and Poverty: Political Argument in Britain, 1605–1834* (Chapel Hill, 1990), pp. 64–5; A.L. Beier, ' "Utter Strangers to Industry, Morality and Religion": John Locke on the Poor', *Eighteenth-Century Life*, 12 (1988), p. 34; R. Wells, *Wretched Faces: Famine in Wartime England, 1763–1803* (Gloucester, 1988), p. 288

55. F. Hervey (ed.), *Suffolk in the XVIIth Century: The Breviary of Suffolk by Robert Reyce* (London, 1902), p. 57.

56. J. Rogers, *A Treatise of Love* (London, 1632), p. 237.

57. Cf. K. Wrightson, *English Society, 1580–1680* (London, 1982), p. 181.

58. Rogers, *A Treatise of Love*, pp. 212–3, 232 (emphasis added).

59. H. Arthington, *Provision for the Poore, Now in Penurie* (London, 1597), p. 11.

2
Social Inequality, Identity and the Labouring Poor in Eighteenth-century England

Peter King

Partly in response to the fragmentation of identities, and to the celebration of difference and diversity, which characterise our times, eighteenth-century historians have become increasingly aware in recent years of the many dimensions that can shape social identity. The detailed research they have done on the now venerable trinity of gender, race and class, and on a range of other sources of identity – nation, ethnicity, wealth, consumption, disability, age, sexual preference, religion, family, locality or mobility – has shown how varied the nature, meanings and impacts of each can be. This has produced some excellent and deeply contextualised histories, some of which have defined as well as reconstructed these categories.[1] However, the huge range of directions taken by this research has itself raised a number of questions. In particular it now seems necessary to ask – have historians become so focused on the plurality of forces that shaped individual senses of identity, that we are in danger of losing sight of the core elements in experiences and ways of thinking (both about self and others) which shaped the lives and actions of people in the eighteenth century? This chapter explores two important aspects of this question in relation to one specific social group – the rural labouring poor. First it looks at the degree to which various forms of social inequality moulded not only the experiences of the labouring poor but also their sense of who they were. Social inequality had many roots, many strands – in eighteenth-century England two central and intimately connected elements being the poor's experience of (often extreme) poverty and their subjection to various forms of subordination. To what extent was the poor's sense of who they were shaped by those inequalities? This leads to a second and related question – to what degree did the labouring poor still have agency? Did these structural inequalities shape the poor's senses of identity so greatly that they felt themselves to have little or no choice, no capacity to act meaningfully to reconfigure their world? What, in other words, were the cognitive consequences of poverty and subjection on the labouring poor's capacity for action?

Recent historical research has done much to restore our sense of the agency exercised by the eighteenth-century poor. Even beggars, Tim Hitchcock's recent work has shown, could often be choosers. The poor adopted many strategies to deal with the fragility and sparseness of their material worlds. Their makeshift economies were often magnificently ingenious. Their threatening letters were highly insubordinate. The letters that those who lived away from their parishes of settlement wrote requesting relief mixed strategic threats of costly and unwelcome returns, with finely tuned pleas of hardship and deferential references to their respectability, their self-help initiatives and their attempts to find work.[2] This chapter will not, however, focus on either anonymous letters or pauper letters, revealing though they are about two completely different sets of strategies used by the labouring poor in their relations with those who held property and power in their communities. Instead it will focus on a potentially rich but methodologically complex source – autobiographies. In particular the essentially private memoir/autobiography produced by the Buckinghamshire labourer, Joseph Mayett will be explored to uncover the ways he defined his world and himself.[3] This essentially hidden transcript will be analysed in the context of other less completely private plebeian writings, such as the autobiographical accounts left by Mary Saxby and John Clare (both of whom, like Mayett, lived out most of their lives in the three predominantly rural East Midlands counties of Buckinghamshire, Bedfordshire and Northamptonshire).[4] The core aim will be to assess how central experiences of social inequality were in the making of plebeian identities during this period, and the extent to which the resulting sense of identity affected individuals' capacity both to take action against those who constrained them, and to develop alternative sources of identity.

(I)

Such a project is, of course, fraught with methodological difficulties. Some of these are common to all studies of autobiography – authorship issues, reliability, deliberate or unconscious misrepresentation, selectivity, genre constraints, typicality or editorial policy.[5] Other difficulties are specific to this particular project and revolve around the nature and definition of social identity, and around the specific issues that arise when an autobiography is used to analyse the writer's social identity. Defining social identity as 'our vision of ourselves in the context of others' or more precisely as, following Jenkins, 'our understanding of who we are and who other people are', along with 'other people's understanding of themselves and others (which includes us)' is not especially difficult.[6] However, using it as an analytical tool is much more challenging. Among the many overlapping issues that need to be kept in mind, perhaps the most obvious is that identity is negotiated. It is a process and yet it can be thought of not only as a dynamic but also as a structure. Moreover, some types of identity are more dynamic and more negotiable than others. (Family and race, for example, are less negotiable.) Since identity is created at the interface of the personal and the social a wide range of further questions inevitably arise when it is used. For example, how much are our identities structured by forces beyond our control, and do some privileged (or simply richer) categories of persons have more opportunities to take up a variety of identities?[7] Equally, at a more complex level – to what extent do we have to identify with an identity in order to be shaped by it, and/or do social structures or discourses themselves recruit people into identities, drawing them in almost subconsciously and structuring their world and the way they see that world.[8]

Other questions about the nature of social identity, and its usefulness as a concept, come particularly strongly into focus when we attempt to use it in analysing autobiographical writings. One problem, for example, lies in the fact that social identity is both internal – what we think our identity is – and external – how others see us. Identities are formed, developed and deepened by the dynamic interaction between these two.[9] Unfortunately, however, autobiographies can, at best, only tell us what each writer thinks about her/his identity. A good autobiography may also record some of the reactions of others to the writer and may even occasionally record the labels they put on the writer, but they never give us a full view of the interaction between the internal and the external. Equally it is extremely difficult to analyse the extent to which the author of any specific autobiography was constrained by the relatively narrow range of discourses available to him or her, or by the specific genres she/he either chose to adopt or was unconsciously influenced by. Did those who wrote plebeian autobiographies feel the need to stay within a specific and established genre or discourse, or did they have the capacity in both linguistic and material terms to break free from those constraints when they felt it necessary to do so?[10] Many of these questions remain very hard to answer. Modern social psychologists have found it difficult enough to uncover the processes by which individuals come to conceptualise themselves in terms of social categories, roles or identities, even when working with subjects who can be interviewed and observed during social interactions. Clearly these problems are multiplied when dealing with the authors of eighteenth- and early nineteenth-century autobiographies. All individuals need social maps which tell them approximately where they are and where others are, but the process by which individuals draw these maps, or have them drawn for them by structures outside their control (or even consciousness) can only occasionally be glimpsed in any detail.[11]

Autobiographical accounts are also difficult to use for more empirical reasons. Many contain very little material that can be used to get any idea of either the writer's sense of their own identity or of the ways their significant others would have described or seen them. The many purely religious autobiographies published in the eighteenth and early nineteenth centuries are a good example of this, as are most of the soldier's autobiographies that survive – the former concentrating almost entirely on spiritual battles and the latter on physical ones.[12] However, a small number of more general, and much less genre-constrained autobiographical accounts have come down to us from rural labouring men and women of the long eighteenth century and these offer a broad range of insights into many different aspects of social identity.

These sources are extremely patchy. Some facets of identity are foregrounded in one autobiography but almost entirely ignored in others. The autobiography of Joseph Mayett, for example, contains virtually no direct insights on race or ethnicity. However, the autobiographies of both Mary Saxby and John Clare contain some very interesting, if isolated, insights into these two issues. On a rare trip to London, John Clare recorded the following encounter, which corroborates Norma Myers' recent suggestion that 'the labouring classes displayed sympathy towards black people'.[13] 'I remember passing by St Pauls one morning', he wrote with his usual erratic spelling and lack of punctuation, 'where stood a poor African silently soliciting charity but the sincerity of his distress spoke plainer than words I felt my pockets but I had only four pence in all and I felt almost ashamed to receive the poor creatures thanks for so worthless a pittance ... I determined the next day to get my pocket recruited if possible and give him a shilling and my first walk was to St Pauls but the poor affican was gone and I never saw him again.'[14] Clare also spent a lot of time with the gypsies who regularly camped in his Northamptonshire parish. He obviously enjoyed their company, and although his description of them was not uncritical he clearly thought more of them than of the local elite. 'I must confess I found them far more honest than their callumniators' he wrote. He was also greatly angered by the prejudices of the propertied towards them. 'An ignorant iron hearted Justice of the Peace ... whose name may perish with his cruelty', he wrote, 'mixd up this malicious sentence in his condemnation of 2 gypseys ... "This atrosious tribe of wandering vagabonds ought to be made outlaws in every civilizd kingdom and exterminated from the face of the earth".'[15] Mary Saxby had a more mixed experience. In late adolescence she met a group of gypsies and, fascinated by 'an exceedingly good dancer' and loving him 'almost to distraction' she 'consented to cohabit with him' having received promises of marriage. However, after a year he 'fixed on another woman' and demanded that Mary perform the role of 'a secondary wife or servant' – a situation that she had great difficulty in escaping from. Thus, although she became deeply involved in the gypsy lifestyle and spent three separate periods travelling with them, during which she 'acquired all the manners of the gypsies ... and was every way like them excepting in colour', Mary remained deeply ambivalent about them.[16]

Given our lack of understanding of plebeian (and particularly rural plebeian) attitudes to such issues, these autobiographies can add considerably to our knowledge, despite the obvious problems raised by typicality and reliability. Some potential sources of identity are, of course, much more difficult to investigate in these sources than others. For example, deep social constraints operating on various levels meant that discussions of sexual preferences are rarely if ever found in the plebeian writings of this period. Clearly the dangers of constructing arguments from silence when using these sources are immense. The lack of discussion of, or apparent interest in, ideas about nation in these three plebeian texts raises fascinating questions, for example, but silence cannot, of course, be read as indifference. This is well illustrated by the different ways these texts approach issues relating to gender.

The male-authored autobiographies of Clare and Mayett are almost completely devoid of any overall discussion of gender roles or hierarchies and give very little space to their relationships with their wives.[17] In the female-authored texts, by contrast, issues of gender loom large, and the roles played by fathers and especially by husbands are described in detail. The early part of Mary Saxby's account describes her escape from her gypsy dancer's attempts to subject her to oppressive household arrangements that were not of her choosing. The later parts not only include considerable information on her husband's drunkenness and violence towards her, they also implicitly and explicitly interweave the themes of extreme poverty and husbandly neglect. 'I was in deep distress of body and mind' she wrote after having twins, 'My ... husband was at the alehouse most of the time; whilst I and my children wanted the common necessities of life.' While she was recovering from the death of one of the twins she describes how her husband 'was all the time usually drinking and swearing at an alehouse and when he did come to me, which was but seldom, it was only to upbraid and threaten to throw me out of the window if I did not get up and do for my family'.[18]

The brief autobiographical sketch left to us by 'the Suffolk cottager', Ann Candler, written in 1801 after 20 years in Tattingstone workhouse, has a similar set of recurrent themes. She writes at length about her husband's drunkenness, lying and deceitfulness, about his regular disappearances in order to try to enlist, and about his fateful attempt to set up house in London with Ann and the children, which resulted in Ann having to sell her few possessions and enter the workhouse where, she records, 'all my prospects of comfort ended'.[19] Moreover her sense that there was always a vital relationship between prosperity/poverty and the character of a woman's husband also comes out in her description of her children. 'My daughter Lucy is married' she wrote, 'and is, I believe, in the true sense of the words, the contented happy cottager! Her husband is a very sober industrious man'.[20] Ann was writing her autobiography as part of a plea for help to get her out of the workhouse, and it would certainly have been tactically useful therefore to blame her troubles on her drunken husband. However, in both Saxby and Candler's accounts a strong sense of the relationship between vulnerability to poverty and the problems created by gendered roles and expectations, as well as by drunken deceitful husbands, form a central thread. Paradoxically another major theme is their husbands' failure at most times and in most places to gain any consistent control over these two women's everyday lives. Ann's experience led her to 'renounce the idea of ever living with him (her husband) again' and she never did so. Mary Saxby continued to go to chapel on Sundays despite the fact that her much-absent husband persecuted her for it and threatened several times to throw boiling water over her.[21] The apparent failure of these two men to construct a meaningful mesh of patriarchal authority in their households, and the complex emotional relationships between these women and their husbands requires a deeper study than is possible here. What is clear, however, is that while their husbands' failings shaped Mary and

Ann's material lives and experiences, those same husbands, despite their resort to verbal or physical violence, found it extremely difficult to exert any consistent authority or influence over them.[22] Fear of want and freedom from male authority may often have appeared like two sides of the same coin to such women. Thus, in a comparison of the autobiographies of Mayett and Clare with those of Saxby and Candler, the men's silence on gender issues stands in stark contrast to the women's willingness to articulate the extent to which gendered expectations and roles shaped their lives. However, the men's silence should not be interpreted as indicating a lack of importance. Rather it reflected, it seems, the relative gender blindness of men in a world of highly unequal wages, work opportunities and role expectations for men and women, which worked so greatly in favour of the former that they took it for granted.

Even from this brief discussion, which has not even touched on other issues such as the roles of age and lifecycle or of mobility and locality, it is therefore clear that the methodological problems associated with attempting to use autobiographies to think about notions of social identity are not inconsiderable. However, if the texts and themes to be studied are chosen carefully and are properly contextualised, these sources also offer a range of opportunities to interrogate key aspects of issues of identity. The rest of this chapter will explore Joseph Mayett's autobiography in order to analyse the extent to which these sources can help the historian to assess certain key elements in the making of social identities, and the extent to which those identities constrain the individual's actions and agency.

(II)

Joseph Mayett's autobiography has four characteristics that make it particularly interesting in attempting to investigate these issues of identity. First, it is essentially a private document. It was not written for publication. Indeed, although penned in the early 1830s it was not published until the 1980s. Thus, for a century and a half after it was written it remained, almost literally, a hidden transcript. There is no indication that Joseph Mayett wished it to be published or designed it for publication. Nor is there any indication that it was edited (as Mary Saxby's was to a limited extent). Joseph did not need to write a text that would be approved by those who were aiding or financing its publication. Nor did he have to kowtow to those whom he was beholden to by patronage links, or from whom he hoped to extract material help in the future. This text was not written with an elite, propertied audience in mind.

There is no attempt to disguise the writer's disgust at the arrogance, stupidity or corrupt motives of his superiors. The squire, the overseers, the constable and the vestry all get short shrift here as they also do in Clare's private writings such as his poem 'The Parish'. This, then, is a private transcript. Joseph Mayett wrote it believing (correctly it seems), that it would not be seen by those who had material sway or significant authority in the community in which he lived.[23]

Second, the text's narrative structure is fairly open. Unlike many nineteenth-century workingmen's autobiographies Mayett's text is not a story of progress or a narrative of improvement. This is no 'ploughtail to Parliament' saga. Nor is it the account of someone (such as Francis Place, William Hutton or Olaudah Equiano) who began their life as a labouring man or a slave but later achieved respectability, property ownership and middling status before writing their autobiography.[24] The narrative has a circular rather than a progressive or unilinear feel. It has been argued that it is a story of decline but this is not the core theme. If it had a title, which it does not, it might well be similar to that used by John Harriott in his equally neglected (though non-plebeian) autobiography – *Struggles through Life*. In part this fluidity is perhaps linked to the fact that the final section of the text is on the borderland between a diary and a reflective biographical memoir. However, it also mirrors the author's deep ambivalence about his life and about the notion that the accumulation of wealth was, of itself, a worthwhile goal.[25]

Why did Joseph write this autobiography? The text contains few clues about this but three themes are useful in exploring this question – vindication, salvation/sanctification and confession.

It may be that the text is at least partly about vindication. Mayett is at pains on many occasions to explain and describe his attempts to act fairly towards other branches of his family and kin (particularly towards his father and brothers), as well as towards other members of the nonconformist and very poor church to which he belonged for a very considerable part of his life. Self-critical in other matters and willing to admit to many failings he stoutly maintained that 'I always in the worst of my conduct abhored dishonisty.'[26] A more important theme perhaps was salvation/sanctification. Mayett's account can certainly be read as, in the main, an attempt to record his spiritual journey. There is much here about his attempts, however unsuccessful, to follow what he conceived of as a Christian path – both as an individual struggling with his own propensity to sin, and as part of a grouping of local believers whose ups and downs are a major thread within the narrative. By the time he wrote his autobiography, religion clearly played an important role in

Mayett's sense of identity and his Christian life comes across as an area in which he made many choices. Kussmaul describes the agenda of the text as 'Joseph Mayett's Trials on the Road to Salvation' and there are parts in which this does become a recurring theme. But this is not the usual tale of a journey from the Wilderness to the Promised Land. In a typical evangelical/nonconformist autobiography, hundreds of which were written in this period, a small group of religious themes recur time and time again – early spiritual education, Sabbath keeping and Sabbath breaking, paths of vice and paths of virtue, conversion experiences, seminal sermons, falling into former ways and spiritual rejuvenation. However, frustratingly for the historian these texts usually contain virtually nothing of worth about other events, work experiences, material circumstances, or wider social relationships.[27] Mayett's autobiography is different. Some of the spiritual elements are there and they are not unimportant. But at the core of the text is a lived life, a sense of struggle, a sense of community, a sense of life's unpredictability – its strange conjunctions, its material problems, its ideological battles, its structures of authority, its small strategic opportunities, its successes and its defeats. It is not therefore primarily, as Kussmaul suggests, 'a late example of confessional writing in the puritan tradition'. The language of Bunyan and the Bible is there and so is youthful folly (swearing, drinking, stealing and whoring) viewed from a later religious perspective. Equally a recurring subtext is the fitful growth of Joseph's core ideology – the hope of salvation by faith. However the text is constantly returning to the material base of Mayett's life and to his social interactions rather than to his purely spiritual journey. Many religious autobiographies, Pascal has argued, 'fail to see the outer world or themselves as persons' but this is not an accusation that can fairly be levelled at Joseph Mayett.[28] The mixed nature of the genres in which Mayett wrote therefore offers substantial opportunities to analyse his sense of who he was and who others were, of his external as well as his internal world.

A third strength of Mayett's autobiographical writings is the large number of occasions on which his story can be authenticated in other sources such as baptism and marriage records, chapel archives and overseers' account books.[29] For example, at the beginning of June 1829 the autobiography records three events in fairly rapid succession. Mayett is discharged by his master, has his parish pay reduced by a third, and then (following his opposition to this) the parish refuses to give him any relief at all. The overseer's account book follows precisely the same pattern. No payments are recorded to Mayett in May. Then a payment of 5*s*. for five days work is recorded on the 6 June. This is then reduced by a third to 3*s*. 4*d*. for five days work on 13 June, following which no further payments are made to Mayett that summer.[30]

A final reason why this autobiography is particularly useful in this context is that Mayett's background and the trajectory of his life journey fit very well with the task chosen here – to focus on the rural labouring poor. Joseph Mayett's father was an agricultural labourer in the Buckinghamshire parish of Quainton, a working man who lived on the edge of poverty. Joseph's mother and father became first partly, and then wholly, dependent on parish relief in their old age, and lived on the cusp of poor relief dependency well before they reached that point in the lifecycle. Joseph himself fared little better. The family's poverty meant that he was put very early to lacemaking with his mother. At 14 he became a yearly servant in husbandry working for various masters until he joined up as a soldier in the militia at the age of 20. He remained a soldier until he was 32, returning to Quainton in 1815. He then did a variety of jobs – mixing general labouring work with other temporary employment as ragman, peddler, yeast salesman, milking man, carter and hayward of the open field. Although he occasionally tried to strike out on his own he effectively remained a wage labourer all his life.[31] He lived and died as a member of the English rural labouring poor.

(III)

Mayett begins his account by locating his family spatially and then describing them with three adjectives. 'I Joseph Mayett was born in the Parish of Quainton in the Vale of Aylesbury in Buckinghamshire', he wrote, 'of poor but I trust of honist and religous parents'. In doing so he was following a fairly standard format for the opening of such a text, but these words – poor, honest, religious – are also expressive of three very important and recurrent themes in the author's account and were integral to his sense of who he was and who he wanted to be seen to be. He clearly acted vigorously to create and sustain a reputation as 'honest' among his family and neighbours, for example. Equally, the autobiography provides much evidence of the importance he attached to his own religious journey, as well as to his deep involvement in the collective enterprise (or 'cause' as he called it) of setting up a new nonconformist chapel in his community. However, this chapter will argue that Mayett's experience of poverty and social inequality, and his reactions to the abiding sense of being 'poor' which surrounded him throughout his life, need to be seen not just as one amongst many factors, but as a central core in the making of his sense of who he was.[32]

Mayett's account is suffused with descriptions of his experiences of poverty and at times of near destitution. The first page makes it clear that he saw poverty as having structured his life-chances. 'Through the narrowness of our circumstances', he wrote, 'I was deprived of ... education, for instead of being sent to school I was set to lace making to provide something of a livelihood.' The first page also locates his family firmly amongst those to whom the avoidance of dependence on poor relief was considered a major achievement. 'My father was a labourer', he wrote, 'and worked ... without any assistance from the parish till I was nine years of age.'[33] From his early teens onwards Joseph was largely sheltered from any direct experiences of want by a long series of hirings as a living in servant, but this was not to last. Mayett first became aware of the struggles ahead when his master dismissed him without reason in the near-famine year of 1800. 'The cares of the world laid hold on me', he wrote, 'and now I began to wonder what I should do for bread'. In the same year this question became a real one. 'Through the dearness of provisions', he wrote, 'I was obliged to live chiefly on barley bread and hog peas.'[34] His 12 years in the army between 1803 and 1815 did not necessarily mean that he was free from the spectre of want. At one point a fraudulent pay sergeant left him 'soon reduced to a state of destress weakness through hungar', but on the whole he was relatively secure from extreme want during his time in the army. Matters soon took a major turn for the worse, however, after his return to civilian life in 1815. Newly married and stuck in an overstocked post-war labour market, he immediately found he 'was out of work' and despite having adopted various strategies this began a period of increasingly acute anxiety and material distress.[35] 'I began to be in very narrow circumstances in life', he wrote, 'Bread was very dear so that poor people could not buy any'. He was forced to think about the 'very few of my goods that I had to sell' and to face the fact that what might be called the terms of trade were set against him. As he ruefully recorded 'there was such a contrast in all sorts of trade at that time so that all things the poor had to sell was very low and all kind of provission was very dear'. By June 1817 when 'bread was three shillings per loaf' and he was earning only 7*s*. a week, he again recorded that 'I was much destressed'. Although after harvest 'things ... began to take a favourable turn' because he got work at 10*s*. a week and bread had fallen to 2*s*., his wages were once again reduced when winter came.[36] The fragile makeshift economy of Joseph and his new wife was vulnerable not only to low wages and underemployment but also to illness and other unforeseen circumstances. When their landlord died in 1820, for example, they were turned out of their house and compelled to take out another tenancy at nearly twice the rent. Things deteriorated even further the next winter when Mayett's master discharged him and the parish refused to employ or relieve him. When he was finally employed it was at only 6s. a week and with more than 3s. going out in rent and fuel and his wife ill and needing a carer, this left him once again with only the price of one loaf a week. He was back on the bread line. Mayett shored things up to some extent by taking a job as a milking man for a local farmer. This involved a 16-hour day (including Sundays) and he hated it, but as he so succinctly put it. 'I was forced to go or starve so I went.'[37]

By the mid-1820s the Mayetts, both in their forties by now, began to suffer increasingly from illness. First Joseph's wife and then Joseph himself needed medical attention. Discharged by his master 'because he had nothing for me to do', Mayett failed to get help from the parish for more than a couple of weeks and could only earn about 5 or 6s. a week in June, July and early August. This, he records, 'brought me into a very weak state for want of the common necessaries of life'. Desperate to make good harvest money he went into Hertfordshire, but after having to sleep in the wet he 'caught a very bad cold and being so weak before it settled in my chest and ruined my constitution.' Attacked by spasms in the chest, Joseph attempted to continue working and found employment for a couple of months on the roads until, as his account records on the 27 November 'I was took with a pain in my left side near my heart and was compeled to give up my work.' Although Mayett went twice to Oxford to seek medical advice and was given free medicines 'as I was a poor man' he did not recover. He was now labelled incurable and declared as 'in a very dangerous state'.[38]

Joseph put down his pen at this point, but although he left us no information about the final decade of his life, the overseer's accounts make it clear he never recovered. As the new decade began he and his wife slid into dependency. As Figure 2.1 shows, from 1828 until the overseers' account books cease with the coming of the New Poor Law in 1835, Joseph Mayett was a regular receiver. At first, as his autobiography records, he received only 2s. 9d. from the parish. However this had increased to 5s. by May 1831, probably because the extensive payments he received at first from his local friendly society were by then being reduced. Joseph and his wife did not, however, manage to maintain this level of relief. By 1834 Table 2.2 shows that their payments had been reduced to 3s. per week. A more detailed analysis of the Quainton overseers' accounts in Tables 2.1 and 2.2 suggest that they may have been particularly poorly supported by the parish. The general profile of

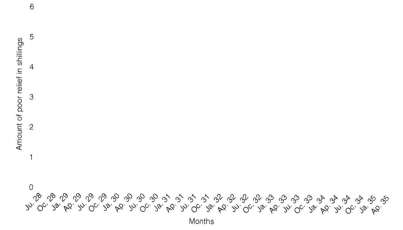

Figure 2.1 Joseph Mayett's monthly poor relief payments, Quainton, Bucks., July 1828–June 1835

Table 2.1 General poor relief levels in Quainton, Bucks., 1833 and 1834 compared to Joseph Mayett's poor relief payments

Amount in shillings given to all regular receivers	Sept. 1833 number	Sept. 1834 number
Less than 1/-	2	9
1/-	11	3
1/6	2	4
2/-	6	6
2/6	8	7
3/-	5	9***
3/6	4***	5
4/-	8	8
4/6	2	1
5/-	3	2
5/6	0	2
6/-	1	2
6/6	0	1
Total	52	59

Note: *** = Joseph Mayett's Level.
Source: BRO PR 169/12/12.

Table 2.2 Poor relief levels for different types of regular receiver, Quainton, Bucks., September 1834

Amount in Shillings given to:	Widowers	'Men and wives'	Widows	Illegitimate children	Families (4–5 children)
<1/-	0	0	2	0	7
1/-	0	0	2	1	0
1/6	0	0	0	2	2
2/-	0	0	3	3	0
2/6	0	0	6	1	0
3/-	2	2***	5	0	0
3/6	2	0	3	0	0
4/-	5	1	2	0	0
4/6	0	1	0	0	0
5/-	0	2	0	0	0
5/6	0	2	0	0	0
6/-	0	2	0	0	0
6/6	0	1	0	0	0
Total	9	11	23	7	9

Note: *** = Joseph Mayett's Level.
Source: BRO PR 169/12/12.

regular recipients of relief in Quainton illustrated in Table 2.1 puts them around or just below the average level of payments but this is very misleading. In September 1834 the receivers were broken down into five groups, as shown in Table 2.2, and from this it is clear that the Mayetts were the lowest paid husband and wife team on the list. This may have reflected the fact that they were still receiving some help from a friendly society or from another charity. Or it may be that Joseph's wife, Sarah, was still able to achieve reasonable earnings. At 55, two years after Joseph's death she was described as a 'lacemaker' in the 1841 census. Finally the low level of payment to the Mayetts in 1834 may reflect the negative attitudes of some vestry members towards them. Whatever the reason, the coming of the New Poor Law makes it very difficult to analyse their situation around the time of Joseph's death in 1839. The union relieving officer's records do not survive for the appropriate union after 1835, but although the Mayetts may well have avoided admission to the workhouse,[39] the union was increasingly stringent in its payments. By 1838 the Quainton rates were down from over £1000 to under £500. After Joseph's death a stray surviving account book records his wife Sarah as receiving 2s. and a six-penny loaf in August of

Table 2.3   Female poor relief levels in Quainton, Bucks., 1839

Amount in shillings given to females	Number receiving
<1/-	2
1/-	5
1/6	5
2/-	4***
2/6	11
3/-	3
3/6	0
4/-	2
4/6	0
5/-	0
5/6	0
Total	32

Note: *** = Widow Mayett's Relief Level.
Source: BRO D/X 118.

that year – a figure which Table 2.3 shows was once again below the usual norm in the parish.[40] The Mayetts' fragile makeshift economy, which had looked so vulnerable even when they remained healthy, had finally begun to break down in 1830 leaving then increasingly dependent on the poor law system in a decade of reform and retrenchment.

Until 1830 the Mayetts were probably not any worse off than the majority of early nineteenth-century Southern labourers caught in the flooded rural labour market of the post-war years. They may have been slightly better off because they never had any children and managed (perhaps because of this) to keep up small payments to a benefit society. However, despite the fact that historians have heralded this period as the age of the consumer revolution, there is very little evidence in Mayett's autobiography that might indicate that patterns of consumption played an important part in shaping his identity. The only goods he describes in his account are the pitifully few household possessions he is forced to sell in order to obtain bread. In 1817, for example, Joseph recorded that bread being 'very dear' his family fell into debt and he and his wife were forced to sell their prized possession – a large bell-mettle pot – and trade down to a tin boiler instead. Labouring men and women were not, of course, excluded entirely from the world of goods.[41] As Beverly Lemire, John Styles and others have recently shown, for example, the poor were substantial consumers of a range of clothing items.

During adolescence and young adulthood, in particular, clothes could be very important to them, performing various social, economic and sexual functions. Like William Hutton, who struggled long and hard in his adolescence to buy a good suit of clothes, Mary Saxby understood the potential usefulness of the right clothing. Taking advantage of a shipwreck which released a large quantity of cheap checks and muslins onto the market, she used her meagre resources 'to get clothed for a trifle' and records that 'having made myself clean and smart' she was then able to join forces for a while with 'a decent woman' who 'sold hardware'.[42] Even in young adulthood, however, Mary had few possessions and she was vulnerable to losing even these when she got into difficulties. When her arm went lame while she was employed in weeding corn, Mary found herself near destitute and recorded that she 'sold what things I had and was forced to bow my stubborn spirit and go to my father, in a poor plight'.[43]

Even those young adults who achieved fairly long periods of relative financial independence could, however, very rarely expect to remain in such a position once they were married. The household economies of the vast majority of Southern labouring families became highly precarious in their late twenties, thirties, and well into their forties, as the number of dependent children who were still at home became significant. Some couples returned to a better financial position in their late forties and fifties, once their children were largely grown up and/or earning some income. For many (and perhaps most) labouring families, however, there appears to have been no such long-term hiatus before illness, widowhood or old age, and the resultant inability to obtain adequate earnings, brought near destitution and increasing dependency.[44] The Mayetts' hampered by illness, never enjoyed a mid-life renaissance of disposable income and semi-luxury spending. Indeed it was in their forties that they gradually slipped into dependence on welfare payments. Nor did either Mary Saxby or Ann Candler enjoy such a period. Ann Candler faced by 'the horrors of extreme poverty in the midst of strangers', and effectively deserted in London by her husband, sold most of her goods, returned home and 'came as privately as I could into this [work]house'. At 45, Mary Saxby faced her widowhood with virtually no possessions at all. Following her husband's death in 1782 she was 'left, a poor disconsolate widow, with five children, four of them young'. 'I was left deeply in debt', she wrote, 'I sold what I had and discharged all our debts ... I then applied to the parish for assistance: and for a short time they gave me three shillings weekly, but soon reduced this allowance.' For the rest of her forties Mary then found herself in a classic poverty trap. At first, having four small children still at home she was given relief and allowed to live in a parish house. However, by the time two of her children had left home her weekly allowance had been cut off and she was forced out of her accommodation by the threat that 'if I did not remove, they would put a man and his wife, and six children into it with me'.[45]

Not all of the labouring poor or those on poor relief lived in houses completely devoid of household goods, as recent work on pauper inventories has shown. Labouring families were not always in debt and some acquired various forms of material goods during better times, by inheritance or during the period of their lives when they were no longer burdened with family responsibilities and not yet too old, isolated or ill to earn a living. However, reading Mayett's or Saxby's accounts in years of crisis can seem rather like being introduced to a dynamic and personalised version of the family budgets collected by Eden and Davies in Southern England in the 1780s and 1790s – accounts that show the fragile, debt-ridden, bread-dependent nature of many labouring families.[46] Many of the adult labouring poor at most stages in their lifecycle were too poor, or too indebted to be significant consumers of non-essentials. They simply did not have ownership of the means of consumption in any meaningful sense. In times of crisis they often lost even the meagre world of goods they had acquired. Hog peas and barley bread were not a lifestyle choice but a badge of poverty and a sign of desperation.

The eighteenth-century poor had considerable experience of brands and branding, but the brands that influenced their sense of identity were the parish brands with which overseers marked the furniture of the poor so that the parish could later retake possession of them in order to recoup some of the relief spent on a pauper household during its lifetime. John Clare's biting satire, 'The Parish', arose out of his direct experience of this brand. His father, already disabled and unable to earn a living, had also suffered another misfortune. The old apple tree in his garden which had 'made shift to make up the greater part of our rent' finally failed and 'as soon as he went to the parish for relief they came to clap the town brand on his goods and set them down in the parish books because he should not sell or get out of them'. Clare was 'utterly caste down for', he wrote, 'I could not help them sufficient to keep them from the parish.' He responded by 'letting loose my revenge' in his poem on the parish, depicting the village constable as:

> Reigning and ruling in the mighty state
> A jackall makeshift for a majistrate

Keeping the tools of terror for each cause
When the starved poor oerstep his pigmy laws
To mark the paupers goods the parish brand
Is in his mansion ready at command.[47]

Mayett's autobiography, like Clare's less organised writings, quietly lays before the reader the stark realities of low wages, insecure employment, and extreme vulnerability to high bread prices, to accommodation costs, to ill-health, to debt, and to the oppressive policies of masters, overseers and farmers. It is possible that Mayett's account overstated his material crises, but since his narrative generally tries to be hopeful and relatively optimistic it is much more likely that he understated them. Closer scrutiny of the specific language Mayett uses in the relevant passages indicates two contradictory forces at work. On the one hand it reveals the extent to which he deeply desired, and strove for, freedom – to 'have the reins of government in my own hands' as he put it. On the other hand it makes clear how deeply constraining he found the structural inequalities of wealth and power within which he found himself having to live out his life. When, very occasionally, he uses more general and reflective terms to describe his life, these structured constraints are presented both as social – as 'this state of thraldom' – and as economic – as 'all my straits in poverty'.[48] The latter theme is particularly reinforced by his use of the word 'narrow'. His autobiography begins by describing his family as in 'very narrow circumstances' and later on he describes his key peer group – the members of his nonconformist church community as 'all poor and in very narrow circumstances'. For a brief period in 1815, after the parish refused to employ Mayett and tried to force him to re-enlist, he was successful enough as a rag-gatherer and itinerant lace, tape and cotton seller to make this language inapplicable. 'I ... At first ... Still enjoyed my liberty', he wrote. However, within a year or two the narrative once again uses the language of straightening and constrictions. 'I began', he wrote once more, 'to be in very narrow circumstances in life'. To Mayett, his low material circumstances combined with the meanness of the local employers and parish authorities deeply constrained him. 'I could not extricate myself', he wrote, 'I was sent ... to work ... I was obligated to do it or have no work ... I was forced to do it ... my work lay very hard upon me ... I was out of work and was compeled.' It is not surprising therefore, that throughout his account his sense of identity is deeply interwoven with his experiences of the structured inequalities, which narrowed, straightened and constrained him. In his own eyes and the eyes of those around him he was first and foremost a 'poor' labouring man.[49]

(IV)

What were the cognitive consequences of this? In what ways did Mayett's experience of poverty and social inequality influence not only his sense of identity but also his capacity for action? He may have seen himself as a poor man whose life was in constant danger of being narrowed down by poverty and oppression, but this did not mean that he deferentially accepted his circumstances and did not push against the constraints. Mayett was not cowed by his poverty. In many ways he was the classic non-deferential worker. His autobiography reveals an impressive range of strategies designed to persuade, hoodwink, cajole, confront or confound the gatekeepers who controlled the key resources he needed in order to survive. Mayett knew how to construct an identity when he needed one. In the Militia, having finally obtained an easier post he made sure he kept in with his superiors by developing a reputation as a sober man even though he was often drunk. 'Such was my craft and pollicy in carring myself upright' he noted, that although he was 'no better in reality than the very worst of men' he managed to give his key superiors the impression that he was extremely reliable. In civilian life Joseph was equally adept at manipulating how others saw him. Faced with a master who would only employ him on a weekly contract rather than as a living-in servant, 'in consequence of the dearness of provision', he succeeded in getting himself a yearly contract after surmising that 'if I beat out after a place and my master heard of it he would sone hire me'.[50]

Mayett could therefore be a master of impression management, manipulating how others saw him to his own distinct advantage. Yet a major theme of his account is the directly confrontational ways in which he faced up to the employers, overseers and magistrates who controlled employment and relief in his community of settlement. For example, faced in 1821 by a combination of problems with the local farmers, overseers and vestry, he did not hesitate to call the law in. 'My master discharged me because the rest of the Parish officers refused to employ their quota of men', he wrote. 'About three weeks after this my old master ... said I did not aught to be employed nor relieved because I had left his service. So the Parish refused to employ me on that account but I went to a magistrate and he compeled them to employ me or relieve me and give me 7 shillings per week till I could get work.' This was not Mayett's only successful use of outside magistrates to squeeze resources out of those who ran the parish state. In 1829 he recorded that 'I mad[e] an application to the overseer for imploy but he refused to imploy me so I Complained to the magistrates in the pettey sessions and they ordered him to relieve me the same as other men'.[51]

Mayett had less success with 'the old squire', in part because he refused to be in any way deferential towards him. In 1829, for example, Mayett led a mini-rebellion in the parish. 'I was discharged and forced to aply to the overseer for work' he records. 'At this time there was many men out of work and the old squire been the Chief Justice in this part of the country he took it upon himself to reduce every mans pay two shillings per week ... So some of us went to the squire to make our complaint but he would not hear a word we had to say but began to swear and abuse us and I reproved him for swearing and told him if he swore again I would make him pay for it this enraged him to such a degree that though he took care that he swore no more in my presence yet he ordered the overseer not to relieve me nor find me a days work.' This attempt to use the laws against swearing, which stipulated larger fines for erring gentlemen, cost Mayett dear. His protagonist was William Pigott. The Pigotts had been the major landholders in the liberty of Doddershall, which formed the southern part of the parish of Quainton for more than three hundred years, and Mayett's attempt to pull off his own version of a linguistic turn against the squire was not appreciated. He eventually got Pigott's decision overturned by going over his head to the local petty sessions, but in the meantime his health had been severely affected.[52]

Four years earlier, in 1825, Mayett had twice been involved in similar clashes. In January, he records, 'I was out of work and was compeled to go into a milking place again the Esquire that lived in the parish and was a magistrate wanted a man that could milk and there being no other man out of work at that time beside me he set upon me and made me go or I should have no employ.' In the same year Mayett had similar problems when he tried to get medical relief. 'My wife was taken very ill', he recorded, 'I aplied to the parish for the docter but they refused to let me have him ... The next morning I went to the Squire and stated the case but he said that I was a good labourer and could get the best of wages and therefore I must pay the docter myself.' Mayett called the doctor anyway, and eventually got the parish to pay up, although not without considerable strategic manoeuvring. Mayett's account indicates that he often had the courage to stand his ground when faced by employers, parish officers or esquires. A few months after the incident just quoted the local squire wanted to hire Mayett at 12*s.* a week – the same price as he gave the rest of his men. But Mayett, rather unwisely, chose to remind the squire that the latter had refused him medical relief on the grounds that he was capable of getting higher than average wages and therefore demanded 13*s.* The squire was not impressed and discharged Mayett who then had to take a job as a hired hayward at little more than half that wage.[53]

For all his strategic sense in some situations, Mayett clearly found it very hard to stop himself from speaking his mind to those in authority. He had a number of clashes, for example, with John Cox, the largest farmer in the parish who fairly regularly acted as overseer. This began when he was Mayett's employer and came to a head in 1822 when Cox touched a raw nerve by calling Mayett a swindler. The latter exploded and 'told him of his faults as well as he did me of mine'. Speaking truth to power in this way is rarely a cost-free exercise for the poor however, and Mayett's family suffered severely for having 'sorely offended' one of the principal inhabitants of the parish – being excluded from their beloved chapel congregation for a while through Cox's influence.[54] The events of 1825 and 1829 already discussed in detail above suggest, however, that Mayett's capacity for resistance was not reduced by this experience. His ability to make his own choices comes through clearly in his responses to the various attempts made to influence his view of the world. In particular two attempts to get him to buy into very different ideologies in his late thirties were singularly unsuccessful.

'At this time', he records, 'there was a great many tracks came out and their contents were cheifly to perswade poor people to be satisfied in their situation and not to murmur at the dispensations of providence for we had not so much punishment as our sins deserved and in fact there was but little else to be heard from the pulpit or the press and those kind of books were often put into my hands in a dictatorial way in order to convince me of my errors for instance there was the Sheperd of Salsbury plain ... the farmers fireside and the discontented pendulum and many others which drove me almost into despair as I could see their design.'[55] These refusals to buy into the religion-based arguments for acceptance and deference to authority put forward by Hannah More and others were balanced by an equally critical attitude to the more radical views More was trying to counteract. When a group of 'deistical' men with whom he walked to work lent Mayett books by Cobbett, Wooler and Carlisle he was initially attracted, 'for these books seemed to be founded upon the scripture and condemned all the sins of oppression in all those that had the supremacy over the lower order of people'.

However, he soon found their atheism unacceptable and rejected both the books and their advocates. Despite his sense that 'most if not all professors of religion did it only for … money', by the time he wrote his account Mayett's core ideas and assumptions were clearly clustered around an egalitarian version of evangelical nonconformist Christianity. His, often stumbling, attempts to develop a bibliocentric view made him neither deferential nor radical. His politics were confrontational but local, focusing on the parish rather than on the political nation.[56]

(V)

Mayett's deeply religious perspective did not make him any less willing to see and oppose the oppression of the local farmers and the parish vestry. His struggles with the parish powerful form a very important strand in his account. It is impossible to say how 'typical' Mayett was, but the theme of struggles against 'thraldom' that comes out so clearly in his autobiography finds many parallels in the other autobiographical fragments examined here. Much of his account of his life experience suggests he would have had a great deal of sympathy with John Clare's view of 'parish oppressors' which comes out so forcefully in Clare's long hidden poem, 'The Parish'.

> Churchwardens constables and overseers
> Makes up the round of Commons and of Peers
> With … cunning deep enough the poor to cheat
> This learned body for debating meet.[57]

Although much research remains to be done on the autobiographies of women labourers and paupers in the eighteenth and early nineteenth centuries, it is interesting that Mary Leaper's poem 'Man the Monarch' has a similar rhythm and content as Clare's. This time however, the perspective is heavily gendered, the unit of oppression being the household rather than the parish.

> Sires, Brothers, Husbands, and commanding Sons,
> The Sceptre Claim;
> And ev'ry Cottage brings
> A Long Succession of Domestic Kings.[58]

As we have seen from Ann Candler and Mary Saxby's autobiographies, it is not difficult to believe that Leaper's poem might have had the same kind of resonance for women such as these as Clare's would almost certainly have had for Mayett (if he had had access to it). The multifaceted relationship between social inequality and gendered identities, as expressed for example in the phrase 'poor women kind' so often used by another labouring poetess Mary Collier,[59] clearly requires separate study. However, to return in conclusion to Mayett's sense of identity, it may be helpful to refer to Harriett Bradley's recent book *Fractured Identities. Changing Patterns of Inequality.*

Bradley argues cogently that our own times are witnessing two paradoxical movements as stratification systems and identities are becoming both more polarised and more fragmented. Economically the gap between the rich and the poor is getting ever greater, while recent social changes have led to increased fragmentation as people become more aware of the multiple sources of identity open to them. In late eighteenth and early nineteenth-century Southern England a fairly similar process of economic polarisation affected the rural labouring poor. However, while that change may have been accompanied by an increased fragmentation of sources of identity among the propertied middling sort – as new issues such as consumption style choices, religious pluralism, racial difference and changing gender roles emerged – the second half of Bradley's modern paradox is surely less applicable to the eighteenth-century labouring poor. Gender issues were very important and for poor labouring women the ways that gendered assumptions overlapped, and interacted, with the structural restraints which poverty imposed was surely central.[60] Equally, for men like Mayett religion cannot be ignored. Neither can neighbourly reputation nor the importance of either neighbourly reciprocity or of associational initiatives such as box clubs can be ignored. However, social inequality surely remains the master key which more than any other factor can help us to unlock how the poor constructed, and/or had constructed for them, their sense of who they were and who others were.

In thinking about the nature and construction of social identities amongst the majority of the people who lived in early modern England, we need, perhaps, to beware of over-fragmentation. As Richard Jenkins has recently commented in his book on social identity the meta-narrative of late modernity is a meta-narrative of fragmentation.[61] In this context it is important to ensure that we do not lose the capacity to give priority to things. Otherwise history will become just one damned plurality after another. In the case of the eighteenth-century rural labouring poor social inequality, poverty and the use of parish-based authority to reinforce the power of the employers were the central issues. 'I have found by experience', Mayett wrote, 'that without money there was no peace'. For Mayett, and surely for the majority of the rural labouring poor, the deep inequality of economic and social relations was the master/mistress narrative, the core foundation of their sense of social identity. They did not lack agency. Many of them, like Mayett, knew how to triangulate – to play off the petty sessions magistrates against the parish officers and employers, and more occasionally to exploit minor differences between the latter two overlapping groups.[62] The huge number of pauper appeals that can be found in the archives of some summary courts indicate that, like Mayett, they often did this with courage, drawing on customary notions such as those concerning their right to relief.[63] Sometimes they did this collectively, as Mary Saxby's daughter did when she led a bread riot in 1800.[64] More frequently they battled as individuals, forming their sense of identity out of the struggle to escape thraldom and achieve some small measure of freedom, or at the very least some room for manoeuvre, in a narrowing world.

Acknowledgements

I would like to thank Elizabeth Hurren and Steve King who kindly read earlier drafts of this chapter, as well as all those who gave comments on the version of this paper I gave at the first Exeter Early Modern England Workshop (EEMEW) on 'Social Identity, Class and Status 1450–1800' in July 2003 and at the University of Oregon in October 2003.

Notes

1. H. Bradley, *Fractured Identities. Changing Patterns of Inequality* (Cambridge, 1996) pp. 5–7.
2. E.P. Thompson, 'The Crime of Anonymity', in D. Hay, V.A.C. Gatrell and P. Linebaugh (eds), *Albion's Fatal Tree* (London, 1975), pp. 255–344; A. Tomkins and S. King (eds), *The Poor in England, 1700–1850. An Economy of Makeshifts* (Manchester, 2003); T. Sokoll (ed.), *Essex Pauper Letters 1731–1837* (Oxford, 2001); T. Sokoll, 'Negotiating a Living: Essex Pauper Letters from London, 1800–1834', *International Review of Social History*, 45 (2000), pp. 19–46; T. Hitchcock, P. King and P. Sharpe (eds), *Chronicling Poverty. The Voices and Strategies of the English Poor, 1640–1840* (Basingstoke, 1997). See also Tim Hitchcock's recent paper on 'Begging in Eighteenth-century London' given at the Institute of Historical Research June 2003.
3. Buckinghamshire Record Office (hereafter BRO) DX/3711 reprinted in A. Kussmaul (ed.), 'The Autobiography of Joseph Mayett of Quainton 1783–1839' *Buckinghamshire Record Society*, 23 (1986).
4. E. Robinson (ed.), *John Clare's Autobiographical Writings* (Oxford, 1986); M. Saxby, *Memoirs of a Female Vagrant Written by Herself* (London, 1806).

5. See, for example, the discussion in J. Burnett, D. Vincent and D. Mayall (eds), *The Autobiography of the Working Class. An Annotated Critical Bibliography. Volume I. 1790–1900* (New York, 1984), pp. xiii–xxxvi; J. Burnett (ed.), *Useful Toil. Autobiographies of Working People from the 1820s to the 1920s* (Harmondsworth, 1977), pp. 9–19.

6. R. Jenkins, *Social Identity* (London, 1996), p. 5.

7. J. Tew, *Social Theory, Power and Practice* (Basingstoke, 2002).

8. Jenkins, *Social Identity*, pp. 1–28.

9. *Ibid.*, pp. 20–1.

10. On the genre see Burnett *et al.*, *The Autobiography*, pp. xiii–xxi; C. Machann, *The Genre of Autobiography in Victorian Literature* (Ann Arbor, 1994).

11. M. Hogg and C. McGarty, 'Self-categorisation and Social Identity', in D. Abrams and M. Hogg (eds), *Social Identity Theory; Constructive and Critical Advances* (London, 1990) pp. 10–27; Jenkins, *Social Identity*, p. 9. Some would go further and argue that the main way in which individual identities are formed is linguistic/textual. 'Persons are largely ascribed identities according to the manner of their embedding within a discourse – in their own or in the discourses of others' J. Shotter and K. Gergen (eds), Texts of Identity (London, 1989), p. ix.

12. Burnett *et al.*, *The Autobiography*, pp. xiii–xv; The soldiers tales were not of course only about battles – R. Palmer (ed.), *The Rambling Soldier* (Gloucester, 1985).

13. N. Myers, *Reconstructing the Black Past; Blacks in Britain 1780–1830* (London, 1996), p. 51.

14. Robinson, *John Clare*, pp. 140–1.

15. *Ibid.*, pp. 69–72; A. Fraser, 'John Clare's Gypsies', *Northamptonshire Past and Present*, 4 (1970–71), pp. 259–67.

16. Saxby, *Memoirs*, pp. 9–17.

17. Kussmaul, *The Autobiography*, p. xxiv.

18. Saxby, *Memoirs*, pp. 10–11, 23–37.

19. A. Candler, *Poetical Attempts* (Ipswich, 1803), pp. 1–17.

20. Candler, *Poetical*, p. 4.

21. *Ibid.*, p. 14; Saxby, *Memoirs*, pp. 30–2.

22. On the problematic nature of constructing patriarchal authority – M. Braddick and J. Walter (eds), *Negotiating power in Early Modern England. Order, Hierarchy and Subordination in Britain and Ireland* (Cambridge, 2001), pp. 17–19.

23. Kussmaul, *The Autobiography*, p. vii; Saxby, *Memoirs*, pp. iii–iv; J. Clare, *The Parish* (Harmondsworth, 1985).

24. J. Arch, *From Ploughtail to Parliament. An Autobiography* (London, 1986); M. Thale (ed.), *The Autobiography of Francis Place* (Cambridge, 1972); W. Hutton, *The Life of William Hutton* (1816); O. Equiano, *The Interesting Narrative of the Life of Olaudah Equiano* (Harmondsworth, 1995).

25. Kussmaul, *The Autobiography*, p. xxvii; On Mayett's ambivalence, see his discussion of the imprisoning nature of avarice at pp. 57–9. J. Harriott, *Struggles through Life* (London, 1816).

26. Kussmaul, *The Autobiography*, p. 48.

27. *Ibid.*, xvii; for an example of a purely religious autobiography see – *The Methodist Magazine*, 27 (1804), pp. 3–9, 49–56, 97–102, 141–7.

28. Kussmaul, *The Autobiography*, p. xvii.

29. BRO, PR/169/12/11-12 and earlier pre-1815 volumes for references to Joseph's father and occasionally to the young Joseph himself. For example he records in his diary that in May 1801 he was taken ill and this can be traced in the overseer's account book PR/169/12/8 – see entry for 9 May 1801, G. Rodwell (ed.), *Overseers Book 1675–1925* (Typescript 1993 in BRO); DX 118; NB/15/11; PR/169/1/5 and 169/1/11.

30. BRO, PR/169/12/11; Kussmaul, *The Autobiography*, p. 92.

31. *Ibid.*

32. For a very similar set of opening lines to Mayett's, which he might well have been familiar with – D. Defoe, *Robinson Crusoe* (1719); Kussmaul, *The Autobiography*, p. 1.

33. *Ibid.*

34. *Idem*, pp. 10–11.

35. *Id.*, pp. 33, 61.

36. *Id.*, pp. 65–7.

37. *Id.*, pp. 71–81.

38. *Id.*, pp. 81, 92–8.

39. We do not know which friendly society he belonged to, but the one we have records of, which met at the White Hart in Quainton from 1812, would have cut his benefits in half after 26 weeks – G. Rodwell (ed.), *Quainton Clubs and Charities* (Typescript 2000 in BRO), p. 97. BRO PR/169/12/11–12. Guardian's Minutes do survive for the Aylesbury Union – BRO G/2/1 indicates the Workhouse system became operational in September 1835. No workhouse records survive. Typescript 'Quainton various documents and 1841 Census' in BRO, p. 66.

40. BRO G/2/3 1833–5=av. £1063, 1838=£495 – Rodwell, *Overseer's*, p. 54; D/X 118. Sarah's payments were around the average for female recipients listed in 1839.

41. Kussmaul, *The Autobiography*, p. 65; N. McKendrick, J. Brewer and J. Plumb, *The Birth of a Consumer Society. The Commercialisation of Eighteenth-century England* (London, 1982).

42. Saxby, *Memoirs*, p. 11; J. Styles, 'Custom or Consumption? Plebeian Fashion in Eighteenth-century England', in M. Berg and E. Eger (eds), *Luxury in the Eighteenth-century. Debates, Desires and Delectable goods* (London, 2003), pp. 103–15; J. Styles, 'Involuntary Consumers? Servants and their Clothes in Eighteenth-century England' and S. King, 'Reclothing the English Poor, 1750–1840', both in *Textile History. Special Issue on the Dress of the Poor*, 33, 1 (2002), pp. 9–21, 37–47; B. Lemire, *Dress,Culture and Commerce. The English Clothing Trade before the Factory, 1660–1800* (London, 1997); B. Lemire, *Fashion's Favourite: The Cotton Trade and the Consumer in Britain 1660–1800* (Oxford, 1991), esp. pp. 96–108.

43. Saxby, *Memoirs*, p. 15.

44. T. Wales, 'Poverty, Poor Relief and the Lifecycle: Some Evidence from Seventeenth-century Norfolk', in R.M. Smith (ed.), *Land, Kinship and Lifecycle* (Cambridge, 1984), pp. 351–89; and R.M. Smith, 'Some Issues Concerning Families and their Property in Rural England 1250–1800' in the same volume;

45. Saxby, *Memoirs*, pp. 51–8; Candler, *Poetical Attempts*, pp. 11–2. B. Stapleton, 'Inherited Poverty and Lifecycle Poverty: Odiham, Hampshire, 1650–1850', *Social History*, 18 (1993), pp. 342–4 suggests by the early nineteenth-century

90 per cent of recipients of charity were being assisted by the time they reached their late forties. For a focus on the forties and fifties in a northern parish see S. King, 'Reconstructing Lives: The Poor, the Poor Law and Welfare in Calverley 1650–1820', *Social History*, 22 (1997), p. 332.

46. P. King, 'Pauper Inventories and the Material Lives of the Poor in the Eighteenth and Early Nineteenth centuries', in Hitchcock *et al.*, *Chronicling Poverty*, pp. 155–91; S. King, *Poverty and Welfare in England 1700–1850* (Manchester, 2000), pp. 94–6 for an even less optimistic northern picture, and p. 135 on cycles of accumulation and dissipation; W. Eden, *The State of the Poor*, 3 vols (London,1797); D. Davies, *The Case of Labourers in Husbandry* (London, 1795); T. Sokoll, 'Early Attempts at Accounting the Unaccountable: Davies' and Eden's Budgets of Agricultural Labouring Families in Late-eighteenth Century England', in T. Pierenkemper (ed.), *Zur Okonomik des Privaten Haushalts* (Frankfurt, 1991), pp. 34–58.
47. Robinson, *John Clare*, pp. 114–5; Clare, *The Parish*, pp. 61–2; King, 'Pauper Inventories', pp. 157–60.
48. Kussmaul, *The Autobiography*, pp. 7, 59, 73.
49. *Ibid.*, pp. 1, 61–3, 65, 75.
50. *Idem*, pp. 47–8, 11–12.
51. *Id.*, pp. 72, 93.
52. *Id.*, pp. xxiii, 92.
53. *Id.*, pp. 81–3.
54. *Id.*, p.73; Cox's landholdings can be traced in the Land Tax of 1829 – BRO Q/RPL 1/50; for his stints as overseer – Rodwell, *Overseers*, p. 73.
55. Kaussmaul, *The Autobiography*, pp. 70–2; M. Scheuermann, *In Praise of Poverty. Hannah More Counters Thomas Paine and the Radical Threat* (Lexington, KY, 2002), p. 135.
56. Scheuermann, *Praise of Poverty*, and for a discussion of his failure to engage in broader political issues, pp. xviii–xxii.
57. For the phrase 'parish oppressors' – M. Storey (ed.), *John Clare: Selected Letters* (Oxford, 1990) p. 73; Clare, *The Parish*, p. 62.
58. D. Landry, *The Muses of Resistance: Laboring-class Women's Poetry in Britain 1739–96* (Cambridge, 1990), p. 32.
59. Landry, *Muses*, p. 59.
60. Bradley, *Fractured Identities*, pp. 11–26.
61. Jenkins, *Social Identity*, p. 12 and Bradley, *Fractured Identities*, p. 102 on 'the risk of a remorseless fragmentation'.
62. On triangulation see P. King, 'Edward Thompson's Contribution to Eighteenth-Century Studies. The Patrician-Plebeian Model Re-examined', *Social History*, 21 (1996), pp. 226–7 and P. King 'Summary Justice and Social Relations in Eighteenth-century England', *Past & Present* 183 (2004). Braddick and Walter, *Negotiating Power*, p. 33.
63. See P. King, 'The Poor, the Law and The Poor Law. The Summary Courts and Pauper Strategies in Eighteenth and Early Nineteenth-Century England', in S. King and R. Smith (eds), *Poverty and Relief in England 1500–1800* (Woodbridge, forthcoming).
64. Saxby, *Memoirs*, p. 74.

3
Honesty, Worth and Gender in Early Modern England, 1560–1640

Alexandra Shepard

In January 1600 Beatrice Swynney, the wife of a Cambridge tailor, was produced as a witness in a defamation case brought by the minister of her parish against a fellow parishioner, the baker John Fidling, in the course of which her honesty, and that of many of her neighbours, was brought into question. Walter House, who was a fellow of Queens' College as well as minister of St Andrew's parish, complained that John Fidling had denounced him as 'a scald and scurvy priest ... a beast ... a Raskall a knave & a troblesome fellowe'. Fidling had also accused House of bringing his parish to 'such a glameringe & troble as never was before', and objected that House had made a presentment against 'one of the honestest men of the parishe'.[1] Consequently, according to the allegations against him, Fidling had wished 'a horne plague' upon House to 'fetche him out of the parishe', adding 'the devill brought him into the parishe & his dame [will] fetch him out', before declaring that 'I will never turne my tonge to my tayle for such a Jack as he is.'[2]

Called to testify on Fidling's behalf, Beatrice Swynney became entangled in a web of consternation that involved not only Walter House and John Fidling, but also several of her co-witnesses and neighbours. Suspecting House's key witnesses were in league against him, Fidling devised a series of questions to discredit them. So, for example, it was asked whether Alice Westgarthe, wife of the parish clerk (who Fidling had also allegedly insulted) and her maid were 'vehemently suspected to live dishonestly', and whether Westgarthe's husband did 'much distrust his sayd wife for her lo[o]se life' having disowned the last child she had borne. Fidling in turn called witnesses of his own to cast doubt upon their testimony.[3] Beatrice Swynney recounted that she had heard Alice Westgarthe coach her co-witness, the widow Elizabeth Bowch, while on their way to court. According to Swynney, Alice Westgarthe had been losing patience with Elizabeth Bowch who could not remember what she had been instructed to say. Bowch was concerned that she would 'have evell wyll of the parish' for speaking against Fidling, but, according to Swynney, she had added that 'yf I had no better meintenance of him for whome I goe to speake the truthe: then I haue of the parishe, I mighte doe full well'.[4]

House in turn lodged his own set of discrediting questions for Fidling's witnesses, which included whether Swynney and her female co-witnesses were commonly reputed as scolds. In addition, Fidling's witnesses were asked whether they had the French pox, whether they were drunkards, and whether they lived 'disorderly and dishonestly ... suspected of Comitting adultrye fornicacion or incontinencye and as it were to keepe Bawdi howses and to have Runn upp and downe from fayre to fayre and from market to markett.'[5] Beatrice Swynney admitted that about ten years previously she had 'hard some speache' that Margery Taylor (one of Fidling's witnesses) had beaten her husband Richard Taylor, who in turn had been charged with fathering an illegitimate child. All Swynney said of her own credit was in response to a question asking how much she was worth and how she got her living: she replied that she and her husband 'have lyved well and honestlye ever since they first came to this Towne to dwell, & have gotten & doe gett theire lyveinges by bothe theire labors, And ... as they owe lytle: soe they are worth lytle'.[6]

This case represents a good deal that is familiar to historians of honesty and reputation in early modern England, yet it also begs questions of the framework in which such material has been interpreted. It has long since been demonstrated that the related attributes of honour, reputation and honesty were not the exclusive preserve of the gentry, and that comparatively humble people went to considerable lengths to protect their reputations by way of defamation litigation in the church courts.[7] One of most striking features of such evidence is the way in which the language of insult was gendered, and it is gender, rather than class, that has emerged as the primary category of identity with which historians have made sense of the substance of slander allegations.

A considerable body of research explores the extent to which concepts of honesty diverged along gender lines, particularly in relation to the sexual double standard.[8] Laura Gowing's pioneering work affords enormous insight into the cultural significance of why there was no male equivalent to the concept 'whore', but her claim that notions of honesty for men and women were 'incommensurable' has been questioned on a number of grounds.[9] It has been argued that men had a great deal staked on their own sexual reputations and were also deeply implicated in the sexual honour of their wives.[10] In addition, it is clear that women's reputations were far more broadly founded than admitted by the narrow jurisdictional parameters of ecclesiastical law, which determined the predominantly sexual content of defamation suits.[11] According to such arguments, concepts of honesty were gender-related rather than gender-specific.

Yet, however nuanced, these are still only partial accounts, for two main reasons. First, the debate rests on a distinction between honesty as a form of sexual honour synonymous with chastity, and 'economic' notions of honesty in terms of plain dealing and trustworthiness. However, these two strands did not exist in discrete separation, and are not easily picked apart, as reflected in the wide range of strategies employed by both litigants in the case above to discredit each other's witnesses. At the request of John Fidling, for example, Walter House's witnesses were asked indiscriminately whether any were suspected of adultery, fornication, keeping bawdy houses, economic flightiness (running from market to market), drunkenness or having the French pox.[12] Chastity and economic trustworthiness were not mutually exclusive categories of identity, but could function as interchangeable components in establishing and disputing honesty. The distinction between sexual honesty and economic trustworthiness also considerably over-simplifies the complexity of concepts of honesty, which combined assorted social, moral and economic meanings and informed notions of honour and reputation in a wide range of contexts.[13]

Second, we will not fully understand the ways in which concepts of honesty were related to gender without also exploring the ways in which they served other status distinctions. As more recent scholarship is beginning to demonstrate, gender was not a monolithic category of identity, and it interacted in subtle ways with many other determinants of status.[14] Honesty was variously invoked, therefore, not only according to gender difference, but also in relation to differences of social status, age, and marital status. In particular, concepts of honesty were as important in policing the divide between the better sorts and their poorer counterparts as to reinforcing gender difference. Distinctions of social status were as instrumental as gender in determining access to and attribution of the varied facets of honesty, and this chapter will argue that the divergence between the honesty claimed by 'able and sufficient' men and the honesty appealed to by labouring men and women was as significant as, and helps contextualise, the gendered distinction between chastity and trustworthiness that has preoccupied historians of early modern England.

This does not require us to jettison church court records as a source for the everyday usage of concepts of honesty, but merely to turn our attention from the slanderous idiom countered by plaintiffs to the subtler tests of credit undergone by witnesses. Rather than approaching early modern concepts of honesty via the language of insult (and therefore assuming that accusations of *dis*honesty were the inverse of notions of honesty), this chapter examines the ways in which honesty was positively claimed by witnesses and litigants as a means of validating their testimony in court. Witnesses in the church courts (and in other courts employing civilian procedure) were often required to respond to a set of interrogatories posed on behalf of the defendant as well as to the plaintiff's allegations. These questions were designed to gauge witnesses' credibility and to assess the weight that should be given to their statements. While sometimes aggressively framed, with questions targeted to undermine particular witnesses (as in the case which opened this chapter), interrogatories were more often highly formulaic. Typically, they began by probing the relationship of the witness to either party (whether as a servant, neighbour, or kin, a debtor, friend or enemy), and then they addressed the credit and social standing of witnesses themselves.[15] Frequently posed questions of the latter category asked witnesses what they were worth with their debts paid, and how they got their living. What was being assessed, therefore, was not only whether the witness was likely to tell the truth in the particular circumstances presented by the case (in attempts to gauge bias), but also whether the witness was trustworthy in *any* circumstances.

The question of a witness's 'worth' is of particular interest here, since it provides access to general statements about a person's own perception of their social standing in the parochial context. Not dissimilar to the concept of 'credit', notions of worth spanned monetary estimates (calculated with reference either to land or goods) and ethical attributes that were often explicitly related to the concept of honesty.[16] In a few cases witnesses were required to assess each other's worth as well as their own, and the multiple perspectives they provide are further illustrative of the terms of reference with which honesty was both claimed and contested in early modern England. Such cases are also suggestive not only of the degree to which identity was subjective but also of the varied levels of control exercised by different individuals over the projection of their own identity, particularly in the court setting.

An investigation of witnesses' responses to the question of their worth, therefore, shifts the focus from the terms with which litigants refuted charges of dishonesty, to deponents' own claims to honesty and the criteria by which they assessed each other's trust worthiness. These must first and foremost be treated as a product of the court setting, not least since the question of a witness's worth stemmed from the legal tradition that a pauper's testimony could not be trusted.[17] However, it seems unlikely that such judgements were exclusive to the courtroom, especially since the concepts of honesty invoked by witnesses involved far more than merely telling the truth. What was principally at stake was a witness's *authority*, and this was related to their standing in the wider community as much as to what they said in court. Many different forms of exemplary behaviour were associated with honesty in witnesses' statements of worth, ranging from hard work and painful industry, to the proper treatment of and provision for household subordinates, to pretensions of civility and decorum related to the concept's classical heritage. Honesty was also invoked defensively to deflect suggestions of untrustworthiness by those whose authority was more open to question. Claims to honesty were therefore determined as much by social position as by adherence to behavioural norms. Each witness had a different purchase on its many components, according to their social status and age and marital status as well as gender, which in turn is suggestive of the ways in which concepts of honesty were involved in status distinctions and the calibration of identity and agency within the wider context of the parish.

Witnesses in court asserted their honesty with reference to a far wider range of behavioural norms than featured negatively in allegations of defamation. While particularly aggressive interrogatories involved insinuations of discredit similar to slanderous insults, witnesses were more often given the opportunity to assert their honesty in positive terms. This involved a subtle spectrum of distinctions, particularly in witnesses' responses to questions of their worth and how they got a living, which ranged from assertions of considerable substance, to lesser claims of self-sufficiency, plain-dealing and painstaking industry.

Although some of these aspects of honesty were gender-related, there was a far greater degree of gender convergence in claims to self-sufficiency and honest industry than the allegations in defamation suits have led us to expect. 'Living of one's own', or maintaining one's self, was often cited as an indication of honesty by witnesses in court such as John Shawe, a Cambridge brewer, who declared that 'he lyveth honestlye of that which he hathe as an honest man oughte to do'.[18] Such general claims were neither gender- nor age-specific, and appeared in the responses of a wide range of witnesses. The 19-year-old yeoman, John Scott, asserted that he was worth £100 5s. and 'a better pennye', taking into account his debts, and that he lived 'honestlye of his owne'. Likewise, William Owldfield, a servant to Queens' College in Cambridge and of a similar age to Scott but of far more modest means, declared that he was worth 40s. and paid four Marks per annum and 'so lyveth of yt honestly'.[19] The key attribute being stressed here was self-reliance and living within one's means, and it was claimed by women as well as men. A 35-year-old Norfolk widow refused to answer the question of what she was worth, declaring only that 'she lyveth of her owne', while another widow from Sussex (aged 47) responded in similar terms when she declared that 'shee livethe of her selfe, and owethe not muche'.[20] Some married women also conveyed a sense of self-sufficiency in response to the question of their worth, such as Mary Vachan of Oxford who replied that 'she is a housekeper & doth live of her selfe by her husbands industrye & her owne'.[21]

Married men claimed their ability to maintain subordinates as well as themselves in a more gender-related form of honesty, in line with the expectation that they should serve as providers for their households. Robert Hilliard, for example, living on a tenement of the Earl of Hertford's worth £9 a year, and declaring himself worth £20, claimed that he 'maintaineth a familie in honest sort and is not in dept'.[22] Although many households were dependent on the contributions of women and children as well as the provisions of a male household head, married women did not appeal to supporting their families as a source of honesty in court, reinforcing the normative assumption that adult men should be providers.[23] Such considerations were also taken into account when witnesses assessed each other's honesty, as suggested by the description of George Austin, a tailor, by one of his co-witnesses as 'a man of an honest life and Conversation, and one that taketh paynes to mayntayne himselfe and his family'.[24]

This form of honesty was also age-related, serving distinctions between young men in service and their householding counterparts – as suggested by the way in which a Cambridge barber chose to insult one Thomas Crawforthe by claiming that he 'was an honest man & did kepe howse, when as he Crawforthe was but a scalde boye'.[25] However much they professed their ability to support themselves, young men and women in service were treated with suspicion because they were dependent, and as a result they were deemed untrustworthy. The Devon labourer Robert Sweet was keen to emphasise his independence when acting as a witness for his employer, John Bennett, by stating that he 'doth at sometymes worcke at husbandry labour at the howse of the said John Bennett for wages, but did never make any covenant with him other then by the day or the weeke as they did agree, and sometymes hath a groate [four pence] a day & sometymes vjd. for his wages'. Joanna

Pittman, another employee in the Bennett household was similarly at pains to emphasise her independence, claiming that she had often spun 'at the howse of the said Joane Bennett & her husband', but that this was for a weekly wage and that she 'but may goe from them at ever[y] weekes end if she please'.[26] Similarly, two witnesses in a tithes dispute brought by a Sussex gentlemen were described by a co-witness as 'honest men and of good name amongest their neighbours and such as live by their labor and not as servaunts to Mr Burcy nor at his findinge'. Another witness added that one of the men 'hath an occupacion and liveth by yt'.[27] The difference between the young men and women in such cases is that many of the men could at least aspire to a far greater level of independence than the women, whose opportunities to 'live of their own' were more likely to have been circumscribed by the strictures of service, marriage, or wage labour.

Adult males were also judged more often than women and younger men on their reputations for plain dealing when appearing in court. Criteria of honesty were applied to their execution of parish offices as well as their business dealings. John Moore, a Sussex yeoman, was described by several of his fellow witnesses as 'an honest man', who discharged his duties as constable 'honestly and faithfully'. Similarly, one David Thickepenie was described by his co-witness as 'a man of honest conversacion and of upright and honest dealing'.[28] Such considerations appear to have been more narrowly commercial when a Cambridge defendant was characterised by one of his witnesses as 'an honest & iust man in his dealings and one that keepe his booke & rekoninges true and iustly'.[29] The avoidance of debt was also deemed 'honest' according to the sexagenarian Bartholomew Chipney of Oxford who claimed that despite being a 'pooreman' he lived 'honestly out of debt and ... by his labor and trade', which was mending shoes.[30]

A far more prevalent form of honesty, however, was claimed by those who emphasised their labour as the basis for their autonomy, in lieu of any concrete worth. The honesty associated with hard work also featured in witness's assessments of each other, such as the description of Peregrine George as 'a very paynefull labourer' and one who lived 'honestly by his hand labour and paynes taking'.[31] Women claimed honesty in the same terms, such as Alice Johns, a midwife, who declared that although she was 'a pore woman dwelling with mr frier' she did 'earne her living by her honest labour & travell'.[32] This was, then, another point of gender convergence – indeed, this was the most common way in which women directly invoked honesty when asserting their integrity as witnesses. The honesty associated with painstaking labour was claimed by dependent as well as independent women, suggesting that even within the context of marriage women could have as powerful as sense of getting a living as men, while nonetheless declaring that they were worth nothing. So Margaret Dodding, the wife of a brewer, declared in line with coverture that she was 'worthe nothinge but that she hathe of hir husband' while adding that she 'liuethe honestlie and trulie by hir labor'; Elizabeth Hills, the wife of a cook, claimed that 'she by & under hir husband getteth hir liveying honestly'; while Margaret Woodward simply told that court that 'she getteth her lyveinge honestlye as a pore woman', without reference to her husband.[33] Although women did not represent themselves as providers, they nonetheless frequently invoked their honest industry as evidence that they were respected and trustworthy.

It is likely that the women and men who emphasised their 'honest' labour as proof of their integrity had a more precarious hold on honesty than their more able and sufficient neighbours, and this becomes clearer in the cases when witnesses disputed each other's honesty in court. Honest living in terms of painstaking industry was frequently posited as a qualifier to statements of poverty in order to confront automatic associations between poverty and dishonesty. The ways in which the integrity of Edward Miles, the sexton of St Mary's Westover (Sussex), was debated by his fellow witnesses in a tithes dispute is illustrative of some of the associations between poverty and dishonesty. While all seven of Miles' co-witnesses confirmed his poverty, they disagreed over whether he could be trusted as a result. One described him as 'a verye pore man ... & a verye ignorante & self willed fellow' – a statement that was reinforced by another's assessment of Miles as 'a simple fellow [who] for wante of discretion maye speake an untruthe'. By contrast, another declared that while Miles was 'but a poore man ... he verylye thinkethe him to be a verye honeste poore man.'[34] Honesty was not expected of poor men and women; it had to be proved.

Besides their purported ignorance, the other major concern voiced about poor witnesses was that they might be tempted to forswear themselves for gain (particularly if they were employed by either of the litigants). When Lydia Tyllet claimed that George Austen, (allegedly reputed to be 'an honest poore man') should not act as a witness in court because he would 'sweare for a meales meate or for drinke', his offended wife retorted 'yow thinke poore folkes will doe anie thing'.[35] This appears, however, to have been one of the presuppositions of the courts, and witnesses were frequently asked whether they had received anything in recompense for their appearance. Deponents and litigants also expressed such concerns. One of the ways in which John Fidling attempted to discredit Elizabeth Bowch, a witness for his opponent, Walter House (in the case which opened this chapter) was to suggest that she had promised to give evidence to support House in return for better relief than she received from the parish. The curate of Laughton (Sussex) similarly deemed several of his co-witnesses to be 'poore needy fellowes of small or noe credit & such as ... may be easily drawne to depose an untruth'.[36] A pauper's testimony, in such constructions, was worth very little.

This issue of susceptibility to bribes was also brought into play when co-witnesses assessed the honesty of Oliver Browning, a shoemaker of Hailsham, Sussex. John Rolf, a husbandman from the same village disputed Browning's claim to be worth £5, declaring that Browning was 'accompted to be a poore manne', but added that he was 'an honest manne and such a one as for gane will not forswer himself'. Another husbandman from the village confirmed that Browning was an honest man who lived by his labour (and not as a servant or retainer to the plaintiff).[37] Like people in service, therefore, labouring men and women aroused suspicion because they were in another person's pay, particularly when they had no other means on which to depend. The greater claims to autonomy sometimes articulated by labouring people in contrast to servants became easily blurred in the light of such assumptions.

The implications of such statements were that poverty rendered its victims either ignorant, greedy, or dependent, and that people working for wages as well as those in service could not be trusted. Working hard for a living was not always sufficient defence against charges of dependency related to being in another person's pay, not least because it was possible that such professed diligence might itself be interpreted as a form of obedient service rather than a sign of intrinsic merit.[38] Witnesses were therefore at pains to emphasise a person's honesty *in spite of* their dependence or poverty. Thus Marian Smith declared that she was 'a pore woman but will speak a truth uppon her oath'.[39] She, and many men and women like her, were clearly aware of the negative associations their relative poverty would arouse, and attempted to pre-empt and refute them – often unsuccessfully.

What was often at stake in such assessments was the divide between the idle and the industrious poor, which appears to have been paper-thin. This is clear from the different terms in which Richard Picknett, an 80-year-old husbandman, and his neighbours described his credit. Appearing as a witness for the defendant, Picknett declared himself worth £5, adding that 'he liveth by his travel & labor & by buienge & sellynge'. This was in stark contrast to the ways in which witnesses for the plaintiff assessed him. Richard Cooper, for example, a yeoman and former churchwarden of the parish in which they both lived (Bexhill), described Picknett as 'a very poore man', who 'liveth altogether by the Almes of the parishe' adding that he got a great deal of his relief from the defendant. He also claimed that about twenty years previously he had been 'suspected to live incontinentlye with one Alice Wardman his servante & was presented before the archdeanarye for the same', and declared that Picknett 'hathe bene verye mutche geven to excessive drinkinge & to lieinge & hathe bene likewise presented for the same'.[40] The suggestion was that Picknett was very much one of the undeserving – and by implication *dishonest* – poor, whose testimony should not be trusted.

With such associations (and long memories) in operation, it is unsurprising that Picknett himself chose not to mention his alms, and that very few witnesses referred to receiving relief. Of 679 statements of worth given by witnesses appearing in the Archdeaconry of Lewes between 1580 and 1631, only two mentioned the receipt of relief. Both were likely to have been considered 'deserving' on account of their age: an 83-year-old thatcher who declared that 'he livethe of the almes of the parish & hathe nothinge of his owne', and a 60-year-old husbandman, who, while admitting to be 'a very poore man [taking] some relief of the parishe', also nonetheless insisted that he lived 'by his labour'.[41] The receipt of relief was used by other witnesses and litigants to cast doubt on a person's testimony. Several deponents appearing alongside Henry Mungay confirmed that he was commonly accounted a poor man, recounting tales of his begging and alms-taking. While some judged him to be 'honest and true' in spite of his poverty, the yeoman George Sheppard declared not only that Mungay was 'an exceeding poore fellowe [who] hath sometymes had relief amongst other the poore of the parrishe by the overseers for the poore' but also that he was 'suspected to bee a lewd fellow'. Another witness added that on account of his poverty, Mungay had been known to break hedges and filch wood for fuel.[42]

In both cases, the receipt of alms by Picknett and Mungay was very quickly linked to suspicions of dishonesty. Even though both men had been considered entitled to relief by their fellow parishioners, neither appear to have been considered particularly worthy of it, which demonstrates the extreme narrowness of the concept of the 'deserving poor'. Doubt was cast on the testimony of both men not by suggestions of bribery, but with accusations of dishonest behaviour. In both instances this involved insinuations of sexual and 'economic' discredit. That the two were related and could be more broadly interchangeable is suggested by a defamation case resulting from one man's contention that Gregory Hills was 'an honest man in that he was forwarde in payinge his tythes & other duties' which was refuted by another's claim that he had 'loved and had yonge fleshe in a bromefeld'.[43] Witnesses, and especially poor witnesses (of both sexes), were therefore vulnerable to a range of charges spanning sexual incontinence of various forms, drunkenness and other spendthrift pursuits, theft, cheating and lying, and causing strife between their neighbours. So a man from Wensleydale, reputed to be in debt, was discredited by a fellow witness as a gamester and 'a man of noe honest estimation reputation or credit'; and John Farneley of West Hoathly (Sussex) was objected to by his co-witnesses on the grounds that he had stolen a knife, 'begot one with Childe in Barcombe', failed to attend church, and been so drunk that 'he vomited as he satt at the table drinkinge'.[44]

Such men may well have had a sense of their own worth and self-sufficiency – even when in receipt of relief – but their neighbours thought otherwise. The highly permeable boundaries between deserving and undeserving, and honest and dishonest, were policed by neighbours whose opinion carried more weight than the self-assessment of the poor themselves. Edward Higgens, a Seaford husbandman, confessing that he was 'a poore man' living from 'the revenew of certen lands which a great while ago was given by will to the poore of this parishe', did not even presume to assess his own worth, adding 'for his credit he referreth him self to his neighboures'. Robert Miles, a ship builder, duly obliged by describing Higgens as being 'of small credit or estimation [with] litle of his owne, and hath monie given him by the Collectors of the parishe'.[45] In the case of those designated poor, it was the assessment of others that mattered. So the Cambridgeshire husbandman Nicholas Morlyn rated Elizabeth and Ann Morlyn to be 'of honest & good conversation & ... well thoughte of amongest theyre neighbors, thoughe they be but poore'.[46] Conversely, John Prance attempted to discredit his father-in-law, Thomas Hodilowe (who he was suing for non-payment of his wife's dowry) by claiming that Hodilowe 'hathe ben & nowe ys accompted of & commonly taken to be an honest man & of good name & fame of & by some men, but not of and by all men'.[47] By implication, the unanimous opinion of one's neighbours was required as endorsement of honesty. Given the many criteria by which honesty might be judged, and the exacting standards that could be invoked, this was likely to have been conflicted and contingent, formed with reference to relative and highly subjective forms of assessment.[48] In addition, in the court setting at the very least, the poor appear to have had far less agency than their wealthier neighbours over the terms of their own worth and identity.

More important than the unanimous verdict of neighbours, therefore, was to be judged honest in the eyes of the honest, which brings us again to the social-status distinctions that were entwined with the concept's usage both in court and beyond. Witnesses in defamation cases were frequently asked whether the slanderous words in question had damaged the victim's reputation amongst their 'honest neighbours' or in the opinion of 'honest and grave persons' – reinforcing the impression that there was a sliding scale of importance attached to different people's words, and that honesty was achieved as much by association as by ascription to social norms.[49] So one Thomas Robucke, a young Cambridge tailor proudly declared that 'he ys conversant with non but ... honest persones.'[50] Ultimately, it was the opinion, if not the company, of the better sort that mattered. So a household servant declared that the defendant in a tithes case brought by his master was 'comonly accompted ... amongst persons of good credite to be a man of good liffe and of honest and quyet conversacion and such a one as will not sweare any thinge contrary to the trueth'.[51] Likewise, a plaintiff in a defamation case (accused of adultery) was described by one of his witnesses as 'ever ... reputed and taken for an honest and well disposed mann amonge the best of the parishe of St Benet'.[52]

Such statements did not refer to a simple meritocracy. It is likely that the man described by John Fidling (in the case that opened this chapter) as 'one of the honestest men of the parishe', was accorded this title because he was one of the better off rather than because he subscribed most thoroughly to behavioural norms. Of those dubbed 'honest and substantiall men', honesty was expected to be *reflected* in their manners, rather than produced by them.[53] Honesty was therefore also a product of wealth and *substance* – the substance associated with landholding, rate-paying and office-holding – and it is in relation to such connotations that gender divergence again becomes more marked. Concepts of honesty for men appear to have been more closely linked with evaluations of their wealth and social status than for women. Furthermore, this may well have been a far more substantial form of gender difference than represented by men and women's relative levels of concern with sexual slander. The greatest divergence between the defamation cases brought by men and women before the Cambridge university courts, for example, involved accusations of social debasement (with a male/female ratio of 5 : 1), rather than sexual dishonesty (with a male/female ratio of 1 : 2).[54]

A man's worth or substance, linked to the ability to pay his debts, was closely related to the value of his word in early modern England, and the honour with which it might be associated.[55] A witness asked to comment on the reliability of Edward Bradley's testimony declared that he was 'of verie small credit and worth litle or nothinge, whose word will skant be taken for the value of a pennie'. Bradley was a servant, who was further discredited by his master's suspicions that he had stolen some of his tools.[56] By contrast, the householding yeoman William Woodward was described by another yeoman of his parish as 'a man of suche credit that he uppon his othe [he] might be taken as a witness or for one witnes with another honest man for the payment of xxx*li*'.[57] It was a sign of respect to trust another man's word, as suggested by Samuel Leadham's response to Nicholas Mackreth's request that he enter into a written bond in return for a loan of 40s. When the scrivener had finished writing the bond, Leadham tore it into pieces, telling Mackreth 'now you shall stick to my curtesye I scorne you will not take my word for xls'.[58]

This form of honesty was so integral to the honour of gentlemen that they mostly did not feel obliged to reveal their worth in court. Instead, they frequently rebutted the question of their worth which they appear to have considered beneath them. So Robert Prance, when acting as a witness in Cambridge, replied that 'he is a master of arte & lyveth honestlye amongst all men [and] refuseth to answere what he is worthe'. Similarly, John Cortope, a gentleman from Ticehurst in Sussex, declared that he did not believe he was legally obliged to reveal his worth in court beyond stating that he was 'a subsidie man & able to live of himselfe'.[59] Such statements were designed to underscore the unquestionable value of a gentleman's word, and were linked to concepts of honour as well as substantial wealth. One of the privileges claimed by gentlemen was that their word could be trusted without scrutiny or question.[60] This stemmed from notions of honesty and civility, but also from the expectation that gentlemen had sufficient means to honour their debts. So the Cambridge gentleman William Albyn responded to the question of his worth by saying that he 'doeth owe noe money to any p[er]son but he is willing to paye it, & otherwyse he sayeth he thinketh he is not bonde to answer to this Interrogatory'.[61]

The inverse also appears to have been the case in instances of discredit, since insults were often deemed to have had a quantifiable impact on the worth of their victims. That discredit was associated with a loss of substance is apparent in the ways in which witnesses referred to the monetary damages claimed by litigants in defamation and other injury suits in the university courts.[62] Estimates of damages served to emphasise the plaintiff's worth and themselves functioned as a statement of credit. So, in a lengthy defamation dispute between two Cambridge gentlemen, Daniel Rogers and Francis Catlyn, one witness asserted that given Rogers' status as a fellow of Christ's College and a minister, and 'in regard of the disparitie of the persons of Mr Rodgers and Mr Catlyn', Rogers had every reason 'soe to esteme his said Injury at lxx*li*'. Similarly, when Sir Richard Hanger of St John's College brought a defamation case against a man who had accused him of being drunk, one of his witnesses claimed that 'Sir Hanger had beine better lost C*li*' as a consequence of the insult.[63] Such logic did not only apply to gentlemen. A witness for the pewterer, Henry Cotton, who sued a neighbouring apothecary for calling his family thieves, deposed that 'Cotton had better have spent a hundred pounds then to be soe wronged'.[64] The suggestion that slander had a direct impact on its victims' worth is a reflection of the importance of social estimation in the brokerage of credit in early modern England, and of what could be at stake when honesty was disputed.

Although some women as well as men sued for damages in the university courts, the links between worth and substance in relation to concepts of honesty appear to have been highly gender-related, if not gender-specific. While labouring women claimed their painstaking industry as a form of honesty in the same way as labouring men, and while there was a high degree of overlap between the forms of dishonesty with which men and women were charged (ranging from sexual incontinence to thieving), the honesty associated with worth and substance was exclusive to men. Women of the better sort had access to such honesty by association alone. So, for example, Ellen Millwarde described herself as 'an honest mans wiffe' in response to the question of her worth – an impression that was confirmed by another witness in the case who also referred to her husband's status as a bailiff and her own as the daughter of a yeoman.[65] Ellen Millwarde was honest in these terms by parentage and marriage rather than in her own right. A similar distinction was in operation when the yeoman Henry Chantler described the wronged victims of a slanderous outburst, Edward Bust and Elinor Harris (respectively insulted as whoremaster and whore) as follows: 'The man beinge a substantiall & honest man accompted & soe shee likewise of good parentage and accompted an honest woman.'[66]

Honesty, as invoked by different witnesses in the church courts, was a highly variable and multifaceted concept. While related to truth telling – and used as its gauge – it was by no means synonymous with truthfulness. It involved far broader claims to trustworthiness in terms of the diligent pursuit of vocation or office; substance, self-sufficiency and the ability to pay one's debts promptly and in full; avoiding strife with one's family and neighbours; and remaining within the bounds of behavioural codes emphasising sobriety, chastity and plain dealing. Men and women's claims to honesty differed according to gender, but also in relation to their age and social status. Servants were perhaps worst placed to make a case for their honesty in any terms other than diligent obedience. Householding men of the better sort assumed honesty as the reflection of their social status, rather than its precondition. Women of the better sort claimed honesty through their behaviour – often, but not always, gauged in terms of chastity – but also by association with men of substance through marriage and parentage. Men and women who were dependent on their labour for their living, however, had a far more precarious hold on honesty, which was won by actively *disproving* the negative associations between poverty, dependence and dishonesty. More narrowly framed in terms of self-sufficiency rather than substance, and industry rather than means, honesty was hard won by labouring men and women in contrast to being automatically claimed by their more able and sufficient neighbours.

Gender difference appears to have been more acutely present in slander litigation over accusations of dishonesty in the church courts than in the strategies for asserting honesty adopted by witnesses in the same forum. In the assessment of witnesses' honesty, the sexual double standard was relegated to a lesser concern by a more complex set of indices based on social status and age as much as gender. A commonly cited standard by men and women of all ages and from different social groups was self-sufficiency, or the ability to live of one's own. Yet this was in turn differentiated according to gender, age and marital status (when the support of a household was involved) and, more importantly, according to the ways in which men and women got their livings. A much broader form of sufficiency – and honesty – was accorded to the minority of men who could live solely by their means without relying too heavily or at all on their own labour. It was assumed that they and their wives would behave in an exemplary fashion, unless proved otherwise, and it was easier for such men and women to present themselves as honest in court, albeit in more highly gendered terms. At the other end of the spectrum were those men and women who laboured for others, either as servants or in return for wages, whose claims to honesty were primarily couched in terms of painstaking industry, and which, rather than being taken at face value, were often deemed to require endorsement by their social superiors. Given the readiness of neighbours to label the poor in terms of dishonesty, the identities of witnesses of little or no means in the context of the court were far less self-determined and far more contingent than those of their wealthier counterparts. Honesty functioned as a form of authority, and, as with other forms of authority in early modern England, access to it was highly uneven and contested. While gender difference may have been temporarily eclipsed in such battles, the gains for women were sadly limited.

Acknowledgements

This chapter has its origins in a paper presented as part of a panel on 'The politics of honesty in early modern England' at the North American Conference on British Studies in 2003. I am grateful to the other panellists (Craig Muldrew, Jennifer Richards, Phil Withington and Keith Wrightson) for their feedback and to Sarah Knott and Naomi Tadmor for their comments on subsequent drafts.

Notes

1. Cambridge University Library, C[ambridge] U[niversity] A[rchive], Walter House c. John Fidling, V.C.Ct.III.8, no. 65; V.C.Ct.II.2*, f.44.
2. CUA, V.C.Ct.III.8, no. 65.
3. Two sets of interrogatories on Fidling's behalf were put to House's witnesses: CUA, V.C.Ct.III.8, nos 67, 70. For the depositions of Fidling's witnesses to his *exceptoria*, see V.C.Ct.II.2*, ff.47^v-54^v, Comm.Ct.II.9, ff.1–3^v.
4. CUA, Comm.Ct.II.9, ff.1^v-2.
5. CUA, V.C.Ct.III.8, no.71.
6. CUA, Comm.Ct.II.9, f.2^{r-v}.
7. J. A. Sharpe, 'Defamation and Sexual Slander in Early Modern England: The Church Courts at York', *Borthwick Papers*, 58 (1980); M. Ingram, *Church Courts, Sex and Marriage in England, 1570–1640* (Cambridge, 1987), ch. 10.
8. See K. Thomas, 'The Double Standard', *Journal of the History of Ideas*, 20 (1959).
9. L. Gowing, *Domestic Dangers: Women, Words, and Sex in Early Modern London* (Oxford, 1996), p.107. See also S.D. Amussen, *An Ordered Society: Gender and Class in Early Modern England* (Oxford, 1988), pp. 98–104.
10. B. Capp, 'The Double Standard Revisited: Plebeian Women and Male Sexual Reputation in Early Modern England', *Past & Present*, 162 (1999); E.A. Foyster, *Manhood in Early Modern England: Honour, Sex and Marriage* (Harlow, 1999), pp.148–64.
11. G. Walker, 'Expanding the Boundaries of Female Honour in Early Modern England', *Transactions of the Royal Historical Society*, 6th ser., 6 (1996); M. Ingram, 'Law, Litigants and the Construction of "honour": Slander Suits in Early Modern England', in P. Coss (ed.), *The Moral World of the Law*

(Cambridge, 2000); A. Shepard, *Meanings of Manhood in Early Modern England* (Oxford, 2003), chs 6–7.

12. CUA, Walter House c. John Fidling, V.C.Ct.III.8, no.71.
13. See for example, A. J. Fletcher, 'Honour, Reputation and Local Officeholding in Elizabethan and Stuart England', in A. J. Fletcher and J. Stevenson (eds), *Order and Disorder in Early Modern England* (Cambridge, 1985); A. Hughes, 'Gender and Politics in Leveller Literature', in S.D. Amussen and M.A. Kishlansky (eds), *Political Culture and Cultural Politics in Early Modern England: Essays Presented to David Underdown* (Manchester, 1995), pp. 176–82. For a discussion of honesty as a component of military honour, see B. Donagan, 'The Web of Honour: Soldiers, Christians, and Gentlemen in the English Civil War', *Historical Journal*, 44, 2 (2001). For the concept's classical heritage and early modern usage, see J. Richards, *Rhetoric and Courtliness in Early Modern Literature* (Cambridge, 2003), ch. 1. For a discussion of the links between gentility, honour and truth-telling, see S. Shapin, *A Social History of Truth: Civility and Science in Seventeenth-Century England* (Chicago, 1994), ch. 3.
14. See, for example, S. Mendelson, 'The Civility of Women in Seventeenth-century England', in P. Burke, B. Harrison and P. Slack (eds), *Civil Histories: Essays Presented to Sir Keith Thomas* (OUP, 2000); L. Gowing, 'Ordering the Body: Illegitimacy and Female Authority in Seventeenth-century England', in M. J. Braddick and J. Walter (eds), *Negotiating Power in Early Modern Society: Order, Hierarchy and Subordination in Britain and Ireland* (Cambridge, 2001). See also E. Barkley Brown, 'Polyrhythms and Improvization: Lessons for Women's History', *History Workshop Journal*, 31 (1991).
15. For a contemporary description of the form of interrogatories, see H. Conset, *The Practice of the Spiritual or Ecclesiastical Courts* (London, 1685), pp. 114–15.
16. For meanings of 'credit' in early modern England, see C. Muldrew, 'Interpreting the Market: the Ethics of Credit and Community Relations in Early Modern England', *Social History*, 18 (1993); *Ibid.*, *The Economy of Obligation: The Culture of Credit and Social Relations in Early Modern England* (Basingstoke, 1998). See also *Idem*, ' "Hard food for Midas": Cash and its Social Value in Early Modern England', *Past & Present*, 170 (2001).
17. See for example, Ioannis Campegij, *De Testibus*, in, *Tractatus Universi Iuris* (Venice, 1584), vol. 4, f.96ᵛ. I am grateful to Prof. R. H. Helmholz for his help with this issue.
18. CUA, Gregory Dawson c. Leonard Glascocke, Comm.Ct.II.6, f.207.
19. CUA, John Swetson c. William and Frances Thompson, Comm.Ct.II.6, f.123; Richard Ellwood c. Henry Mase, Comm.Ct.II.2, f.54.
20. N[orfolk] R[ecord] O[ffice], John Peckett c. Anne Singleton, DN/DEP/32, f.13ᵛ; W[est] S[ussex] R[ecord] O[ffice], John Ashton c. Izard Ashton, Ep II/5/7, f.30.
21. Bodleian Library, O[xford] U[niversity] A[rchives], Office c. Francis Freeman, Hyp/B/4, f.98. See also below, p.135.
22. OUA, William Farr c. John Ringe, Hyp/B/4, f.87ᵛ.
23. Shepard, *Meanings of Manhood*, pp.195–205, 231–45; B. Capp, *When Gossips Meet: Women, Family, and Neighbourhood in Early Modern England* (Oxford, 2003), pp. 42–9.
24. CUA, John Westly c. Gabriel Dugress, V.C.Ct.II.32, f.146.*
25. CUA, Thomas Crowforthe c. Edward Wardall, Comm.Ct.II.2, f.52.

104   *Alexandra Shepard*

26. D[evon] R[ecord] O[ffice], Bennett c. Deymont, Chanter 866, unfoliated, 28 Nov 1634.
27. WSRO, Mr Reginold Burcy c. William Labdall, Ep II/5/2, ff.229, 231.
28. WSRO, Thomas Lord c. John Wildegos, Ep II/5/5, ff.95ᵛ-96ᵛ; Anna Broad c. Goddard Broad, Ep II/5/1, f.46ᵛ.
29. CUA, Daniel Foote c. Peter Norfolk, V.C.Ct.II.32, f.149ᵛ.
30. OUA, Thomas Smith c. Richard Whistler, Hyp/B/4, f.75ᵛ. For the 'honest' repayment of debts, see also CUA, James Huitson c. Will Cotton, Comm.Ct.II.3, ff.157ᵛ-8, 161ᵛ, 164ᵛ.
31. CUA, Edward Tench c. Martin Harper, V.C.Ct.II.32, f.63. See also Christopher Meeres c. Lancelot Harrison, Comm.Ct.II.3, f.181.
32. OUA, Office c. Francis Freeman, Hyp/B/4, f.96ᵛ.
33. CUA, Nicholas Parnbye c. John Wilkinson, Comm.Ct.II.6, f.133ᵛ; Roger Hills c. Richard Stevenson, Comm.Ct.II.4, f.10ᵛ; Robert Prance c. John Carowe, V.C.Ct.II.1, f.42ᵛ. See also A.L. Erickson, *Women and Property in Early Modern England* (London, 1993); P. Crawford, 'Women and Property: Women as Property', *Parergon*, 19, 1 (2002).
34. WSRO, Underdown c. Saxties, Ep II/5/4, ff.146Aᵛ, 126ᵛ, 151ᵛ.
35. CUA, John Westly c. Dorothy Dugress, V.C.Ct.II.32, f.140.
36. WSRO, Robert Constable c. Stephen Pentecost alias Pankeherst, Ep II/5/12, f.15ᵛ.
37. WSRO, Reginold Burcy c. William Labdall, Ep II/5/2, f.229.
38. L.C. Stevenson, *Praise and Paradox: Merchants and Craftsmen in Elizabethan Popular Literature* (Cambridge, 1984), p.194.
39. OUA, Office c. Francis Freeman, Hyp/B/4, f.97.
40. WSRO, Alice Fowle c. Burcombe, Ep II/5/4, ff.58ᵛ, 143.
41. WSRO, Shudd c. churchwardens of Bolney, Ep II/5/5, f.394; Agnes Adams c. Agnes Mathew, Ep II/5/12, f.34ᵛ.
42. WSRO, Churchwardens of Farligh c. Richard Withers, Ep II/5/7, ff.70–86.
43. WSRO, Gregory Hills c. Thomas Pearse, Ep II/5/6, ff.84ᵛ, 93ᵛ.
44. CUA, John Harvey c. Thomas and Joan Wray, Comm.Ct.II.4, f.171; WSRO, Churchwardens of West Hoathly c. James Chamberlaine, Ep II/5/1, ff.126ᵛ-127.
45. WSRO, Ep II/5/1, Thomas Jervys c. Richard Smyth, f.61.
46. Cambridge University Library, E[ly] D[iocesan] R[ecords], John Wastell c. Hellen Baron, D/2/11, f.101.
47. CUA, John Prance c. Thomas Hodilowe, Comm.Ct.II.1, f.59ᵛ.
48. See H.R. French, 'Social Status, Localism and the "middle sort of people" in England 1620–1750', *Past & Present*, 166 (2000); *Ibid.*, ' "Ingenious & learned gentlemen" – Social Perceptions and Self-fashioning Among Parish Elites in Essex, 1680–1740', *Social History*, 25 (2000).
49. CUA, James Borowes c. William Meys, Comm.Ct.II.2, f.78ᵛ; NRO, John Skurrell c. Joanne Campe, DN/DEP/32, f.45ᵛ.
50. CUA, John Simonds c. Robert Leavit, Comm.Ct.II.4, f.75.
51. NRO, Moore c. Peter Woodcocke, DN/DEP/32, f.83.
52. CUA, Richard Nicholson c. Thomas Crowfoote, Comm.Ct.II.5, f.1.
53. WSRO, Churchwardens of Seaford c Gratwicke, Ep II/5/11, f.200.
54. Shepard, *Meanings of Manhood*, pp. 165–7.
55. A. Shepard, 'Manhood, Credit and Patriarchy in Early Modern England, c.1580–1640', *Past & Present*, 167 (2000); *Ibid.*, *Meanings of Manhood*, ch. 7.

56. WSRO, Churchwardens of West Hoathly c. James Chamberlaine, Ep II/5/1, ff.128, 127.
57. CUA, Robert Cropton c. John Towers, Comm.Ct.II.3, f.119.
58. CUA, Nicholas Mackreth c. Samuel Leedham, V.C.Ct.II.32, ff.5–6.
59. CUA, Robert Bowles c. William Stretton, Comm.Ct.II.4, f.242ᵛ; WSRO, Robert and Elizabeth Springett c. Simon Cogger, Ep II/5/7, f.43ᵛ.
60. Shapin, *Social History of Truth*, ch.3.
61. CUA, Thomas Oliver c. Thomas Hobson, V.C.Ct.II.22, f.115.
62. The university courts, while employing the same procedure, were unlike church courts in this respect, since the latter were not empowered to award damages. For accounts of the jurisdiction and procedures of the university courts see M. Underwood, 'The Structure and Operation of the Oxford Chancellor's Court, from the Sixteenth to the Early Eighteenth Century', *Journal of the Society of Archivists*, 6 (1978); A. Shepard, 'Legal Learning and the Cambridge University Courts, *c.* 1560–1640', *Journal of Legal History*, 19 (1998).
63. CUA, Daniel Rogers c. Francis Catlyn, V.C.Ct.II.8, f.25; Richard Hanger c. Paul Tompson, V.C.Ct.II.12, f.2.
64. CUA, Henry Cotton c. John Swetson, Comm.Ct.II.11, f.40.
65. WSRO, Mary Egelsden alias Charpie c. William Awmunde, Ep II/5/4, f.16.
66. WSRO, Edward Bust c. John Harrys, Ep II/5/6, f.319.

4
A Dynamic Model of Social Relations: Celibacy, Credit and the Identity of the 'Spinster' in Seventeenth-century England

Judith Spicksley

> But earthlier-happy is the rose distill'd Than that which, withering on the virgin thorn, Grows, lives, and dies, in single blessedness.[1]

In attempting to gain a better understanding the dynamic nature of social relations in the early modern period, this chapter considers the evolving definition of the spinster in the sixteenth and seventeenth centuries alongside the identity and status of single women over the same period. It draws on a wide range of sources from probate documents to official records and popular literature, recognising the importance of both the discursive and the material in the construction of identity. Moreover, it argues that identity was formed on more than one level. Thus while abstract categories of social description had a prescriptive role in identity formation, the actions and behaviour of the individual within the local context also impacted on subjective and projected images of identity.[2] And while these levels may appear analytically distinct, in practice each continually informed the other, so that shifts in the nature of identity at either level could not fail to have an impact on both.

Historically, research on the subject of identity formation has been approached from two main perspectives: the one seeking to locate the chronological emergence of the individual as a subjective, self-reflexive and autonomous being; the other to reveal the shifting relationship between the self and others within the social setting. Importantly from the point of view of this chapter, many practitioners from inside the disciplines of history and literature have suggested that it was in the early modern period that the individual first became historically significant.[3] There has also been wider interdisciplinary agreement, extending through the humanities and into the social sciences, about the nature of social relations: commentators agree that the identity of the individual cannot be removed from its historical and cultural location, although the extent to which identity is wholly contingent upon culture is still contested.[4]

Within the field of history itself, the historiography of identity in the early modern period reveals a number of approaches. Researchers have, for example, considered contemporary perceptions of the social order; they have examined the distribution of individuals within and through social groups; and they have considered the relationships between social groups. But while a number of earlier studies tended to downplay the creativity of the individual in the shaping of identity – social emulation was once thought to be a significant factor in middling aspirations to gentility, for example – newer studies have shifted the balance in favour of self-fashioning, allowing the individual to emerge as a proactive agent in his or her social make-up.[5]

Neither has history escaped the current penetration of the privileging of language as a mode of social analysis. Since the publication of Gareth Stedman Jones controversial discussion of Chartism in 1983 there have been moves to appreciate the nature of linguistic forms and account for their impact.[6] Language had never been entirely absent from historical analysis – David Cressy's 1976 article, 'Describing the Social Order of Elizabethan and Stuart England', in the third volume of *Literature and History* had been concerned to reveal the great variety of contemporary social descriptions. But Keith Wrightson's more recent study of changing social perceptions seeks in addition to reveal links between language, notions of identity and shifts in social relations.[7] Further investigation of such links forms the focus of this chapter, which opens with a discussion of the evolving definition of the word 'spinster' in the early modern period. It then proceeds to consider in detail the discursive and material factors that were instrumental in the formation of identity in the early modern period, and examines how celibate women may have adapted their actions and behaviour in order to better accommodate their single existence. It concludes with a discussion of the problematic nature of attempts to give single status for women an abstract equality with married status in seventeenth-century England, which reveal themselves most clearly in the post-Restoration literature.

(I)

During the sixteenth and seventeenth centuries the English language in general underwent radical development, witnessing an extremely rapid increase in the number of new words, especially between the 1570s and the 1630s.[8] This increase was achieved essentially in three ways: by borrowing words from other languages; by coining new words; and by zero-morpheme derivation, or the expansion of the meanings of words already in existence without any change in their form.[9] In Görlach's view, a great many factors 'often specific for the individual word, may be involved in the conditions that make change of meaning possible, in the situation that actuates it and favours its spread, and in its acceptance by the speech community'. In the case of 'spinster', however, two factors which he lists appear to have been of especial significance: the continuous interplay of common speech with more specialised jargon, especially legal or medical terms; and the role of psychological factors in the development of disguising or euphemistic terms. The latter is common in areas of social taboo such as sexuality, disease and death, and the specific meaning is signalled by the inclusion of additional contextual material. However, as usage expands, such words no longer provide the intended disguise, and there is a shift in the range of connotative, and often also in the denotative, meaning.[10]

In terms of the three categories of linguistic expansion – borrowing, coining and zero-morpheme derivation – the definition 'spinster' is clearly an example of the latter. First recorded in 1362, according to the *Oxford English Dictionary*, the term 'spinster' originally referred to a female, or more rarely a male spinner, especially one who was fully occupied in the process of spinning. Then from the early seventeenth century at least it was utilised as a legal designation for a single woman, added to official documents to signal that the woman in question was as yet unmarried. Finally, in 1719 it took on what is recognised as its primary modern meaning, coming to be associated with a woman who had remained unmarried, especially one beyond the usual marriageable age – an 'Old Maid'.[11] Such evolutionary activity, and more especially when combined with a static vocabulary, makes the teasing out of intended meanings in historical contexts difficult.[12] Certainly during the whole of the seventeenth century, the definition 'spinster' retained its medieval occupational significance. In 1604, for example, 11-year-old Mary Atwood of Stratford-upon-Avon was apprenticed to Robert Butler, a whittawer (a white leather worker or saddle maker) and his wife Alice for ten years, to serve as a 'spinster or maid servant'.[13] Manuals of guidance also suggest the term remained linked to concepts of work. In the Restoration edition of *The Compleat Justice*, a popular handbook for Justices of the Peace, 'spinsters' were collectively referred to along with 'sorters', 'carders', 'kembers' (wool combers) and 'weavers'.[14] And when John Locke wrote of the impossibility of making perfect mathematicians out of 'Day-Labourers and Tradesmen, the Spinsters and Dairy Maids', at the end of the century, he clearly had an occupational description in mind.[15] Moreover, a number of widows identified themselves on their wills as spinsters as well as widows, presumably to signal their occupational status and the definition 'spinster' was occasionally added to the names of wives in court proceedings.[16] Evidence that the term 'spinster' retained its original occupational meaning throughout the eighteenth and into the nineteenth century is provided by reference to contemporary dictionary definitions as well as other documentation.[17]

But it was also used as a legal term to define a single woman. Indeed in the earliest seventeenth-century dictionaries, largely written to acquaint people with difficult words, new words or unfamiliar legal terminology, its legal definition was its only one.[18] It has been suggested by J.H. Baker that the declining use of the description 'single woman', which had been the definition usually appended to unmarried women in fifteenth-century England, may have been related to technicalities arising out of the law of additions during the reign of Henry V, whereby statutory additions to the names of defendants were required in original writs, appeals and indictments.[19] The usual addition during the fifteenth century, according to Baker was that of 'single woman', but confusion about the ability of this definition to fulfil the conditions of the statute – it did not fall satisfactorily into the category of estate, degree or a mystery – led to a decline in the use of the description 'single woman' and an increasing reliance on the word 'spinster' as an addition for unmarried women in the sixteenth century.[20]

Baker indicated that the Courts of Common Law had begun to use the term 'spinster' in this capacity from the mid-sixteenth century onwards, and examination of printed marriage licence allegations reveals that this was also a feature of the ecclesiastical courts in London and Southampton.[21] Certainly by the time John Minsheu published his *Ductor in Linguas* in 1617, he could rightly claim that the word 'spinster' was, 'a terme or addition in our Common law, onely added in Obligations, Evidences and writings, unto maids unmarried, as it were, calling them Spinners'.[22] But the use of the title expanded dramatically in ecclesiastical courts procedures over the course of the seventeenth century, no doubt aided by the publication of dictionaries and legal handbooks, the expansion of the legal profession and the overlap between the officials of the church and state courts.[23] This is clearly the most reasonable explanation for the use of the title 'spinster' on probate documents. Agnes Dowdney of Uffculme in Devon, for example, was described on her burial record in 1642 as the daughter of John, but on her will she was defined as a 'spinster'. Yet she had no spinning implements, and there was nothing to suggest she involved herself in spinning activity, at least for remunerative purposes; on the contrary she was in possession of at least two annuities, one for 20s. and another for 40s.[24] Business women like Joyce Jeffreys, the Herefordshire gentlewoman, who was also described on her will in 1648 as a 'spinster', were more likely to employ female spinners than join their ranks, and across the inventory sample from the four counties of Cheshire, Lincolnshire, Norfolk and Durham only a small proportion of single women's documents listed spinning implements: in Cheshire only 27 per cent of those designated as 'spinsters' had some type of wheel in their possession; in Lincolnshire the figure was considerably lower at 13 per cent; while in Norfolk and Durham proportions were even lower, at 9 per cent and 7 per cent respectively.[25] In addition, the probate sample as a whole suggests no clear relationship between age, wealth or social position that can be correlated with the adoption of the title; spinsters were old, young, servants, daughters, unmarried mothers, gentlewomen and independent householders, and their inventory valuations varied from the relatively poor to the extremely wealthy.

Indeed the legal definition 'spinster' largely replaced other words commonly used signify female celibacy – 'single woman', 'maiden' and 'virgin' – as the seventeenth century progressed. There was a certain amount of regional variety: in Southampton, Amy Froide noticed an increase in the use of the term 'single woman' in the town court records during the seventeenth century, although 'spinster' remained the most usual term of address and was by far the most common designation for unmarried women in the Winchester and Hampshire church courts; in Cheshire, the definition 'spinster' had already been added to the bulk of probate documents from at least the beginning of the seventeenth century.[26] But ecclesiastical courts across the board appear to have switched to 'spinster' as an addition on probate documents by the latter part of the seventeenth century. In Kent this transition is especially visible. While 'virgin' remained the most common addition to single women's probate accounts in the early part of the century (79 per cent of surviving accounts were annotated with the title 'virgin' in this period), after 1664 the title simply disappeared: if the clerks of the church courts are to believed, there were no more virgins in Kent.[27] Furthermore, from the mid-seventeenth century, the use of the addition 'spinster' was extended to a broad range of other official documentation, appearing routinely in poll tax records, local censuses and parish records to indicate a woman that was not married. But it may have remained unpopular amongst the upper status groups. For while Blount in 1670 noted that the title 'spinster' was 'usually given to all unmarried Women, from the Viscount's Daughter downwards' he noted Coke's earlier comment that '*Generosa*' remained 'a good addition' for a gentlewoman, and that 'if they be named *Spinster* in any Original Writ, Appeal or Inditement, they may abate, and quash the same'.[28]

Interrogating historical identities by means of contemporary social taxonomies is of course complicated by the inability of simplified linguistic categories to transmit complex contextual information. In his *Dictionary of Slang and Unconventional English* of 1937, for example, Eric Partridge claimed that between around 1620 and 1720 the term 'spinster' was a colloquial word for a harlot.[29] Given its links with female singleness, this is not surprising. The construction of womanhood in the early modern period was drawn from the two fundamental discourses of theology and physiology, the former following the Hebraic-Christian tradition of making Eve responsible for man's downfall, and the latter, the Galenic-Aristotelian account of her biological function and natural physiology.[30] This powerful combination facilitated the emergence of a view that held all women to be psychologically and biologically pre-disposed to sexual activity, and thus, as the Bible suggested, in need of male control. William Tyndale's early English Protestant text *The Obedience of a Christen Man*, reflected the full weight of his scriptural influences: woman as 'that weak vessel' should in his view subject herself to 'the obedience of her husband to rule her lusts and wanton appetites'.[31] Such attitudes remained insistent throughout the period. Gilbert Burnet's *A Defence of Polygamy and Divorce* in 1680, for instance, argued against a man having more than one wife on the grounds that 'Women alone of all Animals desires the Male at all Times, even after Conception ... if one Man cannot suffice one Woman, how can he acquit himself towards a Dozen.'[32] Nor were such attitudes gender-specific. Margaret Cavendish, the Duchess of Newcastle, advised that women should be given instruction on how to 'Temper their Passions, and Govern their Appetites', while the 18-year-old Lady Elizabeth Delaval, in the course of her *Meditations*, exposed the powerlessness she felt in the face of her own feelings.[33]

Thus the construction of women in the early modern period was dominated by the view that they were sexually voracious, a view that had considerable ramifications in terms of female self-determination. The notion of the independent single woman had been linked for centuries with prostitution, a view that served to justify the close regulation of single women's working practices and living arrangements.[34] Under the terms of the Statute of Artificers of 1563, anyone under the age of 30 being unmarried with no trade, craft, office or calling, no land or rent to the value of 40s nor goods to 'the clere value of x poundes' could be retained in service 'and shall not refuse to serve accordinge to the tenor of this statute, uppon the payne and penaltie hereafter mencioned'.[35] However, Paul Griffiths has been able to show that this legislation was more commonly applied to the control of single women's activities than those of their male counterparts: of 263 cases of being 'out of service' in the city of Norwich in the late sixteenth and early seventeenth centuries at least 80 per cent (212) proved to involve single women. Moreover cases presented for being 'at their own hand' were almost entirely gender specific: the only case involving a man being found in the records of 1632.[36] This is hardly surprising, given the fact that the same legislation made it possible for two Justices of the Peace or two city officials to compel,

> any suche woman as is of thage of xii yeres and under thage of xl yeres andunmaryed and furthe of service ... to be reteyned or serve by the yere or by the weke or day, for suche wages and in suche reasonable sorte and maner as they shall thinke mete.[37]

Concern over 'masterless' young women is particularly visible in the urban records of the late sixteenth and early seventeenth centuries, when demographic expansion and rampant inflation served to undermine the workings of even the best parochial provision. Complaint was made in Southampton, in 1597, for instance, that

> theare arr in this towne dyvers young women and maidens w[h]ich kepe themselves out of s[er]vice and worcke for themselves in dyv[er]s mens houses contrary to the statute w[hi]ch we dess[ire] may be considered of and reformacon thereof to be had.[38]

In Manchester in 1584, the Puritan town officials announced their discontent with single women who, according to their understanding indulged 'in abusing themselves with young men and others, having not any man to control them ... in consideration whereof the jury doth order that no single woman unmarried shall be at their own hands, or keep any house or chamber within this town, after [Christmas] next'.

Single women selling bread or ale were to have their goods confiscated.[39] Other towns took similar steps to secure female subservience in the following decades.[40]

Given this backdrop, it is not surprising that the legal definition of a single woman as a 'spinster' could have been used, as Görlach has suggested, to disguise concerns about sexual and social independence. By the end of the seventeenth century it is clear from the documentary evidence that the term was not being employed solely to signify or identify an unmarried woman, but instead had become associated with a particular category of single woman. In the Lichfield local census of 1695, which provides details of name, age and marital status, the use of the term was not age-related – the women concerned fell into an age range of between 13 and 66 – but the living arrangements of those described as spinsters suggest the majority enjoyed a measure of autonomy.[41] Of the 53 examples only 2 – the gentry sisters Elizabeth and Ann Lloyd – were still at home with both parents. Seven of the women were living in their own households, 4 were living with their widowed mothers, 17 were living with their brothers, and 23 were listed in residences in which there was no visible relationship with the head. Similarly, the seven spinsters found among the list of inhabitants in Melbourne, Derbyshire, in 1695 appear either to have been living alone, living with a sister, another single woman or a widow, or lodging with a family to whom they appear unrelated (no ages are included in this census).[42] Not all of the local census-type listings that survive for the early modern period contain references to spinsters, even though the Marriage Duty Act of 1695, from which many resulted, required that details of degree or occupation be included.[43] Nevertheless, where the description 'spinster' was used as a title, it invariably referred to a single woman outside the usual boundaries of male authority, that is, not subject to the dictates of either a father or a master.[44]

A better understanding of the range of meanings embedded within particular definitions can often be obtained from a consultation of their literary manifestations, since they frequently contain additional contextual material. Despite the growing usage of the term 'spinster' in official documentation, however, the description rarely appeared in the literature of the sixteenth and seventeenth centuries. In all of Shakespeare's plays, for instance, there is only one example in which the author used the word 'spinster' (in the first act of *Othello*) and the term appears to have been employed in this case in an occupational capacity.[45] The fact that concepts of celibacy were closely connected with those of youth encouraged writers of plays, narratives and ballads to refer to unmarried women rather as maids, virgins or damsels using traditional images of single woman as young, nubile and subordinate.[46] A keyword search on the Eureka database of the *English Short Title Catalogue*, for instance, suggests only four examples of 'spinster' before 1700. In comparison 'virgin' appears 381 times (although some are clearly religious references), there are 423 examples of 'maid' or 'maiden' and 67 examples of 'damsel'.[47]

Of those four examples above, two were trial reports in which the definition 'spinster' was simply used in its legal capacity, while the third, *The New Westminster Wedding, Or The Rampant Vicar. Being a full relation of the late marriage of J-P-, clerk. to E. Hook, Spinster* (1693), lampoons clerical marriage. Since occupation and status designations were common at this point in marital records, there is little unusual in defining single women as spinsters in this context; moreover, the image presented is a traditional one – the woman in question is described as a maid, and fit and ready for marriage.[48] But the final image is very different. The broadside *The Tickler Tickled* (1679), constructed in the form of a mock trial report, purports to be written by 'Margery Mason, spinster'. This is of course a pseudonym, but the characterisation of the 'spinster' is revealing. Margery defines herself as single, a former maid to a 'Lady', now turned sempstress, who is still possessed of cash and beauty, though not in the first blush of youth. The broadside not only implies that Margery may be involved in spinning a story but can also be interpreted to mean that she is selling more than her sewing skills.[49] Here the 'spinster' appears as an adult woman, financially independent, sexually active and prone to gossip – in diametric opposition to the chaste, silent and obedient woman so valued in early modern society.

(II)

While the constitutive role of language in the mechanics of identity formation is linked with post-structural analysis, its descriptive and prescriptive functions have been recognised for some time.[50] Evidence of the descriptive and prescriptive role of language in the formation of identity in the Tudor and Stuart periods is most visible in the contemporary fascination with the idea and importance of estates or degrees, a means whereby commentators sought to highlight not only the *'functional* differentiation of the estates of mankind' but in addition their *'hierarchical* ordering'.[51] This fascination emerges in a variety of linguistic forms: status designations on probate and other official material, for example, dictums on ecclesiastical seating arrangements, concerns with appropriate upbringing and suitable marriage partners, and the desire to be fittingly laid to rest. In addition, the writings of a variety of social commentators and early statisticians from Sir Thomas Smith to Gregory King reflect a view of society largely rendered in terms of a single hierarchy of status groups and occupations, built around the twin notions of gender and age – that is, in terms of adult male rank – divinely ordained and arranged in order of precedence.[52] Such descriptions were probably never meant as accurate representations of the contemporary social order, but rather as a prescription for 'an ideal harmony in social relations', that served to explain and justify social inequality.[53] However, the exclusion of the politically impotent – servants, apprentices, women, and children – reveals the socio-political preoccupations of those who created them.[54]

Susan Amussen has commented that in the seventeenth century, 'English society was finely graded, and villagers lived with a far more intricately ranked society than most historians have acknowledged'.[55] This statement seems to presuppose a number of circumstances: first, that there were many levels of social assessment; second, that everyone was able to recognise where they should stand in relation to others; third, that there would have been some jostling for positions; and fourth, following on from this, that there was room for manoeuvre. Individuals did not seek simply to internalise an identity from abstract social categories, but actively sought to create and fashion their own, by a process of discursive and material negotiation.

Historians have recognised that the abstract notions of identity and status signalled by linguistic categories would have been derived from a complicated mix of social indicators, which included among other factors, birth, title, wealth, occupation, land holding, and any position of authority.[56] Less often discussed in the historiography, but of vital significance were three others – age, gender and marital status.[57] In terms of age, Keith Thomas, for example, has identified the presence of a gerontocratic ideal – the desire to ascribe maturity, self-government and wisdom to increasing numerical age, by contrasting its growing distance from the foolishness and irrationality that characterised youth.[58] Such notions were enshrined in legal practice, with the most significant piece of employment legislation of the Tudor and Stuart periods – the Statute of Artificers – arguing that 'untill a man growe unto the aige of xxiiij^tie yeares, he (for the moste parte thoughe not allwayes) is wilde, withoute judgement, & not of sufficyent experience to governe himselfe, Nor (many tymes) growen unto the full or perfect knowledge of the arte or occupacion that he professeth'.[59] In terms of gender,

Sir Thomas Smith's popular dictum of the wife tarrying at home 'to distribute that which commeth of the husbandes labor for the nurtriture of the children and family of them both, and to keepe all at home neat and cleane' received support from biblical injunctions on women's activity drawn from the Genesis narrative, and physiological understandings of the female mind and body as secondary to that of the male, created for the sole purpose of reproduction.[60]

It is not surprising, therefore, to find that contemporary male opinion regarded marriage as an essential requisite for social completeness. In the course of conducting the marriage arrangements of his daughter, Thomas Ridgeway, gentleman, endorsed the view that no one 'be properly in the world till they be married, before which time they only go but about the world'.[61] 'Married people' Reynel claimed in 1674 'are more honest, economical, and industrious'.[62] The opinions of some men, however, were characterised by a more distinctive gender bias. Thomas Cave, country squire and son-in-law to John Verney, claimed that until they married, women were 'never well settled here in England', and for Samuel Rowlands, the early seventeenth century author and balladeer, marriage represented the completion of a destiny that for women had an especial significance: 'A wif's farre better then a matchlesse maide'.[63] A clear inducement for women to enter marriage stemmed from the knowledge that marriage had the power to modify gendered and ageist political hierarchies and raise social esteem. For despite the fact that men were understood to be superior to women, wives had authority over male apprentices and servants, and hierarchies of age and status could be overturned by marriage: as William Gouge revealingly remarked, 'Among us, if the younger sister be maried before the elder, the preheminency and precedency is given to the younger.'[64]

Marriage also raised the status of adult men, but entry into the world of the married signalled a major transformation in a woman's social position.[65] Her necessary distinctness was marked by the existence of at least two symbolic customary practices. First, she was allowed to wear clothing appropriate to her status, the archetypal emblem of which was the matron's hood and scarf. As the eponymous heroine in Samuel Rowlands' ballad *The Bride* gleefully pointed out to her maiden friends,

> I am your better now by *Ring* and *Hatt*,
> No more playn *Rose*, but *Mistris* you know what.[66]

Second, married women were frequently allocated different seating positions within their parish church. Matrons either sat in front of their single counterparts to mark their higher standing in the community, or were granted access to superior church seating where it was available. In Newcastle, for instance, it was agreed that no church stall 'be letten to any man's daughter, except she be handfast, or asked in the church, or else married with a husband', and in the Essex parish of Burnham, a girl was ushered before the church court in 1617 for sitting in a pew next to her mother.[67] Historians have also been able to demonstrate that married women assumed weightier responsibilities in the local power hierarchy, but more importantly, as wives and later as widows, they were able to penetrate a status-specific adult female culture that allowed them to become privy to a new social world of childbirth, christening and churching, from which the majority, as single women, would have been excluded.[68] Such practices confirmed a woman's social as well as her gender identity.

On the death of her husband, Alice Thornton remarked that she had passed through 'the two stages of my life of my virgin estate, and that of the honrable estate of marriage', measuring the progress of her life against her marital status.[69] It is then likely that, as Crawford and Mendelson have indicated, most women would have conceptualised adulthood 'mainly in terms of being married, with a household to run, and possibly with children to rear and servants to oversee'.[70] During the course of the late Tudor and Stuart periods, however, demographers have identified an expansion in the proportion of women who had not married by their mid-forties, from 10 per cent in the birth cohort of 1566 to reach 22 per cent in that of 1641.[71] As the average age at first marriage stood at around 25 or 26 and was rising, even those who did marry found themselves single for longer than they may have expected. What was the effect of this experience on the identity and status of single women?

Abstract social categories such as gender, age and marital status were not the only significant factors in the creation of identity.[72] Despite the apparent symbolic significance of status-specific clothing and a female culture dominated by married women, the exclusivity of both these factors was being challenged from at least mid-century. According to the diary of Adam Martindale, though the apparel of freeholders' daughters in his youth (in the early seventeenth century) had been confined to 'their felts, pettiecoates and wastcoates, crosse handkerchiefs about their neckes, and white crosse-clothes upon their heads ... [and] the proudest of them (below the gentry) durst not have offered to weare an hood, or a scarfe ... nor so much as a gowne till her wedding day', by the latter half of the seventeenth century such distinctions were increasingly being disregarded: 'now every beggar's brat that can get them [scarves and hoods] thinks [they are] not above her'. Nor was Joyce Jeffreys prevented from attendance at births, baptisms and churchings in the 1640s, despite her single status.[73] Superimposed upon these categories was a secondary level of social understanding of a more malleable variety, in which identity could be shaped by individual behaviour and neighbourly interaction – the extent of an individual's status and 'credit' within the community. Craig Muldrew, for example, has argued for the existence of 'a sort of competitive piety in which householders sought to construct and preserve their reputations for religious virtue, belief and honesty in order to bolster the credit of their households so that they could be trusted'.[74] Concepts of status and credit were interrelated, and were primarily built around the notion of financial solvency, although they relied upon a number of other attendant factors – relationships with neighbours, occupational transactions, charitable activity, personal conduct, wealth and local office holding, for example – in addition to drawing on symbolic social indicators. At this level of negotiation, then, identity as a function of status and credit was much more flexible, although correspondingly more fragile as a result.[75]

Proceeding from the assumption that individuals require a positive image of themselves, social scientists have also argued for a measure of self-fashioning in identity formation. But while symbolic interactionists focus more specifically on the shared norms and values that individuals adapt and develop to achieve some sense of integration and continuity, social identity theorists concentrate on the different forms identity can take.[76] Individuals in the latter view, it is argued, first seek to improve their relative social identity through a process of social mobility, if possible, but if not, through adopting a range of measures to enhance their current social status. This could include seeking to adopt the positive features of the identity they would like to achieve; seeking to create a new identity with an affirmative image that is different from the first, thus reducing the possibility for negative comparisons; or challenging the very basis of the identity or status hierarchy.

Single women can be found adopting such strategies in seventeenth century England. First, they were involved in running households and looking after children.[77] Ellin Stout, for example, took on the role of housekeeper for her brother William, and the role of surrogate mother to two of her brother Leonard's young children.[78] A number of other sources suggest that Ellen's experience was not uncommon. Sarah Lindon, 37, and Sarah Bull, 40, for instance, were both living at their parental homes in Lichfield in 1695 supporting their elderly widowed fathers, and Margaret Litton, another Lichfield spinster, was responsible for lodging John Wattson, ten, and Elizabeth Tippett, nine, probably on behalf of the local parish.[79]

Second, single women as a group appear to have largely dissociated themselves from involvement in activities that could threaten their moral character, in order to present singleness for women in a positive light. In this respect, the form of identity they chose to adopt gained community acceptance because it drew on shared norms and values that signalled respectability and status. Notions of immorality, as indicated earlier, were often embedded in female celibacy, especially when linked to independence, and writers of prescriptive literature were extremely fond of idolising female chastity. William Gouge, for example, argued in 1622, that the experience of being named a 'maid' in itself was an exhortation to chastity: 'The law stileth her that is contracted a maid, to shew that she ought to keepe her selfe a virgin till the mariage be consummate.'[80] In the ballad literature too, dire warnings – addressed to a largely female audience – about the dangers of succumbing to lustful passions prior to the wedding ceremony were a popular subject choice. Chastity therefore remained a cardinal feminine virtue, and invoking a belief in its practice had a strong influence on perceptions of social credit. Thus Ambrose Barnes, merchant and alderman of Newcastle-upon-Tyne, in recalling Elizabeth Sharper, a single woman 'who was well respected by all her neighbours, and lived with her sister to a great age unmarried', implied in his memoirs that her social credit could be and had been re-negotiated favourably at local level: 'It was whispered she bore a child to another woman's husband in her younger years. But the report blew over and she lived with her sister in good credit many years after.'[81] Though pre-marital intercourse is difficult to measure with any accuracy, it seems likely that as a group, single women largely avoided entering into penetrative sexual activity while unmarried. Levels of illegitimacy, though displaying regional variation, fell during the first half of the seventeenth century and remained low until the early eighteenth century, suggesting a strong link between marriage rates and the onset of intercourse, at least as far as women were concerned.[82]

Single women may also have drawn on cultural notions of charity to buttress their case. This is more difficult to argue, since much of the evidence of their charitable activities has been extracted from their wills. Nevertheless, the diary and accounts of Joyce Jeffreys reveal that she provided regular cash gifts for friends and employees as well as relatives during her lifetime: at New Year; for attending the fair; on St Valentine's Day; and for trips to town and city. Rewards were paid to servants who found her spectacle tray on more than one occasion, and Joyce gave generously on the occasions of birth, baptism and marriage.[83] The account book of Sarah Fell of Swarthmoor Hall also records regular acts of generosity by the Quaker sisters, Rachel, Susanna and Sarah. Thus all three girls gave to a collection 'for stocke at Lancaster' in 1673, while Sarah and Rachel gave sixpence between them to 'a Collection for a briefe, for a fire in Southampton' in April 1675. Rachel, Susan and Sarah also made personal donations to individual women: Bessy Bowes, for example, received a total of 2s. in 1676.[84] Both Joyce's accounts and those of Sarah record in addition numerous gifts of small cash sums to the local and itinerant poor.

Such acts fit neatly within the boundaries of the exhortations to charitable practice visible in the literature of the period. Tracts on the value of the charitable gift in early modern England were extensive, largely because the act of charity itself fitted the individual for membership of the Christian church. As Thomas Cooper argued in his book *The Art of Giving* (1615), 'The first and speciall worke of Charity is to provide for the salvation of the soule.'[85] But charity fulfilled a number of other purposes too. While the second work of charity in Cooper's view was the relief of the poor, 'A third kinde of Benefice is where gifts are given betweene parties for civill respects.' This included for 'gratulatory' and 'placatory' reasons, but also 'to procure favour of those of the meaner to the superior' and to 'maintayne mutuall love and friendship'.[86] It may be significant that wives in Cooper's text were listed under the heading of those that could not give, except in regard of goods held in common or held outside marriage, and even then only with the consent of their husbands.[87] The ability to give therefore offered a way for single women to distinguish themselves from married women and raise their status accordingly. Moreover, many appear to have given in accordance with accepted social parameters. William Gouge's sermon on alms recommended a number of ways in which men could exercise their charity, including the setting up of schools, and the support of ministers.[88] Probate records suggest that in addition to setting up annuities for ageing parents or other kin, and providing nieces, nephews and children of friends with cash to augment their portions, single women founded local charities for the training and education of pauper children, and Joyce Jeffreys at least provided funds towards the cost of three local preachers.[89]

It is also likely that wealthy householders would have felt some responsibility towards helping those less fortunate than themselves. An understanding of the social hierarchy as divinely ordained carried with it a system of reciprocal obligations, in which the 'blessed' rich were duty-bound to assist the less fortunate poor.[90] But the wider anthropological significance of the gift as source of moral, social and political power has also been signalled by a number of authors in this context.[91] Thus while it is recognised that Protestantism offered 'novel but still powerful modes of justifications and rewards for charity and good works', such rewards were not purely spiritual. I.K. Ben Amos has demonstrated the capacity of a gift to 'enhance friendships, intimacies, and family bonds – it can authenticate regard'. Moreover, while acts of personal giving could improve the emotional, social and material well-being of both recipient and donor, such acts also 'affected prestige, enhancing and consolidating status, extending the reputation of the members of the elite and, increasingly, of the middle class as well. Informal support affirmed power relations in society at large'.[92]

But in addition to raising their status through the values of chastity and charity, probate evidence from four counties suggests a growing number of single women may have actively pursued adult identities that could deliver economic and social independence, elements of social esteem that were normally associated with male adulthood. Women like Mary Jackson of Stockport, for example, who ran a milliner's shop, and had a female apprentice, and Mary Robson of Ruskington in Lincolnshire and Elizabeth Furnivall of Chelford in Cheshire, who ran busy farming households, used their positions as employers and household heads to signal their independent status.[93] Occasionally single women even gave themselves an occupational title. Ann Bollum of Borrowdone, Alwinton, in Northumberland, for example, referred to herself as 'yeoman' on her will, while Sarah Walker of Sutton in Cheshire defined herself as a 'buttonmaker'.[94]

A more important feature of single women's economic experience in numerical terms, however, was their ability to extend credit.[95] Single women were owed money for a variety of reasons, such as money for wages, for instance or outstanding rent. With regard to money lending proper, however, single women display a mixed portfolio of credit transactions. Some were involved exclusively in the informal extension of money, as identified by references to money held in the hands of others, to 'lent money', 'money owing', money lent 'without specialty', and 'book debts'. This type of lending did not usually attract interest, and may often have been charitable in intent. Others were only lending formally, which generally did attract interest and would have been investment-driven, formal lending being recognised from references to bills, bonds, debts with specialty, mortgages and statute debts. Finally, a small number of women were engaged simultaneously in both. Of the probate sample in total, nearly two-thirds (63 per cent) were involved in some form of credit provision over the whole of the seventeenth century, with well over a third (38 per cent) registering informal debts, and only slightly less recording formal debts (37 per cent). More significantly, however, there was a general shift away from the former to the latter over the period in question, although levels of informal and formal debt underwent considerable fluctuation.[96]

Single women's participation in lending, and more especially in formal lending, had the potential to bring about shifts in levels of access to wealth, status and power. First in terms of wealth, single female lenders as a group saw rises in their personal wealth above the rate of inflation over the course of the period, many of them substantial. Moreover, in every region except Norfolk, those engaged in formal lending were enjoying greater levels of personal wealth by the end of the century than their counterparts who lent only informally.[97] Second, in terms of their status, lending could go some way towards improving the position of single women relative to their married counterparts. In Tim Stretton's work on the Court of Requests, women who appeared in court drew on their money lending activities to signal their honour and self-worth, for example, and the extension of credit clearly linked the borrower with the lender in a network of social obligations.[98] Henry Wilkinson's 1625 tract on debt claimed that whatever the status of the lender and borrower prior to the extension of credit, the fact of being indebted resulted in a type of servility, for 'by Debt a mans state and person is in a maner mancipated to the lender'.[99] And while there were many proverbs that warned against the practices of lending and borrowing, it was recognised that involvement in debt drew individuals inexorably into the community network: 'The world still he keeps at his staff's end that needs not to borrow and never will lend'.[100]

A further aspect of this argument draws on the nature of lending as a charitable activity, for a considerable part of single women's credit provision may have been imagined in these terms. The household accounts of Sarah Fell suggest that she made a number of short-term interest-free informal loans to local men, and at least one single women appears to have viewed her ability to lend exclusively in charitable terms. Alice Wandesforde, later to become Mrs Alice Thornton, recognised that the capital she had inherited 'was faire, and more then competent, soe that I needed not fear (by God's blessing) to have bin troublesome to my freinds, but to be rather in a condittion to assist them if need had required'.[101]

Lending to a neighbour or friend was construed as part of a Christian's charitable duty. In both the Old Testament and the New, Christians were exhorted to lend wherever there was necessity, and without hope of return: 'Every man' in John Blaxton's words, was 'to his neyghbour a debtor, not onely of that which himselfe borroweth, but of whatsoever his neyghbour needeth'.[102] Thomas Cooper even argued that lending was more beneficial than a gift free gratis: 'We must also lend unto him, which steeds him more sometime than giving', a viewpoint that was still in vogue with ministers over sixty years later.[103] The potential returns of such generosity were thus inscribed upon the early modern psyche, and had been for some time. As Thomas Tusser had pointed out in his sixteenth-century household manual, *Five Hundred Points of Good Husbandry*,

> lending to neighbour, in time of his neede, winnes love of they neighbour, and credit doth breede.[104]

Money lending – both as a charitable and profitable activity – had the potential to transfer economic capital into symbolic capital, and thus increase levels of power.[105] This revealed itself not simply in terms of the obligations arising from the extension of credit, but also in terms of the greater freedom of choice increased financial autonomy could deliver. Though lending money was by no means the only way to maintain financial independence, such independence was crucial if marriage was to be avoided. Furthermore, the ability of single women to extend capital in the local credit market may have been a significant factor in authorising extended periods of celibacy. Certainly among the male testators in Lincolnshire there was a move towards allowing daughters to access their legacies at a given age (usually 21) rather than marriage during the seventeenth century, and fathers increasingly chose to leave their unmarried daughters cash.[106]

Like the 'ingenious and learned gentlemen' of Henry French's Essex, single women did not need to draw their identities exclusively from abstract categories of social representation; they were also 'a product of the proximate, contingent evaluations of status made within local hierarchies, where each individual had a "place", and in which everyone was measured by the same scale'.[107] The two were not unconnected, and each had the ability to impact upon the other. By drawing on a range of behaviours that enjoyed a high cultural value, for example, single women could raise their credit and renegotiate their identity and status within their local communities. By doing so, however, they offered a model of the independent celibate female that stood in clear opposition to the model of womanhood currently in existence, and in the process challenged the received notion of marriage as the superior female identity.

(III)

Support for this alternative model of womanhood is most clearly visible in the Restoration literature. Prior to 1640 there had been little serious discussion of permanent celibacy for women in England outside the ecclesiastical sphere.[108] But by the later seventeenth century a number of female writers had taken up the challenge to the Protestant marriage ideal and were experimenting with the concept of female friendship and the single existence.[109] The Restoration was the first time when women as a group began to enjoy financial success as writers, and a noticeable theme, especially in the poetry, was the desire to remain single. Given Janet Todd's view that female fiction began with 'an analysis of female signs and masks, as well as the social and moral effects of sexual desire and manipulation' this is perhaps unsurprising. Certainly in the work of the Duchess of Newcastle it was a recurrent theme, and Jane Barker is perhaps the most notable example of a poet who celebrated the single life for its freedom from male control.[110]

Models of acceptable behaviour in single women reflected cultural concerns about their actions, and offered implicit advice on the circumvention of social notoriety. John Evelyn's 'perfect' example was:

> a maiden of primitive life, the daughter of a poor labouring man, who had sustained her parents (some time since dead) by her labour, and has for many years refused marriage, or to receive any assistance from the parish, besides the little hermitage my lady gives her rent-free; she lives on four-pence a day, which she gets by spinning; says she abounds and can give alms to others, living in great humility and content, without any apparent affectation, or singularity; she is continually working, praying or reading, gives a good account of her knowledge in religion, visits the sick; is not in the least given to talk; very modest, of a simple, not unseemly behaviour; of a comely countenance, clad very plain, but clean and tight.[111]

The work of Jane Barker, in echoing the earlier sentiments of male writers such as Francis Bacon and Sir John Denham, drew on similar classic notions of chastity, charity, neighbourliness and piety in order to justify her call for female celibacy.[112]

> The neighbouring poor are her adopted heirs,
>> And less she cares, for her own good than theirs.
>> And by obedience testifies she can
>> Be's good a subject as the stoutest man.
>> She to her church, such filial duty pays,
>> That one wou'd think she'd lived ith' pristine days.
>> Her whole lives business, she drives to these ends,
>> To serve her god, her neighbour, and her friends.[113]

The key to success appears to have been the ability to demonstrate social value. Although Mary Astell's main focus was the broadening of education for women as a backdrop to marriage, she also argued that knowledge would not 'lie dead upon their hands who have no Children to Instruct; the whole World is a single Lady's Family, her opportunities of doing good are not lessen'd but encreas'd by her being unconfin'd'.[114] From at least the Restoration, then, a number of women writers were experimenting with the concept of celibacy as a function of female choice, but those who championed a woman's right to choose clearly recognised the necessity for financial security. In the Duchess of Newcastle's play *The Convent of Pleasure*, Lady Happy revealed that,

> Women that are poor, and have not means to buy delights, and maintain pleasures, are only fit for Men; for having not means to please themselves, they must serve only to please others; but those Women, where Fortune, Nature, and the gods are joined to make them happy, were mad to live with Men, who make the Female sex their slaves.[115]

Nor was all of this literature aimed at the higher social groups, for even those with little capital to hand recognised they had an element of choice. The West Country maid in 'Tobias' observation' of 1687, for example, rejected the idea that marriage for women was universally desirable:

> For I am a poor Man's daughter, it's known,
> I work for my Living abroad and at home.
> Sometimes Ime at home, to spinning of Yarn,
> And sometimes abroad to reaping of Corn,
> Sometimes in the Field to milk the Cow:
> I get what I have by the sweat of my brow.
> ....
> For I have no fancy to be made a Wife,
> Nor ne'r was concern'd with no man in my Life.

> And for to live single it is my delight
> And so, honest young-man, I wish you good-night.[116]

However, the consequences of attempts to refashion the identity and status of single women laid bare the limitations of self-fashioning in the early modern period. Economic changes may have provided the means by which some women could consider the possibility of a single life in the long term, but allowing women to believe that celibacy and marriage enjoyed equitable abstract status threatened to herald an unprecedented level of social change.[117] Though with hindsight, it is clear that marriage, as an institution, was never seriously under pressure, the spirit of the age was clearly one of concern.[118] Moreover, the proto-feminist literature constituted only one part of the assault on marriage visible in the literature of the later seventeenth century. Some of the more extreme Protestant sects, for example, had toyed with alternative relationship options in the form of polygamy or free love.[119] A declining interest in marriage amongst the gentlemen of the realm was a feature of men's writings, and there was also a revival of the discussion of celibacy for priests.[120] But a more pressing concern from an assessment of a broader range of the published literature reveals itself to be one of female autonomy. The use of money lending as a means of support was linked in popular literature to immorality in women, while favourite images of single independent women for male satirists, the 'embodiments of threatening and castrating female autonomy, were the Amazon, the whore and the witch'.[121]

Indeed the major theme of published material across a range of genres appears to have been the predatory nature of early modern women, an idea that drew heavily on pre-existing notions of female sexuality, and justified their continued subordination within marriage. For marriage provided the cornerstone of religious and social policies, it legitimised gender relations and secured the legal transfer of property. Participation in the world of work was governed by the expectation that all individuals would enter marriage, and the economic and political power of the nation was understood to have been dependent upon it: the true source of national wealth was revealed in the ability of *married* women to reproduce society, both in a literal and figurative sense. The fact that universal marriage had never been achieved was of little consequence – it was the *belief* that marriage was the ultimate aim and choice of all women that had to be maintained.

Janet Todd has argued that the praise of spinsterhood and celibacy in women's writings, which is peculiar to the Restoration and early eighteenth century, may in part be a response to 'the extra-ordinary nastiness of male sexual satire', during this period.[122] Satirists certainly set out to undermine the notion of choice by lampooning the idea that women would ordinarily choose to remain single: the failure of women to obtain sexual satisfaction was held up as the only reason they were likely to have done so. Thus women were *reduced* to consider a preference for celibacy, in opposition to their *natural* desire for marriage. Common tactics involved conflating the failure of women to marry with men's indulgence in two of the popular new vices – tobacco and coffee. The subject of *The Women's Complaint against Tobacco*, for instance, 'being as yet a Virgin (though it may be contrary to my own will)' claimed she was afraid to tie herself to a man who should take tobacco and thereby deprive her of 'those enjoyments and delight which every Woman expects after Marriage'. She further claimed that tobacco would cause many 'to lead Apes in Purgatory' rather than marry a smoker.[123]

The 'true' nature of woman is more directly revealed in other scurrilous material. Thus the sexually deprived maids in *The Maids Complaint* charged young men with being 'more Uncharitable than Beasts and Savages to suffer so many plump *Virgins* to Languish and Pine away with the *Green-sickness*', while the voice of the maids in *The New Parliament of Women* (1683), complained about the greediness of widows in enjoying three or four husbands while they have not yet benefited from one.[124] Ballads such as *Virginity grown Troublesome; Or The Younger Sister's Lamentation for Want of a Husband* (c.1680) may have focused less directly on the sexual voracity of women by listing the recognised problems that prevented a younger sister from gaining a husband – a good old mother at home, the need to travel to find a husband, a small portion – but nevertheless implicitly reinforced the notion that all young women (her age is given as 20) were keen to rid themselves of their 'troublesome' maiden estate.[125]

The construction of female identity was not restricted to the genre of satire. Writers of conduct books, too, attempted to make marriage normal, natural and desirable. The author of *The Batchelor's Directory*, for example, dutifully informed its male readership that,

> Tho' a Maid never asks to Marry, because she has modesty, yet there is nothing she desires with greater passion ... it must be confess'd likewise that it is her true state, and that there is no better party for her to take.[126]

Medical writers were also influential in redefining the saliency, value and superiority of marriage for women as individuals. Again, highlighting women's natural sexual nature allowed writers to insist on the necessity and importance of marriage for women in the maintenance of good health.[127] Further attempts to reassert the validity of marriage involved widening the discussion of women's natural roles as mothers: during the second half of the seventeenth century an expanding number of obstetrical textbooks focused on the role of women as reproductive agents within marriage.[128] In the new genre of erotic cartography, too, epitomised by Charles Cotton in his *Erotopolis* of 1684, women were constructed as a unified and a natural phenomenon distinguishable only by their biological function.[129] Even within the sphere of pornography, women's natural sexuality received increased attention. Roger Thompson's study of late seventeenth-century pornographic material, for example, suggests that, in comparison with earlier examples, the innovation in the second half of the seventeenth century was the idea of women as sexual activists, and men as sexually unsatisfying, or gigolos.[130] For political and economic analysts, however, the significance of marriage for the individual may have been less important than for its wider social necessity. A burgeoning literature underscored by mercantilist philosophy sought to reiterate the value of marriage for national economic and political security, with commentators such as Carel Reynew, for example, arguing that 'Upon this property [marriage], families, and civil government depends, also trade, riches, populacy; and without this a nation crumbles to nothing.'[131]

Finally, alongside the promulgation of marriage as *the* choice for women was a vilification of women who instead remained celibate, through the medium of the Old Maid. When Mary Astell wrote in 1694 of women 'terrified with the dreadful name of Old Maid' who married to avoid 'the scoffs that are thrown on superannuated virgins', she was not expressing a new emotion. The use of the phrase 'Old Mayde' is first recorded in Palsgrave's French-English dictionary of 1530.[132] But by the late seventeenth century the negative stereotype of the Old Maid had been fully articulated. In *The Challenge Sent by a Young Lady to Sir Thomas &c. or, The Female War* (1697), Old Maids were described as 'rank': 'Proud, Prying, Conceited, Curious, Mischievous, Liquorish, Confident, Impertinent, Lazy, Noisie, Empty, Senceless, Ridiculous Creatures', 'forc'd to *poach* for *Lovers*', '*She-Cannibals*', '*Flesh-Crows*', '*Man-Catchers*'. 'Is there anything in Nature so mean, so useless, so contemptible?' Dunton asked his readers rhetorically. If they had any doubt as to the nature of their answer, the author was swift to enlighten them. As he caustically added: 'An *old Maid* in a *Commonwealth* is much such another Impliment as an *Eunuch* in a *Seraglio*.'[133]

(IV)

Over the course of the early modern period the term 'spinster' expanded to incorporate at least two new descriptions. Though it retained its medieval occupation definition, it had also come to signify a single woman in a legal or official context by the sixteenth century, and by the eighteenth century could be used to signify a woman beyond the usual age for marriage, an Old Maid. Furthermore, in the transition from the legal discourse to the social in the seventeenth century the use of the term had attracted in addition a range of embedded meanings indicative of social, sexual and financial independence. These were drawn from two levels of understanding: on the one hand they represented a continuation of long-held discursive images of independent single women as prostitutes; on the other they were affected by economic change. Those who could afford to make wills were relatively wealthy by contemporary standards, and thus likely to have enjoyed some measure of independence. As neighbours, clerks and other officials drew up probate documents, the material conditions of a single woman's life became embedded within the discursive notion of what it was to be defined as a 'spinster'. But if independence was a characteristic that had become associated with the term 'spinster' by the end of the seventeenth century, then the broader dissemination and stigmatisation of the Old Maid was initially a warning to single women of its limits. While material factors could provide the opportunity for them to increase their relative social position, abstract notions of social order – built on the understanding of women as married and rooted within a range of discourses – were significant in countering that challenge. Women were able to choose celibacy in the long term, a fact that was recognised in contemporary advice literature, but the idea that women *would* choose to remain single received scorn and disapprobation, relegating the Old Maid to the margins of society.[134]

How should we interpret the failure of the independent single woman as an abstract category to emerge as an approved social identity in early modern England? This chapter has argued that identity had a constitutive element beyond the boundaries of abstract social representation (though not necessarily unrelated to it), which allowed individuals considerable room for manoeuvre within their local arena. Nevertheless representations of identity in the public domain frequently operated *as if* identity were fixed, allocating to each individual an identity that located them securely within the socio-political framework. This in turn shaped the way individuals perceived themselves and others.[135] Thus questions of identity, as historians, social scientists and literary scholars are aware, are difficult to disentangle from questions of status, and are heavily bound up in notions of power.

Control of single women, especially those with limited access to capital, had been a regular feature of Tudor and Stuart society, and social responses to the problem of poor, independent women continued in much the same vein as had previously been the case.[136] However, the newer problem confronting society was that the main thrust of the challenge did not emanate from within the ranks of the promiscuous poor, but instead appeared to reside amongst the more affluent single women of middling status or above, whose access to capital gave them greater freedom. Convincing such women of the superiority and value of marriage was therefore critical, and may have been achieved to a considerable extent through the use of linguistic suggestion, assisted by a rise in the proportion of women who were able to read, and a parallel expansion of the printing industry.[137] During the seventeenth century, and in particular after the Restoration, the heightened discussion of predatory female sexuality offered a key means by which supporters of the patriarchy could seek to promote and justify notions of universal marriage. For the 'truth' that marriage was the ultimate aim of all women underpinned the social edifice of sixteenth- and seventeenth-century England in its totality. Legal procedures, inheritance practice, religious belief, medical knowledge, occupational training and social custom were all geared to the understanding that adult women would be married.

It is not fashionable now to interpret power in structural or hegemonic terms, but rather as fractured and dispersed throughout the social space, free of any overarching repressive apparatus, and related to the social production of meaning and 'truth'. But the two are not necessarily mutually exclusive: the notion of power as dispersed does not preclude its ability to demonstrate a functional potential, especially if it serves the interests – either knowingly or unknowingly – of the majority. As Geoff Eley and Keith Nield have recently argued, in addition to being 'insidiously dispersed, power is also organized, accumulated, engrossed, stockpiled, put aside for a rainy day, configured into institutions, concentrated into forms of agency, normalized and systematized into a public sphere, naturalized, and made opaque'.[138] The heightened level of value that women sought to attach to the single female identity as a result of shifts in intellectual thought and socio-economic practice proved such a significant threat to the notion of universal marriage for women – and the discourses that were built upon it – that compensatory tactics were deployed to reinstate a sense of equilibrium. In this war for patriarchal survival, a heightened concentration on linguistic categories of identity was perhaps the most visible of the socio-cultural weapons available. But while language may have been a powerful tool in shaping the nature and status of abstract identities, it was successful primarily because it reflected and revitalised the cultural categories that were already structurally embedded within dominant power relations. Avowing and confirming marriage as the superior, indeed the only constructed female identity that was acceptable was then never seriously up for debate.

Appendix 1: Selected definitions of the term 'spinster' in dictionaries printed *c.* 1600–1800

(1) John Minsheu, *Ductor in Linguas* (1617)

> Spinster, a terme or addition in our Common law, onely added in Obligations, Evidences and writings, unto maids unmarried, as it were, calling them Spinners.

(2) Henry Cockeram, *The English Dictionarie or An Interpreter of Hard Words* 2nd edn (1626)

> (No entry for 'spinster'; nor was there one in the 11th edition of 1658.)

(3) John Bullokar, *An English Expositor* 3rd edn (1641)

> (No entry for 'spinster').

> *Ibid.*; 4th edn (1661)
> Spinster. A term in common Law, attributed to every unmarried woman under the degree of a Countess.

(4) Thomas Blount, *Glossographia: or a dictionary* (1656)

> Spinster, a term or addition in our Law-Dialect, added in Obligations, Evidences and Writings to unmarried Women, as it were, calling them Spinners; And this onely addition is given to all unmarried women, from the Viscount's Daughter downward.

(5) Edward Phillips, *The New World of English Words* (1658)

> Spinster, a Law term, being appropriated to unmarried women in all deeds, bonds, and evidences.

(6) Thomas Blount, *Nomo-lexicon: A Law Dictionary* (1670)

> It is the Addition usually given to all unmarried Women, from the Viscount's Daughter downwards.

(7) Samuel Johnson, *A Dictionary of The English Language* (1755)

> 1. A woman that spins.
> 2. [In law.] The general term for a girl or maiden woman.

(8) John Ash, *The New and Complete Dictionary of the English Language,* 1 (1775)

One that spins; the general title of maiden or unmarried women.

(9) Thomas Sheridan, *A Complete Dictionary of the English language,* 2nd edn (1789)

A woman that spins; the general term for a girl or maiden woman.

(10) John Walker, *A Critical Pronouncing Dictionary and Expositor of the English Language* (1802)

A woman that spins; the general term for a girl or maiden woman.

Acknowledgements

I would like to thank the ESRC for financial assistance in the researching of this chapter, and participants at seminars and conferences in Exeter, Reading, Durham and Aberdeen for their help and advice. I also received a warm welcome in the Department of Geography at Cambridge University, and was given much help and support in accessing the local census material held there, especially by Tony Wrigley.

Notes

1. In his reply to Hermia's request to know her fate if she refuse to wed Demetrius, Theseus suggests she must either marry or become a nun, adding his own views on the viability of such an option, and in the process revealing the acceptable face of female celibacy. See *A Midsummer Night's Dream, I, i.,* in *The Complete Works of William Shakespeare* (Ware, 1996), p. 280.
2. In the field of sociology, the notion of two levels of status assignation – the ascribed and the achieved – remains a basic interpretive concept. I am grateful to Dr Anne Byrne, Senior Research Fellow at the Rutgers Centre for Historical Analysis, for allowing me access to her unpublished paper: 'Developing a sociological model for researching women's self and social identities', which provides an overview of the sociological approaches to identity formation that are particularly useful in the study of single women. See also A. Byrne, 'Singular identities: managing stigma, resisting voices', *Women's Studies Review,* 7 (2000).
3. Historians from R.H. Tawney to Christopher Hill have linked early modern England with the rise of individualism; see M. Mascuch, *Origins of the Individualist Self. Autobiography and Self-Identity in England, 1591–1791* (Oxford, 1997), p. 23. Jonathan Sawday has pointed to the emergence of the

prefix 'self-' about the mid-sixteenth century; J. Sawday, 'Self and Selfhood in the Seventeenth Century', in R. Porter (ed.), *Rewriting the Self Histories from the Renaissance to the Present* (London, 1997), pp. 29–30. Porter himself argued that students of Western philosophy often recognise the seventeenth century as 'the point from which rationality could serve as the foundation-stone of the self-determining individual'; see R. Porter, 'Introduction' to *Ibid.*, *Rewriting the Self*, pp. 3–4. A notable exception is Alan Macfarlane's claim that individualism as a strategy had been present in English society from at least the thirteenth century; A. Macfarlane, *The Origins of English Individualism The Family, Property and Social Transition* (Oxford, 1978). See also M. Clancy, 'Documenting the self: Abelard and the individual in history', *Historical Research*, 76 (2003). In literature, the search for subjectivity has encouraged scholars to see the sixteenth century as the period from which there was greater scope for individual self-fashioning. See, for example, S. Greenblatt, *Renaissance Self-Fashioning From More to Shakespeare* (Chicago, 1980); E. Hanson, *Discovering the Subject in Renaissance England* (Cambridge, 1998).

4. For a discussion of analytic debates on the relative autonomy of culture see J.C. Alexander and S. Seidman, *Culture and Society Contemporary Debates* (Cambridge, 1990).

5. Much work has been done on the concept of identity, and from a number of perspectives. Keith Wrightson's article on the three main approaches to the social order of early modern England makes an excellent starting point. See K. Wrightson, 'The social order of early modern england: three approaches', in L. Bonfield, R.M. Smith and K. Wrightson (eds), *The World We Have Gained. Histories of Population and Social Structure* (Oxford, 1986). Significant work on status groups since then includes J. Barry and C. Brooks, (eds), *The Middling Sort of People Culture, Society and Politics in England, 1550–1800* (Basingstoke, 1994); M. Hunt, *The Middling Sort: Commerce, Gender and the Family in England, 1680–1780* (California, 1996); and the work of Henry French, including, H.R. French, 'Social status, localism and the 'middle sort of people' in England 1620–1750', *Past & Present*, 166 (2000); *Ibid.*, ' "Ingenious and learned gentlemen" – social perceptions and self-fashioning among parish elites in Essex, 1680–1740', *Social History*, 25 (2000). For social emulation see Paul Langford's discussion of 'the pursuit of genteel status' by those of middling rank in P. Langford, *A Polite and Commercial People: England 1727–83* (Oxford, 1992), p. 59.

6. Stedman Jones claimed he did not set out to replace a social interpretation with a linguistic one, but argued that 'the ideology of Chartism cannot be constructed in abstraction from its linguistic form'. See G. Stedman Jones, *Languages of Class Studies in English Working Class History 1832–1982* (Cambridge, 1983), p. 94.

7. K. Wrightson 'Estates, degrees, and sorts: changing perceptions of society in Tudor and Stuart England', in P. Corfield (ed.), *Language, History and Class* (Oxford, 1991).

8. M. Görlach, *Introduction to Early Modern English* (Cambridge, 1991), pp. 136–7.

9. Görlach, *Introduction*, p. 138; C. Barber, *Early Modern English* (London, 1976), pp. 67–193.

10. Görlach, *Introduction*, pp. 200–1.

11. See the Appendix for the fuller O[xford] E[nglish] D[ictionary] definition. Dating the emergence of the notion of a 'spinster' as a woman beyond the usual age for marriage in 1719 may be too early. The text quoted in the OED is *The Spinster* by J. Roberts, one that forms part of the debate around the decline of the wool trade in the face of mounting importation of calicoes. The spinsters in question were still unmarried, but not clearly beyond the usual age of marriage, that is, Old Maids. A more suitable text might be *The Old Maid* by 'Mary Singleton, Spinster', first published as a periodical in 1755 and 1756, in which the older 'spinster' is more clearly associated with the 'Old Maid'. Dictionary definitions of the term 'spinster' during the eighteenth century do not suggest that the word 'spinster' as yet had strong associations with the Old Maid.

12. Wrightson, 'Estates', p. 32.

13. J. Jones, *Family Life in Shakespeare's England: Stratford-upon-Avon 1570–1630* (Stroud, 1996), p. 31.

14. Anon., *The Compleat Justice* 7th edn (1661), p. 366.

15. J. Locke, *The Reasonableness of Christianity as Delivered in the Scriptures* (1695), p. 279, cited in M. Astell, *A Serious Proposal to the Ladies Parts I & II* (ed.) P. Springborg (London, 1997), p. xxix.

16. Legal historians have put forward a number of explanations for this. Carol Wiener has suggested that this procedure may have been little more than a legal fiction designed by Justices of the Peace to avoid the uncertainty about criminal responsibility of married women, and apportioning blame between a wife and her husband; C.Z. Weiner, 'Is a spinster an unmarried woman?', *American Journal of Legal History*, 20 (1976), p. 31. Valerie Edwards indicates it may more realistically have been a legal tactic employed by women charged with a serious offence who were using the defence of marital coercion, but whose marital circumstances could not be clearly established; V. Edwards, 'The Case of the Married Spinster: An Alternative Explanation', *American Journal of Legal History*, 21 (1977), pp. 264–5. Finally, J. H. Baker believes it may have been more simply a concern among lawyers with the ability of the term 'wife' to fulfil the obligations of the fourteenth century Statute of Additions; J.H. Baker, 'Male and Married Spinsters', *American Journal of Legal History*, 21 (1977) p. 259.

17. I would like to thank Rod Ambler for pointing out that in 1784 the registers of the Grimsby Methodist circuit in Lincolnshire recorded that 168 married and unmarried women were occupied as 'spinsters', although by 1790 sectoral shifts in employment ensured they had almost vanished from the records. See R. Ambler, *Churches, Chapels and the Parish Communities of Lincolnshire 1660–1900* (Lincoln, 2000), p. 145. The appendix details the evolving definition of the 'spinster' in printed dictionaries.

18. Not all seventeenth-century dictionaries offered definitions for the term 'spinster' and those that did restricted themselves to its legal usage; see examples in the Appendix.

19. Baker, 'Male and Married Spinsters', p. 258.

20. Two factors are held up to account for this. First, since it referred to someone who spun, it was undoubtedly a mystery, and so satisfied the legal requirements; moreover, it was an occupation, or pastime, that was most often associated with women. Second, because it was understood that no

addition was needed for married women and widows, merely a reference to their marital status, the use of 'spinster' as an addition came to be associated with single women in court cases. See P. J.P. Goldberg (ed.), *Woman is a Worthy Wight: Women in English Society c.1200–1500* (Stroud, 1992), pp. xii, pp. 110, 151, 189, 197; Baker, 'Male and Married Spinsters', p. 258.

21. G.J. Armytage (ed.), 'Allegations for Marriage Licences issued by the Dean and Chapter of Westminster, 1558–1699; also for those Issued by the Vicar-General of the Archbishop of Canterbury, 1660–79', *Harleian Society*, 23 (1886). In this volume, 'spinster' first appears in 1568 and thereafter becomes increasingly popular along with other status/occupational titles for both men and women. Similarly, in G.J. Armitage (ed.), 'Allegations for Marriage Licences issued from the Faculty Office of the Archbishop of Canterbury at London, 1654–1869', *Harleian Society*, 24 (1886) though 'widow' and 'gent' appear from the beginning in Volume A, the term 'spinster' does not appear until Volume B begins in 1567. In this instance between 1570–71 and 1575 there are few designations of any sort (two widows and one spinster in 1574). When records begin again in 1632, the use of 'spinster' is commonplace. Finally in G.J. Armitage (ed.), 'Allegations for Marriage Licences issued by the Bishop of London, 1520–1620', *Harleian Society*, 25 (1887) 'spinster' first appears in 1556 ('widow' and 'gent' from the 1520s) but is not used commonly until after 1560, when 'puella' and 'virgin' also appear. Work by Amy Froide on Southampton in the early modern period indicates that the ecclesiastical courts in the Winchester diocese were more likely to record the status of never-married women as spinsters from the mid-1580s. A.M. Froide, 'Single Women, Work, and Community in Southampton 1550–1750' (Duke University Unpubl. PhD Thesis, 1996), p. 373. In Lincoln, wholesale adoption of the term in the ecclesiastical courts seems to have come later. In the volume of marriage licences from 1598 to 1628, 'spinster' does not appear until 1600, and is not common until after 1612, and in the volume of marriage bonds between 1574 and 1626, the description 'single woman' remains the most popular addition, with 'spinster' making its first appearance in 1623; L[incoln] A[rchives] manuscript listings of Lincoln Marriage Licences, 1598–1628 and Marriage Bonds, 1574–1626.

22. J. Minsheu, *Ductor in Linguas; The Guide Into Tongues* (1617), p. 462. Similar definitions can be found in T. Blount, *Glossographia* (1656) and T. Manley, *Nomothetes: The Interpreter* (1672).

23. C.W. Brooks has outlined some of the connections between the ecclesiastical and common law branches of jurisprudence during the seventeenth century. See C.W. Brooks, *Pettyfoggers and Vipers of the Commonwealth The 'Lower Branch' of the Legal Profession in Early Modern England* (Cambridge, 1986), pp. 43–5.

24. P. Wyatt (ed.), 'The Uffculme Wills and Inventories 16th to 18th Centuries', *Devon and Cornwall Record Society*, n.s. 40 (Exeter, 1997), p. 84.

25. Family Record Centre PROB 11/214, Joyce Jefferies; figures from Cheshire and Lincolnshire are taken from J.M. Spicksley, 'The early modern demographic dynamic: celibates and celibacy in seventeenth century England', (University of Hull Unpubl. PhD Thesis, 2001), p. 276; those for Norfolk and Durham have been extracted from current research. More testators could have been employed as spinners by a third party; wheels may not have been

included on the inventory listings because of their low value; or wheels may
have been removed before the inventory was completed.
26. Froide, 'Single Women, Work, and Community', pp. 371–4; Spicksley, 'The
early modern demographic dynamic', p. 277.
27. C[entre for] K[entish] S[tudies], PRC 1/1-PRC 21/15.
28. T. Blount, *Nomo-Lexicon: A Law-Dictionary* (1670). See also E. Coke, *The Second
Part of the Institutes of the Lawes of England* (1642), p. 668.
29. E. Partridge, *A Dictionary of Slang and Unconventional English* ed. P. Beale,
8th edn (London, 1984), p. 1126.
30. K. Aughterson (ed.), *Renaissance Woman: A Sourcebook Constructions of
Femininity in England* (1995), p. 41.
31. W. Tyndale, *The Obedience of a Christian Man* ed. D. Daniell (London, 2000),
p. 34. Concerns about female sexuality were not restricted to English
Protestants. Vives, a Spanish humanist and advisor to Catherine of Aragon,
offered a vision of social order that was heavily coloured by his preoccupation
with the need for men to own and control women's sexuals and reproductive
activity. J.L.Vives, *The Office and Duetie of an Husband* (1555), A5–A6, B2.
32. G. Burnet, *A Defence of Polygamy and Divorce* (1680), p. 13.
33. M. Cavendish, Duchess of Newcastle, *CCXI Sociable Letters* (1664), p. 50;
D.G. Greene (ed.), 'The Meditations of Lady Elizabeth Delaval Written
Between 1662 and 1671', *Surtees Society*, 190 (1978), p. 109.
34. John Stow discussed the link between prostitution and single women as
revealed in the legal restrictions on stew-holders in Southwarke, London, set
down in the reign of Henry II. He also claimed that because prostitutes were
forbidden Christian burial, there was a burial ground appointed for them,
called the 'Single Woman's churchyard, appointed for them far from the
parish church'. See H.B. Wheatley (ed.), *Stow's Survey of London* (London,
1912), pp. 360–2.
35. R.H. Tawney and E. Power (eds), *Tudor Economic Documents*, I (London, 1924),
pp. 339–40.
36. P. Griffiths, 'Masterless Young People in Norwich, 1560–1645', in P. Griffiths,
A. Fox and S. Hindle (eds), *The Experience of Authority in Early Modern England*
(Basingstoke, 1996), p. 153.
37. Tawney and Power, *Tudor Economic Documents*, pp. 344–5.
38. Cited in S. Wright, ' "Churmaids, Huswyfes and Hucksters": the employment
of women in Tudor and Stuart Salisbury', in L. Charles and L. Duffin (eds),
Women and Work in Pre-Industrial England (London, 1985), p. 104.
39. J. Harland (ed.), 'A Volume of Court Leet Records of the Manor of Manchester
in the Sixteenth Century', *Chetham Society*, o.s. 63, (1864), pp. 157–8.
40. In Norwich, for example, in June 1609 the Mayor's Court ordered overseers
to root out maids and singlewomen who 'lyve at their owne handes'. Cited
in P. Griffiths, *Youth and Authority Formative Experiences in England 1560–1640*
(Oxford, 1996), p. 377.
41. Daughters in the same analysis fell between the age ranges of 1 and 37.
42. R.E.C.Waters (ed.) *A Statutory List of the Inhabitants of Melbourne, Derbyshire,
in 1695* (London, n.d.), pp. 12–3, 17–8, 22–3.
43. 7 William III, 1694. The Marriage Duty Act, implemented in 1695 for the purpose of 'carrying on the War against France with Vigour', laid a graduated tax
on births, marriages and burials, but also set a duty on all bachelors over 25

and widowers with no children. See *Journals of the House of Commons*, II, 1693–97 (London, 1803), pp. 230–3.

44. Census listings with references to spinsters include: Chilvers Coton, 1684; London, St Mary le Bow, 1695; Coleham, undated (1695?); Shrewsbury, Stone Ward, 1695 (1698?); Shrewsbury, Welsh Ward, 1698; Leicester, St Mary, 1697–99; Leicester, St Martins, 1695/96; Rothley, 1694; Bristol, St Walburg, 1697/1702. Not all spinsters were financially secure – a number are found amongst lists of almshouse residents. Nor were census enumerators always consistent. Frances Prigg of Bristol St Walburg was described as a 'spinster' in the census of 1695, but a 'widow' in that of 1702. In one case the term could have been used as an occupational designation: two spinsters in Stone Ward, Shrewsbury, were each living in the household of a tailor.

45. In disparaging the military leadership of Michael Cassio, Iago describes him as: 'A fellow almost damn'd in a fair wife;/That never set a squadron in the field,/Nor the division of a battle knows/More than a spinster'. See *Othello, The Moor of Venice*, I, i., in *Complete Works of William Shakespeare*, p. 818. Despite its use in ecclesiastical courts, the use of additions remained uncommon in Visitation Records, lending additional weight to the notion that the term was still uncommon in popular discourse, at least at the end of the sixteenth century. See, for example, D. Shorrocks (ed.), 'Bishop Still's Visitation 1594, and The 'Smale Booke' of the Clerk of the Peace for Somerset, 1593–5', *Somerset Record Society*, 84 (1998), and W.J. Shiels (ed.), 'Archbishop Grindal's Visitation, 1575, Comperta et Detecta Book', *Borthwick Texts and Calendars: Records of the Northern Province*, 4 (1977).

46. Examples in the Pepys collection include: 'The Wanton Maiden's Choice'; 'The Pensive Maid: Or, The Virgins Lamentation for the loss of her Lover'; 'The Amorous Virgin'; 'The Seven London Lasses Lamentations'; 'The Distressed Damsels'; 'The Valiant Damsel'. See W.G. Day (ed.), *The Pepys Ballads*, II and IV (Woodbridge, 1987).

47. See the Eureka on-line database at http://eureka.rlg.org/gateway.html

48. *The New Westminster Wedding, Or The Rampant Vicar. Being a full relation of the late marriage of J-P-, clerk. to E. Hook, Spinster* (1693), relates the story of a lusty vicar who courted a Dutch maid with the promise of clothes, married her and then treated her badly, as a result of which she left him to go and 'patch up her crackt Virginity' for a more deserving Dutchman.

49. *The Tickler Tickled: Or, The Observator upon the Late Trials of Sir George Wakeman and c. Observed: By Margery Mason, Spinster* (1679). In a reference to a Chaucerian couplet, Margery suggests a 'Shop I keep for Countenance But— is my Sustenance'. The misquote is taken from *The Cook's Tale*, the story of a young victualler's apprentice who preferred gambling, wenching and taverns to work: 'And hadde a wyf that heeld [kept] for contenance [appearance]/A shoppe, and swyved [copulated] for hir sustenance'. See G. Chaucer, *The Tales of Canterbury* ed. R.A. Pratt (Boston, 1974), pp. 4421–2.

50. Identity appears to link individual action with social structure. In social psychology identity is seen to be the result of a series of cognitive processes that have their basis in information processing. Through linguistic categories, individuals are able to interpret and negotiate their social world, by internalising the categories – such as age, sex, wealth and status – that are appropriate to themselves. See H. Tajfel and J.P. Forgas, 'Social Categorization: Cognitions,

Values and Groups', in J.P. Forgas (ed.), *Social Cognition: Perspectives on Everyday Understanding* (London, 1981), pp. 114–5. In sociology, identity is predictably more closely related to social than psychological factors, with much of the current theory having developed out of the symbolic interactionist perspective pioneered by George Herbert Mead, in which individuals come to recognise their social roles, become aware of what is expected of them, and judge and evaluate themselves from the perspective of the community. See G.H. Mead, *Mind, Self and Society: From the Standpoint of a Social Behaviourist* ed. C.W. Morris (Chicago, 1934). For an overview of both perspectives see M.A. Hogg, D.J. Terry and K.M. White, 'A Tale of Two Theories: A Critical Comparison of Identity Theory with Social Identity Theory', *Social Psychology Quarterly*, 58 (1995), pp. 256–60.

51. Wrightson, 'Estates', p. 33.
52. According to the Elizabethan homily on obedience, 'Almighty God hath created and appointed all things in heaven, earth, and waters, in a most excellent and perfect order.' See G. Burgess, *The Politics of the Ancient Constitution An Introduction to English Political Thought, 1603–42* (Basingstoke, 1992), p. 132. Thomas Smith and William Harrison both conceptualised this in terms of a four-tier ranking system based around gentlemen, citizens, yeomen and artificers. See T. Smith, *De Republica Anglorum: A Discourse on the Commonwealth of England*, ed. L. Alston (Ireland, 1972), p. 31 and W. Harrison, *The Description of England* ed. G. Edelen (New York, 1968; reprint 1994), p. 94. Richard Mulcaster was of the opinion that 'all the people which be in our countrie by either *gentlemen* or of the *commonalty*', while William Camden, Thomas Wilson and John Cowell developed more complex hierarchies – see D. Cressy, 'Describing the Social Order of Elizabethan and Stuart England', *Literature and History*, 3 (1976), pp. 30–1. But contemporary definitions reached their apogee in the work of Gregory King, whose social tables provide the most formalised and differentiated account of the seventeenth century social hierarchy, in addition to providing an estimate of the size of the social groups outlined. See G.S. Holmes, 'Gregory King and the Social Structure of Pre-Industrial England', *Transactions of the Royal Historical Society*, 5th ser., 27 (1977), appendix.
53. K. Wrightson, *English Society 1580–1680* (London, 1982), p. 19.
54. Thomas Smith, for example, placed all women except queens, duchesses and countesses, who were direct blood descendents to positions of authority, outside the political order. See Smith, *De Republica Anglorum*, p. 30.
55. S.D. Amussen, *An Ordered Society Gender and Class in Early Modern England* (New York, 1988), p. 3.
56. In Wrightson's view, social status (and thus identity) was a compound of 'birth, inherited or conferred title, wealth and the nature of that wealth, occupation, mode of land tenure, legal status, lifestyle and tenure of positions of authority'. See Wrightson, 'The Social Order', p. 180.
57. In a similar way in modern psychological analysis the position of the self within society is thought to be shaped by 'ideal conceptions of what the person ought to be, and these vary by gender, ethnic origin, religion, region, social class, and other kinds of social differentiations'. See J.P. Hewitt, *Self and Society: A Symbolic Interactionist Social Psychology*, 8th edn (Boston, 2000), p. 116.

58. K. Thomas, 'Age and Authority in Early Modern England', *Proceedings of the British Academy*, 62 (1976), p. 207.

59. Tawney and Power, *Tudor Economic Documents*, p. 354.

60. Smith, *De Republica Anglorum*, p. 22. Four reasons were commonly given in order to justify woman's subjection to man: she was made out of man; she was made for man; she was made after man; she was first to transgress. See for example, E. Reyner, *Considerations Concerning Marriage* (1657), p. 14. The writings of Galen, the second century Greek scholar, dominated early modern views on physiology. They also ranked women as secondary to men: 'Now just as mankind is the most perfect of animals, so within mankind the man is more perfect than the woman, and the primary instrument'; Galen, *On the Usefulness of the Parts of the Body*, cited in K. Aughterson (ed.), *Renaissance Woman Constructions of Femininity in England* (London, 1995), p. 47.

61. D. Cressy, *Birth, Marriage and Death Ritual, Religion and the Life Cycle in Tudor and Stuart England* (Oxford, 1997), p. 290.

62. C. Reynel, *The True English Interest* (1674), cited in J. Thirsk and J.P. Cooper (eds), *Seventeenth Century Economic Documents* (Oxford, 1972), p. 759.

63. S.E. Whyman, *Sociability and Power in Late-Stuart England The Cultural World of the Verneys 1660–1720* (Oxford, 1999), p. 113; S. Rowlands, *The Bride* (1617), C2v.

64. W. Gouge, *Of Domesticall Duties* (1622), p. 211.

65. Though marriage remained important for men, bachelors could signal their adulthood through the completion of their occupational training, by becoming the head of a household, and by demonstrating financial independence. However, Alex Shepard has recently argued that the difficulties men experienced in gaining access to the key determinant of masculinity – the patriarchal ideal (originally that of rule by a father as household head) – allowed the attributes of the patriarch to be remapped onto notions of civility and status during the later seventeenth century. A. Shepard, 'Gender and Patriarchy', Conference paper given at the University of East Anglia, April 2002.

66. Rowlands, *The Bride*, A3v.

67. W.H.D. Longstaffe (ed.), 'Memoirs of the Life of Mr. Ambrose Barnes, Late Merchant and Sometime Alderman of Newcastle upon Tyne', *Surtees Society*, 50 (1866), p. 260; Thomas, 'Age and Authority', p. 209. Thomas uses this example as evidence of age hierarchies rather than those of marriage.

68. S. Mendelson and P. Crawford, *Women in Early Modern England* (Oxford, 1998), p. 131.

69. A. Thornton, 'The Autobiography of Mrs Alice Thornton of East Newton, Co. York', *Surtees Society*, 62 (1875), p. 234.

70. Mendelson and Crawford, *Women*, p. 124.

71. R. Schofield, 'English Marriage Patterns Revisited: Once More', May 1998, by kind permission of the author, pp. 6–7. Schofield's unpublished rates for female celibacy are slightly lower than those currently in print. See E.A. Wrigley and R. Schofield, *The Population History of England 1541–1871 A Reconstruction* (Cambridge, 1989), p. 260, Table 7.28.

72. R. Parkinson (ed.) 'The Life of Adam Martindale', *Chetham Society*, 4 (1845), p. 6. Sumptuary legislation did not stipulate the type of clothing single and married women were allowed to wear; this was designated by social custom. For a survey of such legislation see N.B. Harte, 'State Control of Dress and

Social Change in Pre-Industrial England', in D.C. Coleman and A.H. John (eds), *Trade, Government and Economy in Pre-Industrial England Essays Presented to F.J. Fisher* (London, 1976).

73. B[ritish] L[ibrary] Egerton MS 3054, The Diary of Joyce Jeffreys, 1638–49. Keith Thomas has argued that age may have given women increased authority within society. See Thomas, 'Age and Authority', p. 235.

74. C. Muldrew, *The Economy of Obligation: The Culture of Credit and Social Relations in Early Modern England* (Basingstoke, 1998), pp. 148–9.

75. The status of Henry French's 'chief inhabitants' rested 'on evaluations made within the settlement rather than on criteria from outside'; French, 'Social Status, Localism', p. 94.

76. 'A shared set of expectations, sentiments, norms, and values that people use to examine themselves and their conduct enables them to achieve a sense of continuity and integration by identifying with the community'. Hewitt, *Self and Society*, p. 118. For the social identity approach see S. Skevington and D. Baker, 'Introduction', in *Ibid.* (eds), *The Social Identity of Women* (London, 1989).

77. Bachelors were also called upon to provide family assistance. Richard Wicherley of Myddle, who never married, adopted his brother Thomas's son, and 'put him to school', while William Stout took Mary Hall, daughter of his niece Elizabeth into his house 'free' in order to improve her education. See R. Gough, *The History of Myddle* (Ascot, 1979), p. 73; J.D. Marshall (ed.), *The Autobiography of William Stout of Lancaster 1665–1752* (Manchester, 1967), p. 226.

78. Marshall, *William Stout*, pp. 76, 90, 105, 142.

79. Lichfield local census, 1695, pp. 20–1. It was also common to find unmarried daughters living with their widowed mothers, a factor that may have increased the odds of the daughter remaining single. See O. Hufton, 'Women without men: widows and spinsters in Britain and France in the eighteenth century', *Journal of Family History*, 9 (1984), p. 362.

80. Gouge, *Domesticall Duties*, p. 202.

81. Barnes claimed she confessed at the age of 80 to 'bearing a bastard' and in attempting to atone for her sin, 'ript up her belly with a pair of scissars, and pulled her bowells out with her hand'. She was buried in August 1703. See Longstaffe, *Memoirs*, p. 238.

82. R. Adair, *Courtship, Illegitimacy and Marriage in Early Modern England* (Manchester, 1996), pp. 48–64; P. Laslett, *Family Life and Illicit Love in Earlier Generations* (Cambridge, 1977), p. 115.

83. BL Egerton MS 3054, Joyce Jeffreys, ff. 44, 46, 66, 70v. Participating in the custom of giving Valentine's Day presents to male friends also allowed Joyce to signal a token interest in the rites of courtship, despite her advanced age. This may have been another strategy to maintain her credibility, since Anne Byrne has argued that 'demonstrating interest in becoming coupled could arguably offset any stigma accruing from the social identity of "single woman;" ' Byrne, 'Developing', p. 6.

84. N. Penney (ed.), *The Household Account Book of Sarah Fell of Swarthmoor Hall* (Cambridge, 1920), pp. 51, 207, 363.

85. T. Cooper, *The Art of Giving* (1615), p. 2.

86. Cooper, *Giving*, p. 4.

87. *Ibid.*, p. 6. In exceptional circumstances, where the husband was unfit to govern the family, the wife could give.

88. [W. Gouge], Sermon 11, 'After what manner must we give Alms, that they may be acceptable and pleasing unto God?' in *The Morning-Exercise at Cripplegate: or Several Cases of Conscience Practically Resolved, by sundry Ministers, September 1661* (1661), pp. 254–5.

89. BL Egerton MS 3054, Joyce Jeffreys, f.65v.

90. M.H.D. van Leeuwen, 'Logic of Charity: Poor Relief in Preindustrial Europe', *Journal of Interdisciplinary History*, 24 (1994), p. 593.

91. Such ideas have been familiar in anthropological discourse for some time. The best known studies include M. Mauss, *The Gift: Forms and Functions of Exchange in Archaic Societies* (London, 1969) and M. Sahlins, *Stone-Age Economics* (London, 1974). Recent work by historians includes that of van Leeuwen, 'Logic of Charity'; A. Offer, 'Between the gift and the market: the economy of regard', *Economic History Review*, 50 (1997); S. Cavallo, 'The Motivations of Benefactors: An overview of approaches to the study of charity', in J. Barry and C. Jones (eds), *Medicine and Charity Before the Welfare State* (London, 1991).

92. Ben-Amos has suggested that informal support also had the power to solidify the identities of individuals. See I.K. Ben-Amos, 'Gifts and Favors: Informal Support in Early Modern England', *Journal of Modern History*, 72 (2000), pp. 300, 299, 337. In Sandra Cavallo's work on Turin in the later seventeenth century, charity may have been 'motivated essentially by a quest for the symbolic confirmation of the status of the benefactor'; Cavallo, 'Motivations of Benefactors', p. 55. van Leeuwen's charitable logic was derived from its positive effect on social status, political position and the achievement of eternal salvation; van Leeuwen, 'Logic of Charity', p. 611.

93. C[hester] R[ecord] O[ffice] WS 1684, Mary Jackson; LA INV 185A/20, 1684, Mary Robson; CRO WS 1685, Elizabeth Furnivall.

94. D[urham] U[niversity] L[ibrary] DPRI/1/1677/B9, Ann Bollum; CRO WC 1690 Sarah Walker.

95. It may also be possible that money lending by single women, while increasing their social status, served in addition to make them unpopular. However, the usurious spinster does not appear to have been a feature of the contemporary literature. Classic usurer stereotypes – from Jonson *et al.*'s Security in *Eastward Ho* to Wycherley's Alderman Gripe in *Love in a Wood* – were male, not female. See G. Chapman, B. Jonson and J. Marston, *Eastward Ho (1605)* (ed.) R.W. Van Fossen (Manchester, 1979) and G. Weales (ed.), *The Complete Plays of William Wycherley* (New York, 1967).

96. This claim is based on the analysis of the probate records of almost 1500 single women in the areas of Cheshire, Chichester, Durham, Lincolnshire and Norfolk between 1601 and 1700.

97. Figures for personal wealth (minus debts and leases) have been extracted from all the cases for which inventory amounts survive. Deflators have been constructed from the wage/price data series in E.H. Phelps Brown and S.V. Hopkins, 'Seven centuries of the prices of consumables, compared with builders' wage-rates', in E.M. Carus-Wilson (ed.), *Essays in Economic History*, II (London, 1962).

98. T. Stretton, *Women Waging Law in Elizabethan England* (Cambridge, 1998), p. 192.

99. Cited in Muldrew, *Economy of Obligation*, p. 98.

100. M.P. Tilley, *A Dictionary of the Proverbs in England in the Sixteenth and Seventeenth Centuries* (Michigan, 1950), p. 761. In the same volume see also: 'Lend and lose, so play fools', p. 233; 'When I lend I am his friend, when I ask I am unkind', p. 245; 'He that lends gives', p. 376; 'To borrow on usury brings sudden beggary', p. 694.

101. See for example entries relating to Joseph Sharpe, John Holme, William Hathorne, Robert Wailes, James Lancaster and John Cowell in Penney, *Sarah Fell*, pp. 7, 15, 115, 198, 49, 55; Thornton, 'Autobiography', p. 75.

102. J. Blaxton, *The English Usurer; or Usury Condemned by the Most Learned Divines of the Church of England* (1634), p. 11.

103. Cooper, *Art of Giving*, p. 3. According to Richard Kidder, a London rector, it was sometimes 'greater charity to *lend* than to *give*. He that lends a trading man encourages his diligence; and the borrower takes pains that he may repay'. See R. Kidder, *Charity Directed: Or, The Way to Give Alms to the Greatest Advantage* (1676), p. 30. Gouge's sermon on almsgiving argued that one way for men to exercise their charity was 'By a ready lending to such as being in a Calling, want stock, or other means to help themselves in their Trades'. See [Gouge], 'After what manner', p. 255.

104. Cited in Muldrew, *Economy of Obligation*, p. 164.

105. Pierre Bourdieu suggested two ways in which it was possible for an individual to exert power over another – either through gifts or debts. This 'gentle, hidden exploitation' allowed a form of social alchemy, 'the transmutation of economic capital into symbolic capital', through which the power relations between the parties gained social recognition, and thus legitimate authority. See P. Bourdieu, 'Structures, Habitus, Power: Basis for a Theory of Symbolic Power', in N.B. Dirks *et al.* (eds), *Culture/Power/History A Reader in Contemporary Social Theory* (New Jersey, 1994), pp. 185–7.

106. LA LCC Wills, 1565–1700. The study surveyed over a thousand manuscript wills of male testators in Lincolnshire who left bequests to unmarried daughters during the later sixteenth and seventeenth centuries.

107. French, 'Ingenious and learned gentlemen', p. 64.

108. S. Hull, *Chaste, Silent and Obedient English Books for Women 1475–1640* (San Marino, 1982), p. 96.

109. See for example, M. Cavendish, *The Convent of Pleasure* (1668); A. Behn, *The Ten Pleasures of Marriage and the second part, The Confession of the New Married Couple* ed. J. Harvey (London, 1922). The authors themselves were not necessarily single. Margaret Cavendish, Duchess of Newcastle, appears to have benefited personally and professionally from her marriage – see S.H. Mendelson, *The Mental World of Stuart Women Three Studies* (Sussex, 1987), p. 32. Aphra Behn was reputably married to a Dutch merchant who died of the plague in 1665, although he may have been fictional: 'a widow's status gave the best chance of an independent life for a woman'. See A. Behn, *The Rover and Other Plays* ed. J. Spencer (Oxford, 1995), pp. vii–viii.

110. J. Todd, *The Sign of Angellica: Women, Writing and Fiction, 1660–1800* (London, 1989), pp. 2, 42.

111. A. Dobson (ed.), *The Diary of John Evelyn*, III (London, 1906), p. 187.

112. Francis Bacon argued that 'the best workes, and of greatest Merit for the Publike, have proceeded from the *unmarried, or Childlesse* Men'. See F. Bacon, *The Essays or Counsells, Civill and Morall. Newly enlarged* (1625), Number 8, 'Of Marriage And Single Life', pp. 36–7. Sir John Denham's wistful eulogy, 'Friendship and Single Life Against Love and Marriage' (1668) expounded at length on the social benefits of bachelorhood: 'His Life, his Zeal, his Wealth attends, His Prince, his Country, and his Friends'. See G. Greer, J. Medoff, M. Sansone and S. Hastings (eds), *Kissing the Rod An Anthology of Seventeenth Century Women's Verse* (London, 1988), p. 363.

113. J. Barker, 'A Virgin life' (1688), in Greer *et. al.*, *Kissing the Rod*, pp. 360–1.

114. Astell even suggested that 'the Glory of Reforming this Prophane and Profligate Age is reserv'd for you Ladies'. See Astell, *Serious Proposal*, p. 150. Hannah Smith has recently argued that despite the fact that Astell's work is often employed by modern feminist writers to demonstrate how proto-feminists of the late seventeenth and early eighteenth centuries used 'Cartesian, Lockean, rationalist, and contractarian arguments to vindicate women', her work, and those of other contemporary female writers, was a vehicle for 'contemporary religious and political anxieties', geared towards a programme of national moral reform, rather than a plea for female individualism. See H. Smith, 'English "Feminist" Writings and Judith Drake's *An Essay in Defence of the Female Sex* (1696)', *Historical Journal*, 44 (2001), pp. 729–30.

115. Cavendish, *Convent*, p. 7, in Duchess of Newcastle, *Plays, Never before Printed* (1668).

116. J.W. Ebsworth (ed.), *The Roxburghe Ballads Illustrating the Last Years of the Stuarts*, VII (Hertford, 1893), pp. 155–6. The problem of maintaining oneself as a single woman is a theme in the early poety of Isabella Whitney (c.1540–after 1580). See J. Stevenson and P. Davidson (eds), *Early Modern Women Poets: An Anthology* (Oxford, 2001), pp. 48–61.

117. While the notion of social mobility enjoys considerable acceptance – it leaves the status quo for the best part intact – social change, especially where there is a major subversion of the social hierarchy, can impact significantly on the perception of order. See Skevington and Baker, 'Introduction', pp. 2–4.

118. For a taste of the concern about the attacks on marriage in the prescriptive literature see *Marriage Asserted: In Answer to a Book entituled Conjugium Conjurgium: Or, Some Serious Considerations on Marriage* (1674), and F. Barber, *Directions For Love and Marriage. In two Books, translated by a Person of Quality* (1677), A3. In terms of the theatre, Susan Staves has argued that 'the center of interest in the plays characteristic of the seventies and early eighties is closer to skepticism and malaise about marriage than it is to affirming "support for marriage as an institution." ' See S. Staves, *Players' Sceptres Fictions of Authority in the Restoration* (London, 1979), p. 167.

119. See C. Hill, *The World Turned Upside Down: Radical Ideas During the English Revolution* (London, 1972), ch. 15; and D. Cressy, *Travesties and Transgressions in Tudor and Stuart England* (Oxford, 2000), ch. 15.

120. The anonymous author of the pamphlet, *Marriage Promoted. In a Discourse of its Ancient and Modern Practice* (1690), for example, claimed that 'neglect and abuse of Marriage lies most among the Men of *Quality*, and the *Rich*, who partly out of Debauch'd *Principle*; and partly, out of a *Covetous Humour*

forbear to Marry'; *Marriage Promoted*, p. 28. Treatises on the subject of priestly celibacy include T. Hodges, *A Treatise of Marriage. With a Defence of the 32th Article of Religion of the Church of England* (1679); R.H. [Abraham Woodhead], *A Discourse Concerning the Celibacy of the Clergy* (Oxford, 1688); G. Tullie, *An Answer to a Discourse concerning the Celibacy of the Clergy* (Oxford, 1688); H. Wharton, *A Treatise of the Celibacy of the Clergy, Wherein its Rise and Progress are Historically Considered* (1688).

121. See for example 'The Mother and Daughter', in Ebsworth, *Roxburghe Ballads*, VIII, p. 303. In this dialogue, a daughter asks her mother to give her all the bonds of her 'Use-money', to provide for her maintenance. The context of the ballad reveals both women as having indulged in extra-marital sex, the 'Use-money' being a play on words. Todd, *Sign of Angellica*, p. 33.

122. *Ibid.*, p. 29.

123. Anon, *The Women's Complaint against Tobacco* (1675), pp. 5–6. Leading apes in Hell was the proverbial fate for never-married women. See S.S. Lanser, 'Singular Politics: The Rise of the British Nation and the Production of the Old Maid', in J.M. Bennett and A.M. Froide (eds), *Singlewomen in the European Past 1250–1800* (Philadelphia, 1999), p. 298.

124. Anon., *The Maids Complaint against the Batchelors* (1675), pp. 4–7; Anon., *The New Parliament of Women* (1683).

125. Ebsworth, *Roxburghe Ballads*, VI, p. 246.

126. Anon., *The Batchelor's Directory: Being a Treatise of the Excellence of Marriage* (1694), Advertisement.

127. Women who did not have sexual intercourse were thought to be at risk of greensickness or chlorosis, one of the symptoms of which was amenorrhoea. In *The Woman's Doctor* (1652), Nicholas Fontanus proposed that wives were more healthy than either virgins or widows 'because they are refreshed with the man's seed, and ejaculate their own, which being excluded, the cause of the evil is taken away'. Cited in Aughterson, *Renaissance Woman*, p. 61.

128. Audrey Eccles detailed the appearance of only four obstetrical textbooks in English (including the first example, *The Birth of Mankind* (1540)) between 1540 and 1650, but listed at least twenty that were published in the last fifty years of the seventeenth century. A. Eccles, *Obstetrics and Gynaecology in Tudor and Stuart England* (London, 1982), pp. 11–16.

129. B. Orr, 'Whores' Rhetoric and the Maps of Love: Constructing the Feminine in Restoration Erotica', in C. Brant and D. Purkiss (eds), *Women, Texts and Histories 1570–1760* (London, 1992), p. 207.

130. R. Thompson, *Unfit for Modest Ears: a Study of Pornographic, Obscene and Bawdy Works Written or Published in England in the Second Half of the Seventeenth Century* (London, 1979), p. 114.

131. Reynel, *True English Interest*, cited in Thirsk and Cooper, *Seventeenth Century*, p. 759.

132. J. Palsgrave, *Les Clarcissement de la langueu francoyse* (1530), f.lcvi. The first surviving song that ridiculed a never-married woman can be dated to *c.*1557, see J.M. Bennett and A. Froide, 'A Singular Past', in Bennett and Froide, *Singlewomen*, p. 35, fn. 56.

133. [J. Dunton], *The Challenge Sent by a Young Lady to Sir Thomas-and c. or, The Female War* (1697), pp. 139–43.

134. In *The Maidens Best Adorning: Or, A Directory for the Female-Sex: Being, A Fathers Advice to his Daughter* (1687), the decision to marry was not assumed: 'If thou Resolve to change a Single Life, And has a Purpose to become a Wife'.

135. Kirsten Hastrup has claimed that 'social and conceptual order depends on the establishment of discrete categories by means of boundaries between them'; see K. Hastrup, 'The Semantics of Biology: Virginity', in S. Ardener (ed.), *Defining Females: The Nature of Woman in Society* (London, 1978), p. 52. Dirks, Eley and Ortner have taken this one stage further by arguing that 'politics consists of the effort to domesticate the infinitude of identity. It is the attempt to hegemonize identity, to order it into a strong programmatic statement'. Though the authors employ the argument in order to explain the power of the socialist tradition to create a strong concept of the working class in the late nineteenth and early twentieth centuries, the same argument can be applied to explain the ability of the patriarchal tradition to create a powerful image of women as married. Dirks *et al.*, *Culture/Power/History*, p. 32.

136. For details about a resurgence of offences prosecuted under legislation aimed at curbing masterless women in the 1650s when fears about independent women were high, see P. Crawford, 'The Challenges to Patriarchalism: How did the Revolution affect Women?', in J. Morrill (ed.), *Revolution and Restoration. England in the 1650s* (London, 1992), p. 119. For details of single women's problems with the law in the late seventeenth century see R. Shoemaker, *Prosecution and Punishment: Petty Crime and the Law in London and Rural Middlesex, c.1660–1725* (Cambridge, 1991), esp. ch. 7.

137. Estimates of literacy suggest that in the 1550s only one in 20 women could sign their own name, but by 1700 this had risen to one in four. Oral culture was transformed as printers catered for a growing readership of ballads, almanacs, books, devotional works, ballads and chapbooks. See N. Wheale, *Writing and Society: Literacy, Print and Politics in Britain 1590–1660* (London, 1999), pp. 41, 136; M. Spufford, *Small Books and Pleasant Histories Popular Fiction and its Readership in Seventeenth-Century England* (Cambridge, 1981), ch. 2.

138. G. Eley and K. Nield, 'Farewell to the Working Class?', *International Labor and Working-Class History*, 57 (2000), p. 12.

5
Class and Credit: Social Identity, Wealth and the Life Course in Early Modern England

Craig Muldrew

Most historians dealing with social stratification, class, or social structure in the early modern period have generally been concerned with the question of how contemporary society could be divided into different groups or strata. Here the usual strategy has been to adopt the objective gaze of someone observing a past society as an entire group of individuals, and then working on the problem of how to divide them into different hierarchical layers from top to bottom, with those at the top having the most power, wealth, status and those at the bottom the least. This way of seeing was initially adopted in the 1960s and 1970s by the new social historians who began to examine such things from either the Marxist theory of class which provided an historical explanation of how social hierarchy was produced and maintained in terms of wealth and economic power, or sociology which took a more classificatory approach; breaking society into a wide number of groups based on status, occupation, ethnicity and other factors. The most well known instance of the latter approach is Peter Laslett's characterisation of England as a one-class society divided not by conflict but by status in which power was rigidly limited to a small number of elites.[1] In contrast, Christopher Hill sought to interpret English politics and religion in the civil war as manifestations of class conflict between traditional elites and economically rising merchants and tradesmen.[2] But both systems of interpretation are, of course, inevitably limited metaphors in which the group definitions are placed like cookie cutters into the dough of human activity.[3]

Various historians have since tried to deal with this problem, as well as the related problem of describing and measuring social mobility between social groups.[4] For early modern England the most successful attempt to deal with this problem was initiated by Keith Wrightson, influenced by a roughly contemporary shift away from the functional or structuralist nature of post-war sociology and Marxism, to an examination of what Gareth Stedman Jones termed 'the languages of class'.[5] This initiated a more historically based search for how contemporaries sought to describe their own society, which has attempted to explain why they chose the metaphors they did, and how such metaphors changed over time. In a series of articles Wrightson examined how contemporaries divided their society into estates, degrees and sorts, and how this changed over the course of the sixteenth and seventeenth centuries. The simple medieval language of estates expanded in the sixteenth and seventeenth centuries to include a wider variation of degrees of status and occupational groups as the economy grew, making tradesmen, yeomen and professionals wealthier. In addition the word 'sort' started to be used in terms of the better, poorer and middle sorts to designate broad differences based on wealth.[6] Although examples of contemporary use of the term middling sort are hard to find, it has been taken up by historians in the last decade and has been used extensively to refer to those people with wealth and local power, but who were not gentry; roughly equivalent to the modern idea of a middle class. Henry French has continued this investigation into how often the term middling sort was used, by focusing more specifically at the village level to look at what sort of status designations people employed to describe themselves and others, and has discovered that here the terms 'chief inhabitants' (used to refer to officeholders, meaning 'head' from the metaphor of the body politic), and 'better sort' were used more often in the late seventeenth century by those who were not poor, but did not yet have the status to call themselves gentlemen.[7]

It is this line of investigation into social identity which I wish to continue to pursue here, but not so much in terms of how contemporaries grappled with descriptions of social *division*, and attempted to linguistically pin down relations of power in terms of a ladder of status, but rather with the importance of morality in the way individuals viewed self-identity within society. I want to examine how they looked at their own social relations as they were actively negotiating them, and profiting or suffering from such activity, rather than how they attempted to make sense of society as an objective or metaphorical whole.[8] This was a society infused with ideas of Christian love as well as neighbourliness and classical virtue, and the word society was used much more often to describe the condition of living in association with others than as the aggregate of such association. But, it was also a very competitive society in which households strove to be successful in a world where credit relations could easily cause severe financial problems, either through over-spending or through the extension of too much credit to others. This meant that a reputation for creditworthiness was crucial for individuals and households if they were to be trusted with credit, and households could not become wealthy if they were not trusted to pay for what they bought. Reputation was gained through the appearance of virtuous living in which honesty, diligence and thrift had to be balanced with charity and hospitality.[9]

This meant that such a moral language was also used as a means of social judgement. Terms of social description which we have access to were written down by those with the education to write, and were used as an ethics of social judgement produced by the middling sort to justify and define competitive success. To be middling sort, in this sense, was not so much to be a member of a 'class', but a process of continual achievement. The term middling sort was not used nearly as often as were terms of judgement such as 'better' sort, or 'poorer' sort, which divided the successful from the unsuccessful.[10] Thus the successful were praised, and the poorer sort were often generalised as being mean, rude and generally untrustworthy. In this sense there is an element of what I think we could term class formation occurring here with group generalisations being made in moral terms, based on wealth, between the better and the poorer in society. But the problem of mapping this onto stratified hierarchical model of society is that such wealth was very mutable, not only over generations, but very often over the course of lives as well. The metaphor of 'poorer' and 'better' sorts, which was derived form the quality of grain sold at market, could equally be applied to the potential of children in this sense.

In contrast, modern sociology stresses the continuity of power of elites and the middle class through ability to spend on education and to fund political parties.[11] But it is less often noted that such financial power is based on a stable banking system and stock market, as well as eventually much lower mortality rates. Since the nineteenth century it has been possible for middle-class virtues of thrift and security to create savings and investments on a large enough scale so they could be perpetuated through time, unless an entire generation of spendthrifts appeared, or the value of investments was drastically reduced by a financial catastrophe like the Great Depression. Limited liability and more recently bank deposit insurance and more rehabilitative bankruptcy laws have all contributed to such protection.[12] But there was little financial security of this sort in the early modern period before the financial revolution, where much wealth existed in the form of being owed more money than one owed, because there was so little money to save. Thus, people were always vulnerable to unpaid debts, as well as to sickness, fire, bad harvests and other uncontrollable factors. In addition to this, many people found thrift a hard thing to practice when spending was done on credit, and when the only restriction on spending was what others were willing to trust you with. There were no salaries or bank accounts, which could be used to measure what one should have been spending; people only had a rough idea of what total future family earnings might consist of through trade, harvests and odd jobs.[13] Land was, of course, the most important form of 'saved' capital in the modern sense, but it was not liquid capital. It could be mortgaged, and its very existence made one more creditworthy, but attempting to sell it to pay debts could easily violate both inheritance custom and marriage contracts and lead to expensive litigation. If one looks at any family records, or the court of chancery, the inevitability of such problems is evident.

Certain families did manage to perpetuate themselves over generations in positions of local power, but what evidence we have of family survival shows their numbers were relatively low, owing to downward mobility, mortality and geographical mobility (much of which was economically motivated). Certainly this was true in comparison to the statistical studies of the perpetuation of elites by sociologists of the twentieth century. Keith Wrightson and David Levine have shown that in the parish of Terling in Essex in 1671 only 13.8 per cent of the 39 householders with three or more hearths had been resident there for three or more generations.[14] They also traced the fortunes of 14 families from the late sixteenth century through to 1671, and of these, five maintained their social position, either high or low, while five declined, three rose, and one fluctuated.[15] Similarly, a comparison of the surnames of the 26 tenants possessing 1/2 yardland or more in a 1544 survey of the manor of Chippenham in Cambridgeshire with a reconstruction of the manor for 1636 done by Margaret Spufford, shows the survival of only one surname. A further comparison between 1636 and 1712 shows only 3 names out of 13 surviving (23 per cent). In the other manor studied by Spufford, Willingham, 18 out of 33 (55 per cent) names possessing 1/2 yardland or more survived between 1575 and 1603, while 4 out of 28 (14 per cent) survived between 1603 and the 1720s.[16] In the parish of Myddle, David Hey found that very few of the wealthiest gentry families had been resident for more than a century, and that the chance of retaining their possessions at that level of status was only about 50 : 50. He found that families holding smaller tenancies were more stable over time in terms of their ability to survive, but that they did so at the expense of their wealth. Of 13 families examined by Hey that survived for long periods of time, 10 out of 13 became poor.[17]

The most detailed study of the survival of families over time has been done by Anne Mitson for 14 contiguous parishes in Nottinghamshire between Nottingham and the border of Derbyshire. In the majority of these parishes between 7 and 12 per cent of the families could be identified as residing in the same parish for *c*.100 years for varying dates between the late sixteenth and early eighteenth century. The highest rate of survival here was in the two parishes of Wollaton and Attenborough, where it was 20 per cent and 17 per cent respectively.[18] There were also a number of these families who were resident over larger neighbourhood areas, including five resident over the whole area.[19] But, as Mitson notes, few of these dynastic families showed exceptional wealth. Most who appeared in the 1674 hearth tax had only one or two hearths. This is in part due the fact that there were relatively few household rated with three or more hearths, and some of the family members did die leaving inventories worth £200–300, but most were less than £100.[20] Also, in terms of occupation there were as many labourers as yeomen, while the majority were husbandmen. But, as a whole, these families supplied 50 per cent of the churchwardens between 1598 and 1700.[21] A more robust survival of elites, however, has been traced by Henry French in the parish of Earls Colne in the eighteenth century, based on records of land transactions in the manorial courts. There, in 1750, the families of 6 out of 13 vestrymen had held some amount of land for an average of 78 years in comparison to 13 out of 24 officers who had held land for an average of 30 years.[22]

The only comparative work that has been done on towns is Jeremy Boulton's study on Boroughside Southwark where he found that for the four sample years of 1608, 1609, 1631 and 1641 only between 18 and 29 per cent of householders had been in the same dwelling for ten years or more.[23] Work done on urban migration by the Cambridge Group and by David Souden and Peter Clark based on parish registers, shows that simply based on this one factor turnover of elites was high. In addition they experienced much higher mortality rates than in rural areas.[24]

In order to add to these findings I have examined the continuity of elite surnames between a sample of hearth taxes for areas where tax lists exist from both the early 1660s and the early 1670s. I have chosen to examine the simple survival of the surnames in order to capture inheritance from father to son or unwed daughter.[25] Although in most cases first names were the same as well, in some cases they might refer to unrelated families with the same name, so the actual rate of survival is probably somewhat less than these figures suggest. This sample is certainly not exhaustive, and is based on the borough of King's Lynn (the subject of my own research); the county of Huntingdonshire (where the heath taxes are being prepared for publication by Ken Sneath and Mary Carter); as well as various other published sources. To define elite I have chosen to include those rated on four or more hearths. This is based on my study of wealth in King's Lynn, as well as Keith Wrightson and David Levine's analysis of the 1671 hearth tax for Terling in Essex.[26] This cut-off point is somewhat high, as some quite wealthy families could live in houses of three hearths, especially, in the countryside and in the north, where, as Mitson demonstrated, many fewer houses had more than two hearths.[27] This information is presented in Table 5.1, and is divided between rural and urban areas.[28] The information provided here seems to indicate surprisingly low rates of survival over a relatively short period of time. Of course there was a plague in 1666, but such epidemics were fairly regular occurrences in the preceding years.[29] It also seems to indicate that, as might be expected, survival rates were 11 per cent lower in towns than in rural parishes. In King's Lynn, however, there is evidence that the very rich had a greater percentage of survival. There, of 20 individuals rated on 7 or more hearths in 1664, 70 per cent were still present on the 1672 list.[30] In Lynn the town aldermen and councillors were almost all members of wealthiest 10 per cent of the town's population, and between 1680 and 1687 the survival rate of aldermen was 7 out of 13 or 54 per cent.[31] Thus, it might be thought that, perhaps, town office holding could bolster a family's security over time. In order to test this, Table 5.2 lists the reappearance rate of individuals who composed the 'twelve' the town council of the manorial borough of Lewes in Sussex and Table 5.3 records the same for the aldermen of High Wycombe in Oxfordshire. From these tables it can be seen that, in fact, the reappearance rate of aldermen was not significantly different from the survival rates recorded in Table 5.1.

What all this information demonstrates is that at the level of the parish the social structure was anything but stable for most families over time. It is true that there must have been much short distance local movement of families, but recent work has stressed that it was the parish where middling identity was formed.[32] This indicates that the structural model of elites, at the level of the middling sort, being able to perpetuate themselves over time is not applicable to sixteenth and seventeenth century. Mortality, economic migration, as well as economic uncertainly due to credit made the expectation of such certainly untenable. It was impossible to look at society as something which could be cut up in neat

Table 5.1 Continuity of surnames of individuals rated on more than four hearths between 1662 and 1674[1]

Places	County	Total number of hearths 1662–64	Numbers of householders (4 + hearths) 1662–64	Same surname on 1670s lists 1671–74	Percentage of same surnames on 1670s lists 1671–74
Urban					
King's Lynn (6/10 wards)	Norf.	569+exempt	170	41	24
Faversham	Kent	281+exempt	137 (1662)	69 (1671)	50
Dudley[2]	Worcs.	172	11	6	55
Stourbridge	Worcs.	219	33	13	39
Newport	IoW	228	52	22	42
St Neots	Hunts.	144	49	18	37
Huntingdon	Hunts.	160	45	20	44
St Ives[3]	Hunts.	263	47	15	32
Average					37
Rural					
Hagley	Worcs.	55	9	8	89
Yarmouth	IoW	36	15	12	80
Motteson	IoW	58	8	4	50
Gatcombe	IoW	35	9	5	56
S. Shorewell	IoW	34	8	6	75
Northwood	IoW	45	8	2	25
Norton	IoW	45	3	2	67
Arrton	IoW	51	9	4	44
Bowcombe	IoW	36	6	2	33
Brixton	IoW	44	7	1	14
Lewerston	IoW	28	6	3	50
Throwley	Kent	48	11	8	73
Baldesmere	Kent	26	6	4	67
Normancrosse Hundred	Hunts.	984	95	47	49
Leightonstone Hundred	Hunts.	1033	128	56	43
Toseland Hundred	Hunts.	1195	134	63	47
Hurstingstone Hundred	Hunts.	1373	99	42	42
Average					48

[1] The dates for the King's Lynn hearth taxes are 1664 and 1672; for the Dudley and Stourbridge hearth taxes the dates are 1664 and 1674; for Faversham the dates are 1662 and 1671; for Huntingdonshire the dates are 1664 and 1674; and for the Isle of Wight the dates are 1664 and 1674. Public Record Office, E179 154/697, 238/119, 367/13; P. Chandler (ed.), *Hearth Tax Returns for Dudley and Stourbridge, 1664–1666–1674* (1992); P. Hyde and D. Harrington (eds), *Hearth Tax Returns for Faversham Hundred, 1662–1671* (Faversham, 1999); P.D.D. Russell (ed.), *Hearth Tax Returns for the Isle of Wight 1664–1674* (Isle of Wight, 1981).

[2] By 1674 the number of 41 hearth households had jumped to 24, an unusually large rise.

[3] Mary Carter has traced 31 core families of St Ives and its urban hinterland who remained in the areas for a long time, which represents only 4 per cent of the whole urban society. Furthermore, only three families saw their influence in the administration of town affairs last more than two generations. M. Carter, 'Town or Urban Society? St. Ives in Huntingdonshire, 1630–1740', in Phythian-Adams, *Societies, Cultures and Kinship*, pp. 110–12, 115–17.

Table 5.2   Survival of surnames among members of the 'Twelve' in Lewes, Sussex, 1591–1741[1]

Dates	Number of 'Twelve' at first date	Number surviving at second date	Percentage of surviving surnames
1591–1618	18	5	28
1618–33	17	7	41
1633–47	19	13	68
1647–57	24	14	58
1657–63	21	16	76
1663–74	20	3	15
1674–84	11	6	55
1684–95	20	7	35
1695–1710	19	4	21
1710–19	15	2	13
1719–29	22	3	14
1729–41	16	7	44
Average			39

[1] L.F. Salzman (ed.), 'The Town Book of Lewes 1542–1701', *Sussex Record Society*, 48 (1945–46); V. Smith (ed.), 'The Town Book of Lewes 1702–1837', *Sussex Record Society*, 69 (1972–73).

Table 5.3   Survival of surnames among aldermen of High Wycombe, Bucks., 1650–1710[1]

Date	Number of aldermen at first date	Number surviving at second date	Percentage of surviving surnames
1650–1661	13	5	38
1661–1670	11	5	45
1670–1683	9	4	44
1683–1691	13	5	38
1691–1700	12	8	67
1700–1710	14	6	43
Average			46

[1] R.W. Greaves (ed.), 'The First Ledger Book of High Wycombe', *Buckingham Record Society*, 11 (1947), pp. 142–271.

segments in which the same families would generally continue to occupy the same stratum over time. Mutability was too obvious, and caused too much anxiety. Change in fortune and the moral and uncontrollable causes of such change in fortune, was probably the most important lens through which society was seen. There is a great deal of evidence of this anxiety in diaries and autobiographies. Oliver Heywood, a Lancashire clergyman writing in the late seventeenth century wrote that God had laid his father Richard, a fustian weaver, low by bringing him and his wife 'into debt and danger' soon after their marriage, which was

> occasioned by his answering anothers debt, wherby he was often forced to skulk in holes and flee, they removed one year from his house to the walk-mill at water-side, for secrecy and security ... it was a sad and afflictive year, partly for poverty, partly for debt.

His father, however, managed to recover from this by being 'thrifty and carefull' and opened up a trade by selling fustians to a merchant in London, through which he got out of debt and 'grew to a considerable estate, and things succeeded comfortably' as his family grew in size. His profits were obviously considerable for he purchased land worth £800–1000 and spent £200 on a paper mill; sent his children to university; and set up two sons in business in London. But after encumbering himself with all of these expenses the fustian trade declined, and he 'unawares was cast into 1200li debt'. As a result for the next 13 years his father was 'battered with anxious thoughts' because of his 'continual entanglement in the law'.[33]

This instability suggests that it was reputation or credit for good behaviour which would allow one to be given the responsibility for upholding the ideals, or civic virtues of what Jonathan Barry has described as bourgeois collectivism, or the political culture of the 'chief inhabitants of parishes' described by Hindle and French, and which were crucial in the creation of social identity.[34] If the familial composition of the middling sort changed so much, it stands to reason that the behaviour of those with the necessary wealth would perhaps be the most important factor in their acceptance as one of the better sort. The importance of such reputation is obvious in the way Richard Gough chose to construct the narrative of the history of his parish of Myddle in Shropshire. This remarkable local history of all of the families holding pews in the parish church was written in 1700–01 when Gough was 66, and although he researched old records to provide a history of the customs of the parish, most of the work was based on his own memory and the oral transmission of the parishioners about what had been passed on to them about their ancestors, sometimes as stretching back over a century.[35] Gough was a successful yeoman and also antiquarian, having received a thorough grammar school education in the classics, and a subsequent legal training while clerk to Robert Corbett, a local JP and Master in Chancery.[36]

What is most fascinating about his work, apart from the immense amount of local detail about people's lives it contained, is the way in which he chose to structure his narrative around the success or failure of different branches of families through time. Although he began with the customs the parishioners had in common, and while the traditions of the old community obviously still existed, and were respected by most including Gough himself, the defining factor for Gough when discussing his neighbours was not so much the adherence to custom, as the continual moral evaluation of the success or failure of familial competition. For someone of Gough's middling status, neighbourliness, charity and other liberal values were important, but the impression one gets from the narrative is way that they were used to judge individuals and households, and not the community as a whole.

Gough described one of the more successful yeoman families, that of William Watkins, in this way:

> ... it hath pleased God to give him such skill, care, and industry in good husbandry as his grand-father and father had ... Hee is alsoe happy in a prudent, provident and discreet wife who is every way suitable for such a husband. They live loveingly togeather, very loveing to their neighbours, and very well beloved by theire neighbours ...[37]

A blacksmith was described as having got a great estate 'by his owne labor and industry', and another 'carefull, laboriouse person' 'lived plentifully'.[38] The terms repute, laborious, and honest were repeated by Gough in numerous other similar contexts to describe persons of 'good quality', and in the best families these qualities were also coupled with good hospitality.[39] A tailor named Richard Taylor was described as, 'soe famouse in that trade, that hee was of good repute in his time, and that hee had much custome, and lived in a handsome condition'. In contrast, his son was described as 'very unlike in moralls to his father, for the sone was an idle drunken fellow, and for debt and some petty misdemeanors was compelled to leave his country'.[40]

The History of Myddle was filled with many such moral contrasts, and the number of individuals and families who declined through imprudent or extravagant living were much more prominent in Gough's memory than the success stories. Such downward decline was inevitably described as a process of increasing indebtedness, and the loss of reputation. One man who became an expert and profitable shoemaker declined once he began spending 'a groate beefore hee had gott two pence'. He also spent much in law to get lands worth £30 per annum from his wife's family, and borrowed more to buy more land. His brothers stood sureties for him, and before long they were all sued, and he and one brother were imprisoned, and two others he owed money to had to flee the country one leaving behind a wife and child.[41] Most often Gough attributed indebtedness to bad husbandry, as in the case of one smallholder who wasted his stock and his wife's portion of £50, could not pay his rent, and was turned away by his landlord, and had to remove himself to a cottage in the town of Myddle and work as a day labourer.[42] Another man had to sell his estate because his wife's daily drinking ran up scores at the alehouse of £10 or more at a time.[43]

Anxiety about reputation and self-identity can also be found in contemporary diaries. But most examples we have are for those who were successful, such as Samuel Pepys or Thomas Turner.[44] Fortunately, though, the memoirs of John Cannon offer lengthy and enormously detailed comments on the local communities where he lived, and he was someone who earned enough to be moderately successful but never was for various reasons. He suffered serious poverty at one point in his life, and also wrote many petitions on behalf of the poor. Cannon was born in East Lydford in Somerset, just south of Wells, in 1684. He spent the whole course of his life described in the 'Memoirs' in the West Country, apart from one trip to London, finally settling in Glastonbury. The 'Memoirs' are some of the most comprehensive we have for the early modern period. In total length they run to many hundreds of very full pages and cover his whole life from his birth in 1684 until 1742. Although he termed it a memoir, only the first part of his text until 1735 is actually written up as a memoir, after this it is really a diary, although the daily entries were composed from rough notes in the same way that Samuel Pepys wrote his diary, so that the form and spelling are generally very polished. His description of events is interspersed with local histories, as well as commonplace book entries taken from his voluminous reading on themes such as virtue, riches, the lives of great men and local families, and descriptions of local towns and places.[45] It is a much fuller examination of his own and others' lives than, for instance, the diary of Ralph Josselin. It contains much of a sexual nature, which has been investigated by Tim Hitchcock, as well as merry pastimes such as shitting and pissing contests.[46] Although he was clearly concerned with morality, he was not a puritan. It seems likely, however, that he became more moral as he grew older. He went to church increasingly regularly and took the sermons seriously and expressed guilt at his pre-marital sex, and some of his gambling. But this did not stop him from attempting to discuss such matters, even if he did formulate them as a narrative of youthful folly. Like Pepys, his love of literate culture and his desire to be a part of it led him to be very frank in his description of things. His motivation for writing, however, was not puritan self-examination, but his learning and participation in the expanding world of letters, or public sphere, through his reading. In many ways he was like a much poorer Richard Gough, eager to display his local knowledge combined with a much wider range of assorted learning.

Cannon began his working life learning husbandry on his father's farm, and he worked as an agricultural labourer, before becoming an excise officer, but was dismissed from this position for debts he owed to those he had to assess. He attempted to set himself up as a maultster, but went broke and survived school teaching, doing accounts, writing letters and doing small legal work in and around Glastonbury. For most of his life he was poor despite being very literate. The major reason for his poverty was ironically his love of reading and buying books, which continually drove him into debt despite the fact that he was earning £50 a year as an excise man when he was single. When his wealthy uncle died in 1715 he inherited a close of four acres called Butmoor (which was later sold to his cousin Elizabeth Pope for £100) but he soon secretly mortgaged part of it for a loan of £30. He only inherited a house and garden from his father's estate in 1723, where his wife and daughters continued to live when he went to work in Glastonbury.[47] He probably earned between £30–60 when he was older from his school teaching, scrivening work and account keeping.[48]

His own interpretation of his troubles focused on his lack of thrift, what he termed his 'extravagant dealing in books', even though he suffered financially, as we shall see, because of his stubborn inability to compromise with his father's wishes and his inability to get along with his brother, as well as the failure of others to pay their debts to him.[49] In an uncertain world thrift was seen as the main means of controlling spending, thus retaining the liquidity to pay one's own debts when they came due, especially if earnings were curtailed or delayed because of some unforeseen circumstance.[50] He bought into the morality of thrift and mentioned his inability to practice it in this area of his life, and continued to buy expensive books despite the heavy toll it took on his life. One of the most striking examples of this was his dismissal from his steady employment as an excise officer in 1720. Although his dismissal was generated by a complaint resulting from a quarrel with a maultster he had to survey, the complainant informed his supervisor that he was in debt to some of those whom he had to assess for the excise and it was alleged that he had under-assessed them. As Cannon stated; 'it hath been said often that by my purchasing books etc. [I] had reduced my circumstances, that to keep up in my reputation I often borrowed money, and that of Some with whom I Surveyed, and it being not a close Secret it began to be muttered About.'[51] He then tried to set himself up as a maultster in Bridgwater at a cost of £10, but because his customers did not pay on time and because he had to buy his barley on credit, it soon brought him into 'Straits, Trouble and Charge'.[52] But even so, Cannon continued to buy books: 'Notwithstanding my Necessity of money in my business I, blinded in my zeal for books, Still gave orders for more of a great value, ... and was trusted, and failing payment according to order I Suffered Charges for the Same.'[53] In 1723 his father died leaving him encumbered with debts of £150 to pay off, leading Cannon to comment, 'I had nothing but the dog to hold, or worse Not so much as a hair of his tail.'[54] He was forced to sell most of his father's land as well as half of his own small meadow to his cousin Mrs Pope.

Soon after this he became totally insolvent, and was forced to shift by doing odd writing jobs. He spent some time as an estate steward, but without any authority the tenants and servants opposed him and he was never paid for his work. He also sold ale at fairs, while his wife baked bread for very little profit.[55] During this time, as well as for the rest of his life he was continually being threatened by lawyers, or arrested at suits of debt, so that law charges ate up a huge amount of what he earned. It caused his wife to accuse him of neglecting his responsibility as a husband;

> poverty came on very fast, And to encrease my dolor my wife murmured because I could do nothing, which fretted to be much, on which words did often Arise, but once more particularly to a vast height that she said that she and the Children must Spin only to Support Such a lazy, indolent fellow as I was (and She would not do it) who ... took no further care than for the present time, and that I riotously wasted that which might have been treasured up for future Support, and further said that as poverty came in at one door, so love hastened out at the other.[56]

After this he endured a period of sickness in which he says his relations and good neighbours sent in necessaries and 'helps' such as wheat cheese and apples. He gradually recovered his health and got temporary employment as an excise man replacing another who was sick, and in this way managed to regain his reputation.[57] Then in 1732 he moved to

Glastonbury at the age of 48, while his wife and children remained in his house in Lydford, seven miles away, whom he continued to support sending them money and goods when he visited them, most often on foot. He remained there for the next ten years at least, when the diary ends, teaching school, keeping accounts and doing enough scrivening work to support himself and his family, although he remained constantly short of money and continued to be arrested for debts.

During his troubles he described the course of his life: 'from a Schoolboy I became a plowboy, from a plowboy an Exciseman, from an Exciseman a Maltster, from a maltster to an almost nothing except a Schoolmaster, So that I might be called the Tennis ball of fortune'.[58] At the beginning of the 'Memoirs' Cannon also provided a history of both his mother's and father's families going back until the late sixteenth century which he describes in terms of social mutability which are very close to those used by Richard Gough. Although the detail he has of dates is rather sketchy, his knowledge of their fortunes is quite remarkable, and his stories are generally told in terms of economic failure or success in relation to moral virtue, just as Gough's had been. He related that his grandfather on his father's side had been left destitute along with all his siblings when their parents died of smallpox. One son 'wandered up and down till Providence directed him to London,' like many in the early seventeenth century.[59] There he avoided the new trade of kidnapping (to be taken as an indentured servant to the colonies), and was bound apprentice to a tailor who proved a good master and 'by frugality and Gods Assistance Saved a round Sum of Money, with which he again (not liking his first Trade) put himself a second time Apprentice for a Term to a waterman'.[60] Here he prospered and became master of a whole barge. Cannon's grandfather also wandered around to seek some honest employment and became a butcher, which he followed according to his mean circumstances at first, 'but in process of time, Strength Encreased, [and] he followed it with Successful gains and growing wealthy became at length to be the most noted of that Trade in all those parts'. It was said at his marriage that he and his wife could 'hardly Advance Money enough to buy One Calf to carry on their Trade, but the Omnipotent God raised them up a friend one Mr. Craddock, who constantly in a Generous way Supplyd his wants without Interest'. He became wealthy enough to hire day labourers and bought land worth £30 per annum. Cannon described him as a 'good benefactor and upright honest dealer and a liberal advocate for the poor being Merry facetious and pleasant in his Deportment'.[61] For Cannon honesty and frugality were the key reasons for success. Another relative 'being frugal ... acquired a Competent Estate' Another was 'a resolute blustering swearing man given to Excess of drinking, yet honest in his dealing', and one other 'a rattling man yet frugal in his affairs'.[62]

But, the wealthiest person whom Cannon was related to, his uncle Robert Walter on his mother's side, who by Cannon's estimation became worth more than £5000, was described as very moral. A baker by trade he was described as being 'a very Industrious young man, of an honest and indifferent family' who married Cannon's mother's sister. They lived 'lovingly together many years very prosperously and Increased in riches, wealth and reputation'. He was also described as 'honest and upright in all his dealings, Charitable to the poor and a good Master'. (Cannon, however, also called him stubborn and opinionated when they quarrelled later.)[63] In contrast, he described his maternal great-grandfather as someone who was 'once very rich but thro' misfortune Idleness or voluptuous living, he with his Sons ... wasted and sold their patrimony'.[64] One relative who was honest and had integrity, however, married a 'haughty Clamorous woman and withal very Expensive and costly in her apparel when she attended the Markets, which pride of hers occasioned a great decay in their Circumstances'.[65] Also, very interestingly, although Cannon described one of his great uncle's estates having been 'honestly and labouriously gotten', he did not trust his brothers or children with it, but rather committed all his money and effects to a neighbour called Broker Hole, 'who made it his Sole business to put out other persons Moneys on Security to himself and in his own Name ... by which indirect practice he gott great Substance and ill Name and odious to all who knew him. This Hole had at last his deserved End, for falling from his horse at a gate in the road (since called Hole's gate) he break his neck.'[66] According to Cannon his descendants who enjoyed this ill-gotten wealth were attended with misfortunes such as lunacy and vagabondage. This story is very significant in terms of Cannon's attitudes because, although it describes a tale which probably took place in the Jacobean period, Cannon's attitude, written over 100 years later, mirrors almost exactly the morality against usury and deception found in city comedies such as Jonson's *Volpone*. Cannon certainly accepted the practice of charging interest, which was common in his time, and borrowed from attorneys who lent money for others. What he objected to here was the dishonesty of the broker's deception in using others' money as if it was his own.[67] Cannon reflected with the proverb: 'what is gotten on the Devils back is Spent under his belly. But goods and wealth honestly gotten will Endure to all posterity according to the words of Solomon – The righteous shall never be removed but the wicked Shall not inhabit the Earth.'[68] This is also the first of many instances when he saw the workings of providence in the social order. If somehow wealth was gained or used without some sort of virtue – the most important being honesty – then God helped to correct things through providence.[69]

Cannon's own father John seems to have been a moderately successful husbandman with a copyhold estate (which he converted to leasehold after a serious illness which affected both he and Cannon's mother, to circumvent the custom of the manor which seems to have been that if both parents died the land would go to his brothers rather than his children in their minority).[70] He had, however, had a bastard child by one of his servants during a year when Cannon's mother was confined to bed after a bad childbirth.[71] He owned two ploughs and left the farming of his own estate to a servant in husbandry and Cannon while he undertook agricultural work for other people. He was wealthy enough to indulge his wife and Cannon's sister in the cost of a large flower garden with walks and imported plants and flowers, the expense of which Cannon was always envious of and called a needless cost.[72] In this he was not without justification, for, as mentioned, when his father died, Cannon, as eldest son, inherited his considerable debts. He was also jealous of his younger brother, because when his father left off business in 1705 at the age of 57 he left the younger son to manage his estate.

The exact reasons for this are unclear because Cannon did not directly address the issue, but it is clear from the memoirs that as the eldest son Cannon's parents intended him to inherit the farm and its operation. They trained him in husbandry and he became skillful enough at it so that his father could trust him to work his farm while he was employed elsewhere. Cannon, while proud of his skill in husbandry, at the same time resented this destiny, and was jealous of the more expensive schooling his parents provided for his younger brother, with the intention of setting him up in trade. Whatever his skill in husbandry, Cannon claimed his heart was not in it and he much preferred book learning, describing how, instead of working in the fields, he spent his time under hedges reading, which resulted in regular reprimands from his parents.[73] This resentment eventually lead to a major falling out between Cannon and his brother as well as his parents. As a result in 1705, at the age of 21, he was sent to work for his uncle Robert Walter as a 'hynd and Servant' but without a contract or wages because of his kinship relations, while his brother replaced him on the family farm.[74] Here he did well for two years, reading only at night or on holidays as he put it, but his relationship with his uncle broke down primarily over an argument about the best way to plough a field together.[75] Cannon told Walter since he had been raised as a baker, while Cannon had been trained by his father as a ploughman, he knew best. This led to a fight in which they struck each other with their tools, after which Cannon was immediately dismissed from his service.

This led him to plan to go overseas as a bookkeeper to a Bristol merchant, but his mother and sister intervened by sending someone ahead to give a bad report of Cannon's reputation and ability. This enraged Cannon to 'such a passion' that he swore at his mother and vowed to find employment outside of any kinship obligations. Although he later helped Walter again when his daughter was sick, it was this desire, which led him to become an excise officer. When he came to write the *Memoirs*, Cannon clearly regretted this falling out and claimed that the relative duties of parents and children 'are the first Steps to a fair character in the world', but he still maintained that parents should have flexibility to allow their children to follow an honest calling suitable to their skills so as to prevent a breach like that between Cannon and his parents. He wrote, 'if a Separation should thus happen and either party dye before a reconciliation be brought about it must needs follow that grief and Sorrow must be ye portion of the Survivor'.[76] Cannon had justification for feeling sorrowful from the standpoint of his adult years, for in terms of his fortune it probably directed the course of his life to a greater extent than anything else, because in the same year Walter's daughter Mary had died leaving him childless, and had Cannon continued working with him he might have been adopted as his son and inherited much of his fortune, which instead went to his cousin Elizabeth Pope, who once she became a widow was Cannon's patroness, and helped him financially on many occasions.[77] Also, Cannon's brother received most of his father's land before he died in 1723, leaving Cannon to deal with his debts, forcing him to sell what land had been bequeathed to him.[78]

Here we can see that although Cannon condemned quarrelling in others, he was as easily roused to a passion as those he described, and was constantly getting into fights, and found it especially difficult to show deference when it was required, because of the value he placed in the superiority of his learning. His stubbornness also meant that he was not given to reconciliation. This, combined with his lack of thrift in regard to books, meant that his credit and reputation often suffered. We only have his viewpoint on events, but he often indicates that his debts for book buying were public knowledge, and he constantly complained of being slighted by everybody but his cousin Elizabeth Pope. Although, in his own view, he suffered from the same stubbornness, as well as malice, at the hands of others, his bookkeeping skills, education and obvious intelligence should have meant that he was much more successful than he was. There must have been many like Cannon whose appetites and passions and desire for independence prevented them from fashioning a reputation for good credit that someone like Samuel Pepys achieved through eager attention to social conformity.[79] His disagreement with his parents was probably also not exceptional, as hundreds of thousands of young men left home and migrated to London and the New World, or became soldiers in the seventeenth and eighteenth centuries. After going broke he did manage to regain his credit in time, but he did not set himself up in business. Instead he was forced to employ his skills in service of those less educated than himself, but was never able to elevate himself to their level because he could not accept that he would have to build his credit on the terms of those neighbours whom he held in contempt.

Despite his continuing failure, Cannon continued to believe in thrift and the possibility of upward mobility, and the circumstances of the other lives he describes, indicates that this was probably a sensible view of the world. Near the beginning of the memoirs he provides a series of 'Examples of mean beginnings ... although not parallel to my case only, yet as an Instruction to futurity and a leading Card to the progress of these Memoirs.' Here he gives examples of various historical and local figures including Thomas Cromwell, whom he claimed when he was young borrowed 40s. from a poor woman whom he later saw in the street while he was travelling in a coach with the Archbishop of Canterbury, and called to her and asked if she was not his creditor and settled his debt with interest.[80] He then went on to say that his own ancestors had as low beginnings as any of his examples, but that providence and 'their Industry provided Handsome substances for their respective posterity of most of them. Yet as in Most families, Indolence and Supiness, or Neglect crope in and Infected Some of them of which last Some people may be apt to Charge the Author hereof in reading the whole Sequel yet weigh me truly and Judge me right and impartial, they could never find me idle, negligent or given to loose Company.'[81] But his praise for such success was always coupled with the value of honesty and virtue. Later on he claimed that 'Every Man (as Says the Proverb) is the builder of his own fortune and most miscarry for want of the lucky gale. For ye good that proceeds from heaven requires patience and that which comes from the world, Care and prudence, to keep one from [being] baffled by Impertinence and folly', and that modesty is a chief virtue because it creates an utter dislike for what is offensive, foolish or ridiculous.[82] He also praised the virtue of frugality despite being unable to practice it:

> A Spirit of Frugality is the Strongest and most efficacious remedy against Corruption. A man who knows how to manage his fortune prudently will be Independent tho' that fortune will be but Small, for having once acquired the Art of governing himself and his affairs there will be no temptation Enough strong to induce him to give up the liberty which he thereby possesses.[83]

In contrast to such virtues he opposed the value of gentility and wealth earned without honesty or charity;

> It is more honour to raise than to be [the] ruin of a family. Of all vanities and fopperies to boast of, Gentility is the greatest, for what is it they boast So much of and challenge so great Superiority over those they think their Inferiors that a man must forfeit his ear to the pillary for his tongue taking the Liberty to tell them the truth, Birth *Tantane vos generis tenuit fiducia vestui* It is a meer *non eus*, a flash, a Ceremony, a Toy, a thing of no real value. Consider its beginning, present estate progress, deceit, knavery, Usury, pimping, Murder and Tyranny were the beginning of many Ancient families.[84]

He also related the story of a 'rich old Blade' in his neighbourhood who told his son not to mind religion, but to 'get money and wealth no Matter how or which or what way, So thou gettest it'. This the son did according to Cannon by amassing £100 000 through speculation in the South Sea bubble, and ignoring charity, leading him to comment that 'Muck and Money no matter how gott was the rise of thy gentility and nobility'.[85] On another occasion in 1738 after doing the accounts between the Viscount Weymouth and his bailiff and finding the former indebted to the latter for about £250, he claimed that the Gentry through 'indolence or weakness of intellects' allowed bailiffs to control their weak masters through debt, who would then amass lands and exceed their masters in wealth and riches laying a foundation for their families to become JPs, MPs or mayors, while the former became 'so degenerate' that he would not be fit 'for the most servile place or station of the latter. Such is the pride, arrogance, grandeur and haughtiness of most of these upstart gentry or Nobility (or rather mobility)'. This instance led him to comment that 'as Idleness is the rust and bane of all human virtues so on the contrary Industry and diligence in business are conquerors in all difficultys', before going on to give more examples of upward mobility.[86]

Such comments make him sound almost like a proto-Marxist advocating middle-class virtues against an economically out of date aristocracy, but his belief in economic virtue was a commonplace of the time and echoes Daniel Defoe, Richard Steele and others whom he could have read, as well as comments in magazines. But he goes much further than someone like Defoe in lack of respect for inherited gentility, and his view might well be unique in being the most articulate expression by someone so low on the social scale. Although he was a royalist and had no sympathy for Cromwell and the Commonwealth and considered Charles I a martyr, he was very critical of any inherited wealth (which he was denied himself) and power, other than that *earned* through virtue. He had a lot to say about politics in the diary; it is clear that he disliked Walpole intensely, and regarded much politics as nothing but corruption. His views seem to have been that of a little man who could only observe what went on above him. But as a view of society the dividing lines were clearly drawn between the virtuous and the corrupt. He praised the humility of elites who remember their mortality, and identified with the less fortunate, but in general one gets the impression that inherited power and status were nine times out of ten a corrupting influence, while continued upward mobility through economic competition was a corrective to the encrustation of inheritance.

In regard to the petty commonwealth of local officeholding Cannon's views were similar. Although he never held office he did pay rates on his close at Butmoor, and house in Lydford, but more importantly he kept overseers accounts for Glastonbury for a time and wrote many letters and petitions and checked other parish accounts. Cannon clearly thought himself superior to most in his world because of his literacy and expressed this in his diary. For instance, he claimed the major part of the inhabitants of Glastonbury were 'gross and illiterate', and,

> That when a Choice is made of one to bear the office of a proctor or Mayor, it happens Sometimes on such who perhaps has Some Small Substance in the World but without Learning, and it is so Notoriously gross that they cannot Read a Warrant nor Sign their name Altho' writ by a Clerk or penman whom they will Imploy as their Clerk (which Sometime have been my fortune) ... in this Grand Office [mayor] comes in their turn other Mechanicks such as Black Smiths, Tanners, Taylors, Chandlers, Woolcombers etc. whose learning is so

rife that they could as well distinguish the wrong end of a Warrant uppermost as the right way.[87]

On another occasion at Lydford when the parishioners were meeting to pass the annual accounts and elect new officers, Cannon 'as a small payer only took up the Poor book to see how the accounts stood, as a freedom inherent to all that are payers thereto; and some of the company as illiterate, ignorant, impertinent as they were, demanded how I liked it'. This led to a man whom Cannon called 'the great Mr. Taunton', someone whom 'none must object against or control' because they owed him money, to fall into 'ill manners and rude expressions, swelling and pouting calling [Cannon] flick gutted fellow and other unseemly epithets'. In the privacy of the diary Cannon compares him to Walpole and states:

> In Some parishes Some overgrown and Self-interested persons ... not for the common good but purely to Aggrandise themselves and trample on their Inferiors make themselves demi Gods for their own ends and purposes monopolize all affairs within the precincts.[88]

Cannon often used the epitaph self-interested to describe the competition for office which he saw as the essence of local politics, and rarely praised local office holders but rather characterised them as ill suited by reason of poor literacy or industry.

This was especially true of the Glastonbury vestry whose meetings he had to attend in his role as bookkeeper. He considered them quarrelsome and inconsiderate to the needs of the poor, and more interested in saving themselves from paying rates. His opinions were very similar to those of Thomas Turner who used the same terminology to characterise the vestry in his parish in Sussex. They were equally quarrelsome and tried to avoid paying their proper rates.[89] But Turner was clearly wealthier than Cannon, as he was an overseer himself, and a successful if small shopkeeper, and while Turner was sympathetic towards the poor, Cannon at one point in his life clearly was poor, even if his wealthy relatives meant he did not need relief.[90] Fortunately for us, if not for him and his family, this meant he was someone poor who commented extensively on the nature of poverty. Some who are most diligent, he says, emigrate and 'leave no port or creek in the habitable or unhabitable world unsearched with the hazard of their lives'. Others not so courageous damn their bodies and souls by turning to cheating robbery and murder to avoid the yolk of poverty.

Those who remain at home and stay honest however, retain,

> A reputable Character and among good men they are objects of commiseration and charity but here the world is too generously faulty; for if A man be necessitous in his circumstances he is called a poor Devil, and contemined and neglected, Tho' never So well born, honest, wise, learned and well deserving … he is forsaken of all or Employed as a footstool for every man to trample on, or a wall to piss against. … The misery of poor men compels them to cry out and make their moan to rich men, who give a Scornfull Answer to their Misfortunes. Instead of comfort, they threaten and miscall them and aggravate their Miserys by ill language, or if they do give good words what's that to relieving their Necessities?[91]

The only comfort Cannon says is hope and the knowledge that riches are the gift of heaven and that, while they are often the rewards of virtuous actions, they should not be esteemed one's only happiness, 'For men in the greatest prosperity are often like trees laden with fruit that breaketh with the weight of thir boughs and are ruined by their own greatness.'[92]

Cannon continued to work for the vestry, not only doing accounts, but was also a key person in facilitating interaction between the poor and the vestry. He often drew up petitions for poor individuals and made lists of the deserving poor, and was usually present when doles were given out. He seems to have been generally sympathetic to the views of the poor, describing their fears that the workhouse was too similar to a house of correction, and defending their not wearing of the poor badges.[93] He also once described himself as 'a friend to one Joan Harvey, A poor Widow and her child, in getting her weekly pay'.[94] At the same time though he also complained about those who were addicted to 'horse racing, backsword, cudgels, bull baiting, et cetera' despite the great number of poor and greater number of indigent people of both sexes having no employment. He claimed many of these unemployed were slothful, ignorant and proud, but were able to find enough time and money to ride about to such entertainments while their families starved. He argued that if such money was employed in charity and piety and the poor sought honest labour the nation would be in a flourishing condition.[95] At another point in 1738 he complained of the excess and luxury of weavers and manufacturers in Wiltshire whose great wages made them proud and given to voluptuous living causing them to riot against their masters, contrasting them with 'the poor husbandman that toils in the dirt weary and hungry and thirsty … for lower wages'.[96] The former example probably reflects his reading, combined with the reflections of an older man, and the latter his training as a husbandman, rather than strongly held beliefs about the poor or the desire to associate himself with the better sort. After all, he sold ale at such pastimes and revels, and had participated in them as a youth. Most often, his view of the poor was sympathetic in contrast to his dislike of the parish elite.

Looking at the circumstances of Cannon's life it is very difficult to categorise him into any clear-cut division between the middling sort and the poor. His earnings of about £50 a year in good times would have put him into the same league as Thomas Turner, and his literacy would clearly seem to signify him as a member of the middling sort as his cultural horizon was clearly very wide. He read newspapers and the Gentleman's Magazine, followed foreign affairs and detested Robert Walpole and the Whig oligarchy. He was obviously enormously proud of his skills and intelligence, and the diary was his major means of expressing this. He was continually scathing about the illiteracy and innumeracy of those he worked with. But he probably never would have been termed a chief inhabitant, or one of the better sort because he did not hold high enough office. It is difficult to know how well he lived in the 1730s when he was earning money because his accounts have not survived. He did however list many of the things he took from Glastonbury to his family in Lydford, which often included sugar, meat and spices. But in his time of poverty he clearly survived on much less. The less indebted Thomas Turner, in comparison, reduced himself to eating meat only two days a week, and tried a cheap soup recipe intended for the poor, when grain prices were very high in the winter of 1758.[97] In terms of attitudes, Cannon was certainly less censorious of bastardy than a chief inhabitant like Turner, as both he and his father had illegitimate children, although he paid support for his child. This was another aspect of his life that divided him from those who held office, and marks a clear-cut divide between him and others in his community, and shows how the politics of reputation were part of the politics of the parish.

It is much more difficult, however to direct our gaze in the other direction down the social scale to determine if Cannon's neighbours differentiated him from families such as day-labourers and cottagers who remained poor over generations. Cannon himself, as we have seen, often identified with poor householders, but we do not have any reports of his neighbours on his status in regard to his poverty and indebtedness. Cannon did use the term poorer sort on occasion, but it was always in a positive not negative sense. The terms poor or poorer sort could be used in a simple descriptive sense to described as those only earning enough to support their families and not pay rates or taxes, but not dependant paupers, or they could be used in a more positive Christian sense as those deserving the charity of their richer neighbours, which is the sense adopted by Cannon.[98] But increasingly the poor were also described *en mass* in negative terms as the 'meaner', 'thriftless', 'poorer', 'baser', 'ruder', 'vulgar' or 'common' sorts of people. But when used collectively in this negative fashion, rather than individually, it was usually done to equate some form of group disorder with ignorance, whether this was going to alehouses on Sundays or rioting. This was the many-headed monster – the crowd, which in humanist eyes acted without the self-control of reason, which was the product of education.[99] The poor were also generalised as having less credit and blamed for spending too much on beer rather than paying their debts, as those with uncertain earnings were more likely to spend too much on the cheapest form of leisure (drink), and earn too little. Certain groups of the poor, such as the weavers described by Cannon, or miners, could be described as riotous or disorderly.[100] But in detailed local accounts such as Cannon's or Richard Gough's most poor families were described individually rather than as a group, and the morals used to judge the poor were the same as those used to judge middling-sort failure.

If we look at Richard Gough's characterisation of the poor in Myddle he does not generally distinguish between families with varied fortunes and cottagers and day-labourers. He rarely, if ever, describes the poor as a group separate from the rest of the community.[101] He looks at the poor often with as much attention as he gives to families of variable fortune, and the same moral judgement which he used to determine who was most creditworthy was also used to judge which poorer families were the 'honest poor'. Gough described an old man with a blind wife, who was an object of charity, but who 'built a pretty liytle house ... and lived in a good condition for many years' because 'Hee was alwayes a sober man, and a painefull laborer'.[102] When describing the poor man Michael Braine, who was expelled from the community for stealing meat, Gough claimed this was unfair because he only stole out of want, and had always behaved 'himselfe as an honest man' and was peaceable amongst his neighbours. Gough also called one of his sons 'an honest and laboriouse person' who married 'a fashionable, modest woman' and he judged 'they were likely to live well' as a result.[103] One poor family is also described in terms of variable wealth as thriving at one point and then being reduced by the husband's death.[104] Many poor cottages are described without any adverse commentary on their poverty.[105] It is interesting to note that most of his comments on poor families concerned whether or not they were a charge on the parish.[106] The descendants of one day-labouring cottager were described as remaining poor, but never becoming a charge on the parish, as were the 11 children of a weaver.[107] In contrast the cases of some poor families who caused disputes with neighbouring parishes over bastardy were accounted in some detail.[108] Here the poor are praised by family rather than by group for not falling into dependence, whereas the poor in families of variable wealth were judged much more harshly for wasting their families' estates.

Unfortunately we lack any sense of whether continually poor families thought of themselves as the same or different from downwardly mobile poor families, or whether they too divided themselves up as honest, dependant or disorderly. There are too few sources to get a sense of their self-identity apart from complaints about the lack of charity of the wealthy. One source, however, which has been examined by Adam Fox, libellous popular ballads, does tellingly show how the poor could use the same moral language when they wanted to criticise their betters. Although anonymous ballads were used as a means of criticism by all classes in society, they were, as Fox has shown, an accessible means by which the humble could damage the reputation of those with 'riches and authoritie' by making rhyming verses about their alleged moral lapses such as adultery or fathering bastards. Such criticism could indeed damage the reputation of those of the better sort attacked in this way, ruining their credit and trade to the extent that many were willing to spend a great deal of money defending themselves in the court of Star Chamber.[109] One ballad made in the summer of 1607 in Northampton – a time of many enclosure riots in the Midlands – against the 'knights and justices of the county' complained of one dignitary that:

> He snappes poore people by the nose,
> And scornfully from them doth turne.[110]

This language, in fact, echoes that used by the privy council against engrossers in times of dearth, who acted 'without pitty towards poore men', and although this does not tell us about what the continually poor thought of themselves and the use of terms such as the baser sort, it does demonstrate that the poor writers and singers of ballads, at least, accepted the same practice of judgement on the basis of moral action.[111]

Although it is unfortunate we cannot learn more about those continually poor, their use of moral judgement to criticise betters does demonstrate that this formed an important part of self-identity and the negotiation of reputation. Further, recent work on the importance of the concept of character for the Victorian middle class, and the willingness of working-class families to save in friendly societies to pay for funerals in order to maintain their credit and respectability shows that moral judgement played an important part in way the languages of class were formed.[112] But, returning to John Cannon, what is most striking about his memoirs is how much insecurity and contestation there was over status based on reputation. It was this more than group labels, which mattered to early modern people. Cannon, like Turner, and other diarists used his memoirs as a means of justifying his own reputation to himself when it was challenged by others, just as he constantly questioned the reputation of others.

Acknowledgements

I am grateful to John Money, Helen Weinstein and Keith Wrightson for their helpful comments.

Notes

1.   P. Laslett, *The World We Have Lost Further Explored* 3rd edn., (London, 1983), ch. 2; K. Wrightson, *English Society 1580–1680* (New Brunswick, NJ, 1982), ch. 1.
2.   C. Hill, *The World Turned Upside Down: Radical Ideas During the English Revolution* (Harmondsworth, 1972), chs 1–3; C. Hill, 'A One Class Society?' in *Ibid., Change and Continuity in Seventeenth Century England* (London, 1974), pp. 205–18. Some of Hill's followers who see class as important element of social structure include R. Brenner, *Merchants and Revolution* (Cambridge, 1994), and in more localised sense, A. Wood, *The Politics of Social Conflict: The Peak Country, 1520–1770* (Cambridge, 1999), p. 18.
3.   The historian of nineteenth century France, Theodore Zeldin has said 'Rather than begin with preconceived views about the groupings one should use to study men, I have used as my point of departure the individual and the attitudes with which he faces the world'. He has used the metaphor of pointillism to describe how he has done history; letting the reader build up the larger picture through juxtaposition. T. Zeldin, *France 1848–1945; Anxiety and Hypocrisy* (Oxford, 1977), pp. 392–3.
4.   The initial debate on social mobility was actually over whether the gentry was falling or rising in status and wealth compared to the aristocracy. This was initiated by Lawrence Stone, who also wrote one of the first articles on early modern social mobility in general. Although we know a considerable amount now about social movement into and out of the gentry, social mobility below the elite is difficult to investigate. L. Stone, *The Crisis of the Aristocracy, 1558–1641* (Oxford, 1965); L. Stone, 'Social Mobility in England', *Past and Present*, 33 (1966). Some of the findings on the gentry are summarised in Wrightson, *English Society*, pp. 24–6. For a recent article on the middling sort

see C. Brooks, 'Apprenticeship, Social Mobility and the Middling Sort, 1550–1800', in J. Barry and C. Brooks (eds), *The Middling Sort of People: Culture, Society and Politics in England, 1550–1800* (London, 1994), pp. 52–83.

5. G. Stedman Jones, *Languages of Class: Studies in English Working Class History 1832–1982* (Cambridge, 1983), p. 7.

6. K. Wrightson, ' "Sorts of People" in Tudor and Stuart England', in Barry and Brooks, *The Middling Sort of People*, pp. 28–33. K. Wrightson, 'Estates, Degrees, and Sorts: Changing Perceptions of Society in Tudor and Stuart England', in P. Corfield (ed.), *Language, History and Class* (London, 1991), pp. 30–43.

7. Wrightson, 'Sorts of People', p. 42; H.R. French, 'Social Status, Localism and the "Middle Sort of People" in England, 1620–1750', *Past and Present*, 166 (2000), pp. 66–99.

8. R. Jenkins, *Social Identity* (London, 1996), ch. 8.

9. C. Muldrew, *The Economy of Obligation: The Culture of Credit and Social Relations in Early Modern England* (Basingstoke, 1998), ch. 5.

10. See below pp. 249–50.

11. J. H. Goldthorpe, with C. Llewellyn and C. Payne, *Social Mobility and Class Structure in Modern Britain* (Oxford, 1987), ch. 12.; J. Porter, *The Vertical Mosaic, An Analysis of Social Class and Power in Canada* (Toronto, 1965).

12. P. Hudson, *The Genesis of Industrial Capital, a Study of the West Riding Wool Textile Industry c.1750–1850* (Cambridge, 1986); J. Smail, *The Origins of Middle Class Culture: Halifax, Yorkshire, 1660–1780* (1994), ch. 4; L.S. Pressnell, *County Banking in the Industrial Revolution* (Oxford, 1956), p. 162; By 1873 the value of bank deposits, bills of exchange, coins and bank notes and securities in England Wales and Scotland amounted to £3345 million, or about £129 per person. S. Quinn, 'Money, Finance and Capital Markets', in R. Floud and P. Johnson (eds), *The Cambridge Economic History of Modern Britain, Volume I: Industrialisation 1700–1860* (Cambridge, 2004), pp. 147–51.

13. Muldrew, *Economy of Obligation*, ch. 9.

14. K. Wrightson and D. Levine, *Poverty and Piety in and English Village, Terling 1525-1700* (New York, 1979), p. 83.

15. Wrightson and Levine, *Poverty and Piety*, pp. 106–7.

16. M. Spufford, *Contrasting Communities, English Villagers in the Sixteenth and Seventeenth Centuries* (Cambridge, 1974), pp. 66–71, 135–45.

17. D. Hey, *An English Rural Community: Myddle Under the Tudors and Stuarts* (Leicester, 1974), pp. 117–18, 141, 126–42.

18. A. Mitson, 'The Significance of Kinship Networks in the Seventeenth Century: South-West Nottinghamshire', in C. Phythian-Adams (ed.), *Societies, Cultures and Kinship, 1580–1850: Cultural Provinces and English Local History* (Leicester, 1993). This is based on the numbers given on pp. 36–37, divided by the population figures on p. 74.

19. Mitson, 'Kinship Networks', pp. 42–50.

20. *Ibid.*, pp. 42–3, 51.

21. *Idem*, p. 51.

22. French, 'Social Status', p. 91.

23. J. Boulton, 'Neighbourhood Migration in Early Modern London', in P. Clark and D. Souden (eds), *Migration and Society in Early Modern England* (London, 1987), p. 119. I. D. Whyte, *Migration and Society in Britain 1550–1830* (London, 2000), ch. 3.

24. E.A. Wrigley and R.S Schofield, *The Population History of England* (Cambridge, 1989), p. 48; P. Clark, 'Migration in England During the Late Seventeenth and Early Eighteenth Centuries', *Past and Present*, 83 (1979), pp. 63–5, 78. See also, D. Souden, 'Migrants and the Population Structure of Later Seventeenth Century Provincial Cities and Market Towns', in P. Clark (ed.), *The Transformation of English Provincial Towns* (London, 1984), pp. 99–132.

25. This, of course, will not capture the transfer of wealth through a daughter's dowry to the son of a poorer family, but if the family's aim was to maintain power it would be more likely they would attempt to marry the daughter into a wealthy family.

26. Muldrew, *Economy of Obligation*, pp. 69–78; Wrightson and Levine, *Poverty and Piety*, pp. 34–5.

27. Spufford, *Contrasting Communities*, pp. 38–44; S. Hindle, 'The Political Culture of the Middling Sort in English Rural Communities, c.1550–1700', in T. Harris (ed.), *The Politics of the Excluded, c.1500–1850* (London, 2001), p. 134.

28. The selection is unfortunately quite arbitrary and is not meant to be a proper survey, but only an indication of what might be done with these sources, since many hearth taxes survive for both periods in the Public Record Office. What we now know about the relationship of geography and disease has not been considered. M.J. Dobson, 'The Last Hiccup of the Old Demographic Regime: Population Stagnation and Decline in Late Seventeenth and Early Eighteenth-Century South-East England', *Continuity and Change*, 4 (1989), pp. 395–428.

29. P. Slack, *The Impact of Plague* (Oxford, 1985), p. 58.

30. See above, note 22.

31. Of 44 individuals who either sat as aldermen or town councillors from 1683 to 1686, and which can be identified in tax records, only two were less wealthy than this. C. Muldrew, 'Credit, Market Relations, and Debt Litigation in Late Seventeenth Century England, with Particular Reference to King's Lynn' (Cambridge University Unpubl. PhD thesis, 1990), pp. 99, 101. Norfolk Record Office, KL/C7/11–12.

32. Hindle, 'The Political Culture of the Middling Sort', p. 134; French, 'Social Status', p. 75.

33. J. Horsfall Turner, (ed.), *The Rev. Oliver Heywood B.A., 1630–1702: His Autobiography, Diaries, Anecdote and Event Books* (Bingley, 1883), I, pp. 19–32.

34. J. Barry, 'Bourgeois Collectivism? Urban Association and the Middling Sort', in Barry and Brooks, *The Middling Sort of People*, pp. 84–112. On the link between wealth and reputation see Muldrew, *Economy of Obligation*, ch. 6.

35. R. Gough, *The History of Myddle* ed. D. Hey (Harmondsworth, 1981), p. 11.

36. Gough, *Myddle*, p. 14.

37. His ancestors had much improved the farm. *Ibid.*, pp. 113–14.

38. *Idem*, pp. 126, 132. Although this estate only lasted a very short time, leading Gough to suspect that the blacksmith was not really an honest person.

39. *Id.*, pp. 97, 126, 113, 136, 138–9,145, 159, 166, 183, 234.

40. *Id.*, p. 232.

41. *Id.*, pp. 128–9.

42. *Id.*, p. 92.

43. *Id.*, pp. 198–9.

44. Muldrew, *Economy of Obligation*, pp. 167–72.

45. For a fuller description of the diary, see J. Money, 'Teaching in the Market-Place, or "Caesar adsum jam forte: Pompey aderat": the Retailing of Knowledge in Provincial England During the Eighteenth Century' in J. Brewer and R. Porter (eds), *Consumption and the World of Goods* (London, 1993), p. 347.

46. T. Hitchcock, *English Sexualities, 1700–1800* (London, 1997), p. 28; Somerset Record Office DD/SAS/1193/4 'John Cannon's Memoirs', pp. 134, 150.

47. Cannon, 'Memoirs', pp. 157–8, 185, 197–8, 215.

48. Unfortunately it is impossible from the dairy to work out how much Cannon was earning and spending because the memoirs in the version which has come down to us is the third transcription which Cannon made from rougher versions. It is clear from an incident while he was working as a bailiff for William Peirs in 1726, when he was asked by Peirs' wife to produce his accounts that they were kept with his journal – which was examined and helped to lead to his dismissal. In this he was like most other diarists such as Pepys who used their diaries as a sort of daybook of expenses and earnings. *Ibid.*, p. 175.

49. *Idem*, p. 147.

50. Muldrew, *Economy of Obligation*, pp. 159–65.

51. Cannon, 'Memoirs', p. 152.

52. *Ibid.*, pp. 152, 154–6.

53. *Idem*, p. 156.

54. *Id.*, p. 158.

55. *Id.*, pp. 157–61, 172–4, 181.

56. *Id.*, p. 182.

57. *Id.*, pp. 186–7.

58. *Id.*, p. 161.

59. *Id.*, p. 9.

60. *Id.*, p. 11.

61. *Id.*, p. 12.

62. *Id.*, pp. 17–18.

63. *Id.*, p. 20.

64. *Id.*, p. 11.

65. *Id.*, p. 15.

66. *Id.*, p. 8.

67. *Id.*, pp. 8–9.

68. *Id.*, p. 8.

69. A. Walsham *Providence in Early Modern England* (Oxford, 1999). pp. 8–32.

70. Cannon, 'Memoirs', p. 28.

71. Cannon himself also fathered a bastard to one of the girls he was having sexual relations with while an excise officer in Watlington in 1712. She apparently attempted to procure something to induce an abortion, but a surgeon stated that the pregnancy was too far advanced. As a result Cannon had to hurry to the town where she lived to defend his credit as 'the Town was full of the Lascivious and Wanton Conversation of Devon and the strumpet'. But by this time he had returned to West Lydford and when the child was born, Canon arranged for a friend to the child's maintenance on 1s. a week on behalf of Cannon until it died in 1716. *Ibid.*, pp. 21, 101–3, 108. Hitchcock, *English Sexualities*, pp. 35–7.

72. Cannon, 'Memoirs', p. 34.

73. *Ibid.*, pp. 33–4.
74. *Idem*, p. 54.
75. Cannon, however, was also at the time beginning a relationship with Walter's maid servant Mary Brown which involved 'kissing and toying when together in private'. *Id.*, p. 57.
76. *Id.*, pp. 58, 32–3.
77. *Id.*, pp. 61–2.
78. *Id.*, p. 157–8.
79. Muldrew, *Economy of Obligation*, pp. 167–71.
80. Interest was illegal at this time, but Cannon does not mention this. Cannon, 'Memoirs', pp. 34, 36.
81. *Ibid.*, p. 37.
82. *Idem*, p. 62.
83. *Id.*, p. 377.
84. *Id.*, p. 36. Roughly the Latin translates as 'How much does the cut of your clothes guarantee the credit of your pedigree?'.
85. *Id.*, p. 37.
86. *Id.*, pp. 421–2.
87. *Id.*, p. 211.
88. *Id.*, p. 464. See also pp. 447, 323.
89. D. Vaisey (ed.), *The Diary of Thomas Turner* (Oxford, 1985), pp. xxxiv–xxxv, pp. 83–4.
90. At least he does not mention receiving it.
91. Cannon, 'Memoirs', pp. 182–3.
92. *Ibid.*, p. 184.
93. *Idem*, pp. 260, 340, 349, 421, 306.
94. *Id.*, p. 239.
95. *Id.*, p. 495.
96. *Id.*, p. 551.
97. Turner, *Diary*, pp. 131–2, 143.
98. K. Wrightson, "Sorts of People", pp. 34, 45: S. Hindle, 'Dearth, Fasting and Alms: The Campaign for General Hospitality in Late Elizabethan England', *Past and Present*, 172 (2001), pp. 44–86.
99. Wrightson, "Sorts of People", pp. 37–9; K. Wrightson, *English Society 1580–1680* (New Brunswick, NJ, 1982), pp. 168–70, 205, 216–21; C. Hill, 'The Many-Headed Monster' in *Ibid.*, *Change and Continuity*, pp. 181–294.
100. Wood, *Politics of Social Conflict*, pp. 230; Wrightson, *English Society*, p. 172.
101. Similarly, Thomas Turner, despite his many lengthy dealings with poor individuals, especially concerning cases of bastardy, as overseer of the poor for his parish, rarely described the poor as a single group. Also, when he did so it was more often in a positive rather than negative way, such as one instance when he complained of the vestry members succumbing to the 'cankerworm of self-interest' in trying to avoid paying poor rates on their full rent, thus, 'withholding from the poor what is their just right'. Turner, *Diary*, pp. 91, 238–9, 267–8.
102. Gough, *Myddle*, p. 145.
103. In contrast to this story of honesty achieved in difficult circumstances, he told the story of a man, (whose bastard daughter married one of Michael's other sons) who ran away to London as a result, and there became a wealthy

timber merchant worth thousands of pounds, but who eventually broke, went to prison and died in poverty. As a moral comment on this life of wealth gained by escape from one's responsibilities Gough added in Latin that the 'hidden woodworm devours the wealth of adulterers'. *Ibid.*, p. 101, 316.

104. *Idem*, pp. 246–7.
105. *Id.*, pp. 225, 231, 244, 247–8.
106. *Id.*, p. 146.
107. *Id.*, pp. 108, 132.
108. *Id.*, pp. 251, 243.
109. A. Fox, *Oral and Literate Culture in England 1500–1700* (Oxford, 2000), pp. 325–34.
110. Fox, *Oral and Literate Culture*, pp. 332–3.
111. J. Walter and K. Wrightson, 'Dearth and the Social Order in Early Modern England', *Past and Present*, 71 (1976), p. 31; Hindle, 'Dearth, Fasting and Alms', pp. 44–5.
112. M.C. Finn, *The Character of Credit: Personal Debt in English Culture, 1740–1914* (Cambridge, 2003), pp. 18–20; P. Johnson, *Saving and Spending: The Working Class Economy in Britain 1870–1939* (Oxford, 1985), pp. 43–7.

6
Sense and Singularity: The Social Experiences of John Marsh and Thomas Stutterd in Late-Georgian England

Helen Berry

Changing economic and social circumstances in the last quarter of the eighteenth century brought new discussions regarding the relationship between the individual, the family and the state in the evolving language of political philosophy and in the broader debates that were articulated in the popular press of the day.[1] On one hand, in the half-century after 1750, we find evidence of unprecedented social and economic change, accompanied by the growing political agitation of the emergent middle classes, the dissenting voices of a groundswell of Protestant nonconformists, and the radical press, some of which went so far as to articulate Republican, even feminist ideologies. The term 'class' itself, anachronistic in its application to much of the period under discussion in this volume, began to have currency, as an accurate descriptor of the political consciousness and solidarity which emerged at this time between groups of the same status.[2] Indeed, it is to the Georgian period that some historians have looked in order to trace the roots of modern identity, as a time when certain defining features of modern society, such as burgeoning technology, the rise of mass communication, economic opportunity and education, were made available to a growing number of people.[3] An unprecedented degree of social mobility was now possible, in theory, if not in practice.

However, in spite of the changes that were taking place, late-Georgian society was one which in many respects encouraged and rewarded 'sense' in the manner evoked by Jane Austen's *Sense and Sensibility* (published in 1811, but first devised in 1795): that is, a pragmatic evaluation of life's opportunities and risks, trammelled according to gender and rank, and considered, not independently, but through sensitivity towards family duty and the needs of 'friends' and kin.[4] One example of the prevailing dictates of 'sense', this chapter proposes, were the contemporary comments evoked in response to what was called 'singularity', a contemporary term popularised in the eighteenth century, which was applied to anyone who, by expressing their own individuality, indirectly resisted or openly challenged communal patterns of behaviour or opinion. 'Singular' when applied to an inanimate object, such as the architectural form of a building, was used in a straightforward sense to denote uniqueness; for example, the unusual, asymmetrical design of Claremont House, the seat of the Duke of Newcastle (designed and built by Vanbrugh) was described in a late-Georgian guidebook as 'singular'.[5] When applied to a naturally occuring phenomenon or event, 'singular' denoted the unprecedented nature of the subject under discussion; one global traveller in the eighteenth century described the diseases to which he fell victim on long-distance voyages as 'most *singular* and unaccountable of any that affects the human body'.[6] The label of singularity, when applied to a person, however, expressed more than just unprecedented or unusual behaviour: it carried with it the implication of criticism, and was in effect a polite way of impugning someone's character. One notable example of this was that 'singular' was a favourite eighteenth-century adjective for describing those who descended from respectable society to an unconventional, even criminal, path in life: those 'remarkable highwaymen, swindlers and other daring adventurers', like the moneylender and pettifogging attorney John Innes, described in one contemporary account as a 'singular character', who was brought before the King's Bench in 1794 for perjury and fraud.[7]

Only the very rich and famous could afford the luxury of singular behaviour. It was excusable, even requisite, for example, in metropolitan 'artistic types' such as writers, for whom the usual rules of behaviour did not apply: Dr Johnson's 'habitual incredulity with respect to facts, of which there was no reasonable ground for doubt', as noted by both Mrs Piozzi and Hogarth, was described by an eighteenth-century biographer as 'a *singular* trait in his character'.[8] In the wider population, for those below the ranks of the nobility, a more precarious fortune and concern for reputation were powerful mitigating forces against the exercise of unconventional habits and autonomous choices. Here, the lead was provided by no less a figure than Pitt the Elder, who was praised after his death for keeping to the general standards of his day, neither exhibiting too much zeal in either his virtues or vices ('He did not pretend to be *singular*').[9]

If the hypothesis stated at the start of this chapter is correct, is there evidence that an increasing number of people at this time were willing to risk exercising 'singular' opinions on the road to greater individualism and freedom of expression? This chapter provides case studies of two late-Georgians of the same generation, John Marsh and Thomas Stutterd. The careers and personal lives of Marsh and Stutterd are a study in contrasts: both men were aware that they lived in an era of profound change, and have left fascinating parallel commentaries of the momentous political events of the 1770s and 1780s from vastly different social viewpoints. Marsh was a man of profession, a lawyer, but also an amateur musician; Stutterd was a middling-sort nonconformist bookkeeper for a Huddersfield wool merchant. By these definitions of status, religion, gender and occupation, we begin to think we can sketch their social identities. Yet if we read accounts of their lives in their own words (Marsh's extraordinarily detailed diary, and Stutterd's extensive correspondence) their histories become more complex.

In their own ways, both John Marsh and Thomas Stutterd's lives contained an admixture of sense and singularity.[10] Marsh was deeply reactionary in his politics; his singularity was that he had a love of music that went beyond the level of the usual polite accomplishments. This admiration for musical talent led him into unconventional notions of meritocracy that brought him into conflict with his social peers. Thomas Stutterd was more obviously 'singular' than John Marsh in his nonconformity: his Baptist faith left him at odds with both his employer and neighbours. Each man in his own way ultimately remained bound, as will become evident, by his social circumstances, and his own sense of duty towards a network of local ties and family relationships. Although the idioms that they used in their written records were different, reflecting the purpose of each document and its author's social background and frame of reference, their common admiration for 'men of sense' reflected their own desire to be viewed as such themselves.

(I)

The extraordinary 37-volume diary compiled retrospectively by John Marsh from his own pocket books reflects upon his long life, from his birth in 1752 until his death in 1828. It first received widespread attention in academic circles with the publication in 1998 of John Brewer's *Pleasures of the Imagination. English Culture in the Eighteenth Century*. Brewer's magnificent volume contains an entire chapter on Marsh, whom he presents as the epitome of an amateur gentleman-musician of the eighteenth century, his diary the finest surviving source on Georgian provincial music. Hitherto, Marsh's contribution to the cultural life of an English cathedral city (Chichester) had been almost entirely forgotten. After his death, the volumes of Marsh's diary were scattered; one ended up in New Zealand, believed lost, before it was rediscovered in 1996, when it was reunited with the other volumes at the Huntington Library in San Marino, California.[11] An edited transcript of the diary in seventeen volumes, compiled by Marsh's son, Edward Garrard, was deposited in Cambridge University Library, suggesting that there had been a plan (which was never realised) to publish part of the diary in the nineteenth century. In the same year as Brewer published his *Pleasures of the Imagination*, Brian Robins' edition of the diary, *The John Marsh Journals. The Life and Times of a Gentleman Composer* was published as part of the Pendragon Press's Sociology of Music series. The editor was himself a musician, interested largely though not exclusively in references to Marsh's musical career as a composer, conductor and performer, up to the age of 50. Though we must be grateful for this sustained work of scholarship, which is the only published version of the diary to date, a close comparison of the text with the original manuscript reveals the extent and richness of the material that Robins (of necessity) edited out.[12]

The unedited original version of the diary of John Marsh has much more to offer, especially since Marsh's sustained record of his experiences offer us especially vivid insights into everyday life, in such diverse areas as childhood and education, the power dynamics within Georgian society, and the experience of ageing. More especially for our purposes, there is also an acutely observed study of the finely attenuated social hierarchies of provincial life; first in Romsey, where Marsh received his training as a lawyer, then among the country gentry of Kent after he inherited an estate at Nethersole; and finally in his city of choice, Chichester, where he was content to spend 40 years, his desire for the company of fellow-musicians satisfied by the cathedral organ and choir, militia bands, and the balls, concerts and assemblies that supplied the needs of local polite society. Like Brian Robins, the editor of Marsh's diaries, I disagree with John Brewer's interpretation that the diaries are a dispassionate account of the society to which Marsh belonged.[13] The unedited pages are riddled with petty grievances, biased accounts of internecine warfare, and judgments upon his own and others' conduct.

The early volumes of Marsh's diary are a detailed retrospective account of his childhood and upbringing. The son of a ship's captain, he was educated at Greenwich; his earliest memory was from the age of four, 'walking with my Father & Mother to Gosport (being then in

Petticoats) & going to a Presbyterian Meeting there, where Mr. Williams was Minister (my Mother being a Dissenter)'.[14] He also recalled being 'measur'd for my first Suit of Cloaths', and was 'much disconcerted at being set upon at Table & handled by a rough looking Man, & especially at his taking off not only my outer Garment, but my *Stays* also, which it was then the fashion to lace up Children in'.[15] He discovered at a very young age that he loved music beyond anything else; he remembered as a boy of six hearing the organ in the Chapel at Greenwich Hospital, and being transfixed by the 'celestial tones' issuing from its gilt pipes.[16] He learned how to play the organ as a child, and continued to pursue his musical interests throughout his life, although there never seems to have been any question that he would take up the career of musician full time. His mother died when he was only seven, after which time the influence of Dissenting religion upon him appears to have declined. He was educated at 'Messrs Swinden & Bracken's Academy at Greenwich', and was later apprenticed to an attorney in Romsey.

As a member of the professional classes by birth, upbringing and occupation, Marsh's diary gives detailed and various insights into the sense of social identity of someone of his rank. Much more than his professional life as a lawyer, there is explicit and lengthy attention in his diary to the various leisure activities wherever he lived, the judgements upon which he provided commentaries about the other members of his local community, and his sense of place within society. He found Romsey wanting, for example, due to the town's relative lack of 'Exercises or Amusements', which he anticipated the reader of his diary would judge to be 'not very elegant or genteel'. His main pastimes there as a young man were bell ringing and playing a form of darts in his local pub, which he favoured over 'Skittles or Nine pins & Quoits', since the Skittle & Quoit Grounds were resorted to by 'all the Riff raff of the place'.[17] In spite of this comment, Marsh was not overly prejudiced against his social inferiors; indeed, he had a tendency to assess the character people he encountered according to whether or not they were musical, and whether they were 'men of sense'. On a visit to Nottingham, he took tea with Mr Hunt, a stocking manufacturer, whom he described as 'a very pleasant, sensible Man'.[18] Marsh's privileging of both sense and musical talent led him to disrupt status hierarchies by promoting certain members of his acquaintance who were inferior to him in rank, a 'singularity' which tested the limits of social mobility in the narrow orbit of provincial society.

The most striking example of John Marsh's singularly meritocratic attitude towards the musically talented was at local assemblies in

Romsey, where he was appointed Master of Ceremonies at the young age of 17. This appointment placed him at the centre of negotiating the status hierarchies of the neighbourhood, and required all the diplomacy and tact of a statesman, since it was he who had to decide whom to admit to the assemblies, and which order of social precedence to observe in the company of dancers. Marsh adhered to the original spirit of Richard 'Beau' Nash, the Master of Ceremonies at Bath whom all provincial towns with polite aspirations attempted to emulate. Nash placed dress and comportment above the traditional ranking by birth, and thus created a new model of politeness against which members of local society were judged.[19] In keeping with this tradition, Marsh allowed a Mr Day, who was 'something of a Beau & always fashionably dress'd & a very well behav'd Man' to subscribe to the Romsey assemblies in the winter of 1770/01, even though Day had been excluded from the public balls at neighbouring Southton, '[he] being Organist & ranking in their opinion with Tradespeople'.[20] What was worse was that Day's companion was Mr Burgat, a 'Dancing Master'. Many provincial assemblies admitted tradesmen, but Romsey, it appears, was not ready for such a radical piece of social inclusivity.[21] Objection came from Marsh's own guardian Mrs Daman, who was 'surprized to hear that Day the Shoemaker's Son (as she call'd him)' had been allowed to subscribe, and said that she feared all the shoemakers and cobblers would now be admitted to the Romsey assemblies. 'As I told Mrs D. what we had to do with the Son's Pedigree, who was only known in general as Organist Music Master in which profession he had always acquitted himself perfectly well.'[22] The social barriers to painters, actors and other singular characters becoming acceptable members of polite society may have been stormed in London, but in the smaller world of provincial towns and cities, social memory made it less likely that someone could escape his roots and be judged according to merit, not birth.

By 1782, at the age of 30, Marsh was newly married, and took possession of a country estate, which he inherited at Nethersole in Kent.[23] This episode of his life, when he moved his family from Romsey to Nethersole, has much to reveal about his sense of social identity in relation to those who were above him in rank and fortune, but whom he judged critically for their lack of musical appreciation. His inheritance provided him with an income of nearly £1000 a year from rents. Viewed in purely material terms, Marsh and his family went up in the world: he acquired a great house, complete with servants, which was refurbished at considerable expense in consultation with his wife to reflect their status and identity as people of taste.[24] However, in spite of his elevation to the rank of a country gentleman, with the income and trappings to suit, Marsh's diary reveals that he was but a minnow in his local area, and felt his inferiority keenly. The principal family 'in Rank and Fortune' in Marsh's neighbourhood was a baronet, Sir Henry Oxinden, whom Marsh described as 'a pleasant goodhumour'd, convivial, unaffected Man; his Lady very much of a Gentlewoman, & their Son ... one of the greatest Foxhunters in the Country'.[25] The Straceys, 'people of considerable fortune' were their nearest neighbours, who lived a mile away. 'Had they therefore been people whose Notions & Manners were at all congenial with our own', reflected Marsh, 'it wo'd have been very fortunate for us, but on the contrary, they *both* in the 1st. place *hated* Music, and he was a very unpleasant overbearing Man, much dislik'd by the country people in general'.[26] Mrs Stracey was no better 'a bookish Lady [who] valued herself upon her Masculine understanding'. The Derings were slightly more agreeable, although the husband was fond of card playing (anathema to Marsh) and his wife was obsessed with rearing poultry 'having always quantities of Turkeys Guinea Fowls etc. parading before the House, on ye Lawn'.[27] Assorted baronets, military men and clergy were also in the area, many of them well connected, such as the Plumptre family, whose senior member was 'a fine venerable old Gent[lema]n (in a great Wig)'.[28] John Marsh and his wife received the condescension of the greater gentry and nobility in his neighbourhood, who adhered to the traditional tokens of good neighbourliness and patronage by sending them an annual gift of venison.[29] Marsh describes many of his neighbours as 'pleasant', 'sensible' or even 'Elegant', but his particular praise for Mr and Mrs Paylor, 'very pleasant people & having a large young family' illustrates his own identification with their values: they 'were very domestic & not such *High Flyers* as the generality of the Barham Down Neighbourhood'.[30] Here, we find evidence for the ongoing relevance of Henry French's model for considering status as a relational concept, entirely grounded in the social profile of local communities, well into the late-eighteenth century.[31]

Marsh articulated his own sense of removal from those whom he describes as 'country people' both above him and below him on the social scale; he abhorred the common crowd, whose tastes were exhibited in their preference for 'spiritous liquors, cakes etc.' at public executions, just as he eschewed the hunting and shooting lifestyle of his rich neighbours at Nethersole.[32] By instinct, he retained the opinion and manners of a professional man of middling rank, even when his lifestyle became rather grander. His neighbours the Plumptres were fond of the organ, and had a liking for sacred music; but for Marsh this was as charming, yet as old-fashioned, as the 'great wig' worn by the family patriarch. Miss Eleanor Pujet and her sisters played and sung, but only so that they could exhibit fashionable accompaniments (by her own admission, she 'only liked *pretty Music*').[33] 'As to the others' records Marsh disapprovingly, 'expensive Dinners Fox-hunting & Cards seem'd to be their princ[ipa]l amusements'.[34] Here was Addison's Man of Taste, washed up among a host of real-life Sir Roger de Coverleys. Marsh found his neighbours' lack of musical appreciation depressing, for which his trips to London (including the great Handel commemoration of 1784) could not compensate.[35]

At the end of the second year of residence at Nethersole, Marsh was beginning to consider moving again. The focus of his anxiety was the cost of living – the expenses incurred by keeping a carriage, the high cost of estate maintenance and feeding livestock during two harsh winters, propelled him to take sensible measures to 'lessen our general Establishment'.[36] What was never far from his mind was his situation in comparison with those of his neighbours:

> I much doubted whether my little fortune of from £900. to £1000. a Year we co'd with any comfort for any length of time associate principally, continue to vie with Families of from about £1500 to £3000 or £4000. a Year, w'ch possess'd most of ye adjoining Estates and Seats in our Neighbourhood.[37]

It was not only the fact that he lacked the means to emulate his richer neighbours that troubled him, but that he was not sufficiently wealthy to fulfil the expectation of reciprocal hospitality. Keeping up with the gentry had been more than he could afford, but, just as importantly, it was not what he desired; the estate was eventually sold, and his family removed to Chichester, and a society and way of life in that Cathedral city which was more felicitous to his musical interests.

Although his rejection of a socially advantageous inheritance and the forfeit of the life of a country gentleman was singular in purely material and status terms, Marsh did not see himself as a radical in any sense. He made unusual choices, but, like many men of his rank and fortune, he had a profound dislike of party and religious schism, favouring instead consensus and 'harmony' in society, even though at local assemblies, as John Brewer observed, 'Harmony was the object but discord was often the result'.[38] In his travels around England, Marsh's musical interests brought him into contact with people from various walks of life, with whom a common interest in music overcame other, often quite serious differences of outlook and political opinion. In December, 1785, for example, on one of his many visits to London, Marsh stayed at Joe's Coffee House, Mitre Court, Fleet Street, and visited 'Philosopher Walker', whose son he had met on a previous visit to Canterbury. This Mr Walker, with whom he held an impromptu concert, played the bass:

> tho' a very pleasant & agreeable Man, & certainly very eminent in his Profession, was I found very *singular* in his opinions as to Religion, Politics, & Music; as if it was necessary that as a Man of Sense & Abilities he shod. make a point of thinking for himself in every thing & differ *at any rate* from the vulgar in all common receiv'd opinions – Accordingly as to Religion, he as a Deist, laughing at all religious Establishments & abusing the Clergy of *all* determinations for their pretended Infallibility ... As to Politics he of course sneer'd at the existing Government as if he knew much better than any of the Ministry to manage the Helm of ye State. In Music his chief *Singularity* appear'd in his indiscriminate abuse of Handel, whom he wod. not allow to have excelled in anything, except in the art of making a great Noise.[39]

If Walker was tactless in his free expression of anti-ministerial opinions, his criticism of Handel was singularly unforgivable to Marsh, who was a lifelong fan of the most popular composer of the eighteenth century.

The toleration and consensus Marsh favoured and sought to promote among polite society once he had moved to Chichester was noted by John Brewer in his commentary upon those volumes of the diary that cover the 40 years of his life in that city. Certainly, there are some fascinating illustrations of the range of moral philosophies, religious convictions and domestic arrangements that were cognizant among the middling sorts. Among his friends, Marsh numbered nonconformists and High Church Anglicans. He did not shun having dinner with Mr Hayley, who lived with his wife and bastard child, the result of Hayley's liaison with a female servant.[40] As the musical svengali of his neighbourhood, and a respected member of his community, his was a peculiarly influential position, and was genuinely aggrieved that others among his peer group did not share his values on this matter. Marsh detested having to 'dumb down' his concerts; many of his fellow-performers had a style of playing that 'was quite equal to the Taste of the *generality* of our Audience' at public concerts in Romsey and Chichester, but he himself belonged to a more aesthetically superior elite who could appreciate 'a better sort of Music'.[41] Marsh was always at odds with those who participated merely for reasons of social prestige; he detested going to concerts in London where 'Ladies of Quality' distracted him from the music with their chattering.[42]

Marsh's arbitration as Master of Ceremonies at local assemblies and balls indicates the extent to which the cultivation of order and civility at polite public gatherings was an unstable endeavour, under constant threat from the 'lord of misrule' (as John Brewer points out) when people were slighted and took offence, or got drunk, or flouted the rules. Brewer's astute observation underplays, however, the extent to which Marsh was an *agent* in challenging social norms through his insistence upon the primacy of musical talent above considerations of rank.

(II)

The Stutterd family correspondence provides an insight into another provincial community, but a world that would have been entirely unfamiliar to John Marsh and Chichester society. The letters to and from Thomas Stutterd, his wife and brothers, form a richly detailed collection that span the period 1776 to 1815, although the surviving letters are most prolific for the two decades from 1776 to 1796.[43] They provide a synchronic commentary to many of the national and international events chronicled by John Marsh, but from the perspective of a much humbler, though (on the whole) confidently literate stratum of society.[44] Thomas was bookkeeper to W. and J. Whitacre of Woodhouse, who were among the chief merchant-manufacturers of Huddersfield.[45] He and his wife Mary lived with their growing family at Allison Dyke; their kinship network and community of fellow-Baptists with whom they corresponded lived in Yorkshire and Lancashire. The letters were written since Thomas's work required him to be almost constantly on the road, travelling to Oxford and Banbury and Buckinghamshire to the markets. In this, he followed the pattern of middlemen in the Halifax and Huddersfield area who since the sixteenth century had travelled between fairs buying wool and securing orders for finished cloth. In the late-eighteenth century, improvements such as turnpike roads expanded the horizons of the middlemen, whilst the impact of new technologies and potential rivalry from cotton manufacturing was beginning to have an impact in the Colne Valley.[46] Thomas purchased raw wool from as far afield as the Cotswolds and Ludlow, which was sent back to Yorkshire for manufacture, and took orders for the supply of manufactured cloth from as far away as Northampton, and (eventually), London.

The Stutterd papers are interesting not least because within this single family there were contrasting fortunes. John, the eldest brother, was a schoolmaster and Baptist minister in Southfield. His penmanship was more accomplished, and his letters contained more narrative detail than his brother Thomas's, with frequent references to the books he was reading, which were mostly of a spiritual nature. Both brothers earned a reasonably comfortable living, and were respected members of the Baptist community. By contrast, their younger brother Jabez scraped a living as a weaver, and was in constant ill health. His letters suggest in their style and content a man ill at ease with a pen, and were written usually to ask for money from his elder, more prosperous siblings.[47] If Thomas and John were of middling status by virtue of their occupation, Jabez barely subsisted as a skilled worker.[48]

The insights which the Stutterd papers provide into the experience of social identity may be traced through the family's exchange of information about their work, family life and meditations upon the unfolding political events of the 1780s and 1790s. These, it should be said, are entirely from the perspective of the male members of the family; unfortunately, Mary Stutterd's letters to her husband have not been preserved. Like John Marsh, Thomas Stutterd struggled whilst still a relatively young man to find a vocation in life, presented with an overweening boss whose preferred mode of address was to criticise and bark instructions. The hard-headed business acumen of the Whitacres, and lack of niceties in their search after profit, was pithily expressed by William's son John, who wrote to Thomas at Banbury in November 1788, 'I hope there is no great Danger of his Majesty dying, this Mornings Paper seems to speak more favourably of his [illness] being abated, your Sale of ... Goods I think will depend upon that very much'.[49] Early on in his career, Thomas wrote to his brother for advice, and considered giving up his job to take up teaching instead. Unlike John Marsh who had the luxury of choice of residence, and the financial means to pick and choose his employment, Thomas received counsels of caution from his brother on the subject of a change of career, in a manner that reveals much about the influence of one brother upon another, and the prevailing attitude at this level of society towards self-advancement and social mobility:

> I have the Unhappiness to disapprove of the important Affair you mention. An aspiring Spirit ruined our first parents, and is the Bane of true Contentment – I greatly fear Speculation will deceive you; and that abandoning your present Situation will one day be put down, by you, among the greatest Misfortunes of your Life.[50]

Thomas eventually stayed at Whitacre's, although a brief (and unsuccessful) attempt at setting up in business on his own as late as 1796 is suggestive of the fact that he never gave up a secret ambition to leave his employer.[51]

Although there is no explicit mention of Thomas Stutterd's wealth, we may judge from the comments he makes about the fortune of a distant relative who was a London innkeeper, that £100 a year was a larger income than his own.[52] Thomas's family to some extent enjoyed a middle-class lifestyle; they were comfortably accommodated, first at Allison Dyke, then, upon the death of his employer, in a four-bedroomed apartment on the ground floor of Woodhouse, a mansion bought by John Whitacre, his heir. Due to Thomas's occupation, they were never short of clothes, and their dress was of better than average quality. Thomas' children wore striped waistcoats, and his relatives were supplied with the new kerseymere, a high-quality fine-twilled cloth that was exported to London and America from Huddersfield in the 1780s.[53] He sent his wife printed cloth 'for a new Gown', his taste for a well-wrought piece of cloth bound up with his esteem and affection for his wife, 'I thought the Colours exceedingly bright & well done I hope you will wear it for my sake'.[54] A nephew who became a news-seller in London supplied him with newspapers and tea. But these were some of the few luxuries that the Stutterds allowed themselves. As Baptist 'professors', the distance that they put between themselves and the rest of society was in part self-imposed, in part a result of enforced discrimination. The continuing existence of the Test and Corporations Act was an injustice of which Thomas and his correspondents were only too aware. That this sense of difference cut across the usual social hierarchies was expressed by John Stutterd to his brother Thomas thus: 'An interest in *your* prayers at the divine throne is much more valuable and satisfactory to *me* than if I had the acquaintance, friendship and favour of all the courtiers of King George.'[55] In another letter from 1786, John revealed something of his attitudes towards the prevailing fashions of his time when he commented favourably upon Mr Sharp, a Baptist preacher from Manchester, who was 'A *sensible* Man. No Foppery about his person.'[56] In matters of material goods, Thomas Stutterd held a similar philosophy to his brother. As someone who was an active participant in trade, Thomas considered it providential that God had put him in the position to be able to provide for his family, but he found it a constant struggle to reconcile material and spiritual concerns, especially when he was travelling on business and found his mind preoccupied with worldly things. Letters sent home while he was away were full of maxims to his wife and children, such as 'Set your affections on things above, not on things below'; 'Eternal Concerns are certainly the most weighty and of infinitely greater Importance than the Trifles of this World.' Not without humour, Thomas's letters expressed considerable affection for his wife and children; 'I hope thou does not forget to pray for thy *other half*', he added, as he scolded Mary for not writing to him more often.[57] His identity was bound up not only in his religion, but as the father of sons. 'I sometimes think as I ride along', he reflected in a footnote to one letter to his wife, 'what 2 fine lads I have [in] Jabez and John, & hope the[y] will be good & great men sometime'. He bought them Banbury cakes, and a copy of the instructive book 'A Young Man's Companion'.[58] Indeed, so pleased was he that 'my dear lads are fond of reading', that he invested in a copy of 'Rapin's Hist' (i.e. Rapin de Thoyras's *History of England*) 'for my self and Sons' since, as he expressed it, 'My Father used to commend it very much, as the most impartial History of England – And my Father was a man of better parts & more learning than his son Thomas'.[59] This transmission of knowledge from Thomas's father through to his own sons was one aspect of the responsibility which he felt was incumbent upon him as a father; his admiration for his own father, perhaps even a sense of inadequacy, was matched by his high ideals for his own sons.

Thomas's reflections upon English society provide a rather different take on the idea that all Georgians participated enthusiastically in the provincial 'English urban renaissance': visiting Salisbury on business, he commented 'I do not envy the Inhabitants of this gay City their carnal Pleasures but rather pity them'.[60] Peter Borsay made no claims for universality in his seminal work *The English Urban Renaissance*, but its subsequent popularity and enduring influence has tended to eclipse pockets of resistance such as we find among the members of the Stutterd family. John also reported to his brother that 'Uneasiness' had taken place in the church at Barnwoldswick, occasioned by 'the Introduction of [a?] Musical Instrument in Divine Worship'. 'Is not this an Innovation?' asked John.[61] It is unclear whether John's sympathies here are with the musicians or the 'bretheren' who were offended by this innovation; his arch question regarding the innovative nature of music in Baptist worship suggests that this was not something which troubled him deeply; he observed the conflict it caused with some diffidence.

Several documented incidents serve to illustrate the moments when middle-class Baptists found their 'singular', religious values at odds with others'. In 1785, John Stutterd wrote to his brother Thomas, for example, about another Baptist couple, Mr and Mrs Adamson, who had caused a stir in their church by going to an Assembly at the 'Red Lyon' in Colne, near where John Stutterd lived. Mrs Adamson, he recorded, had gone so far as to dance, and this was after Mr Adamson had explicitly sought the deliberation of the dissenting ministers to see 'if there would be any Harm in his going to the Assembly, if it was only for Half an Hour'. The reply he received from them was unequivocal, 'They Answered – there would'.[62] The same Mr Adamson was still causing a stir among Baptists at Colne in 1792, when he added his name to the list compiled by what John Stutterd called 'the Gentlemen of this Neighbourhood' for the purpose of establishing a circulating library. The exact cause of John's disapproval is evident from the exclamation mark next to the fee for participating in this venture ('Entrance is to be £1..1 ... !').[63]

In 1788, we find Thomas on the road, witnessing the comings and goings of his social betters in the Cotswolds with detachment ('There is a strange Bustle in this Country – Many Gentry [are] going to Cheltenham Spa where the King is – Carriage after Carriage').[64] In an account of a rare pleasure trip he made to Blenheim Palace whilst passing through Woodstock in 1790, Thomas recorded the view of Marlborough's seat, 'the largest House, I suppose in the Kingdom'.[65] He observed that there was a 'fine large piece of water & delightful row of Trees' in the grounds at Blenheim. While contemplating this charming scene on that early autumn day, he chose to share his thoughts with his companion, another traveller, commenting that 'the decaying leaves put me in mind of decaying nature, that we must also fall ... This pleasant place will one day, be demolish't & utterly consumed in the General Conflagration ... '.[66] Thomas was genuinely surprised to find that the other gentleman 'did not seem disposed to enter into such serious Conversation'. Never was there better illustration of how his world-view differed vastly from that of polite society. His opinions of the common people were no less critical, and often read like the diaries and correspondence of John Wesley (at Worcester, Thomas lamented the small congregations he found worshipping in that city, and the fact that the inhabitants seemed to 'love darkness, rather than Light').[67]

(III)

With the unfolding political events of 1789, religious affiliation often marked the division between those who welcomed the French Revolution, among whom were prominent dissenters like Josiah Wedgwood and Richard Price, and Anglican moderates like Edmund

Burke, who denounced the Revolution and its advocates.[68] Here, singularity in the matter of political affiliation was a serious and potentially dangerous matter.

Some more profound challenges to the social order than his own modest stand in favour of talented, yet socially obscure friends, were intruding upon John Marsh's consciousness by the 1790s; the Chichester Book Society, of which Marsh was a founding member, obtained a copy of Paine's *Rights of Man* in April, 1790, at which our subject was 'much disgusted with the Author's Treason, Impudence and Scurrility'.[69] Whilst on holiday in Devon in September 1792, he read newspaper accounts of the 'melancholy details' of massacres in France whilst drinking tea in a public room in Sidmouth.[70] Calling on Mr Jackson, the organist at Exeter, in the hope of having a 'Musical Conversation', international politics again intruded, since the talk among clergymen and ladies present was all of the 'late Atrocities of the Jacobins'. In response to this, Marsh was galvanised into action by enlisting as a volunteer in his local militia (and commented disparagingly in his diary upon the 'Democratic Party' at large in the country). He was pleased that the presence of the Sussex Militia in Chichester gave a temporary boost to the concert life and assemblies of that city, although this was only a short hiatus in their long-term decline.

By contrast, Thomas Stutterd undoubtedly mixed in pro-revolutionary circles, but, like John Marsh, was shocked to read in the newspapers of the bloodshed that took place in France in the early years of the 1790s. Unlike Marsh, Thomas at this moment found himself forced to decide between loyalty to his religion, and loyalty to his king. Between 1792 and 1794, the letters exchanged between Thomas and his fellow-Baptist and co-worker at Whitacre's, George Dyson, are particularly vivid articulations of the experience of religious persecution in England, and the violence directed against Baptist Republican sympathisers. Thomas witnessed the burning of effigies of 'Tom Payne' in Northampton, and an arson attack upon a Baptist Meeting House at Guilsbury ten miles away, a consequence he thought, of the 'prejudices of Churchmen', so that many Dissenters had been 'insulted and abused in the streets by the populace'. In September 1792, one of Stutterd's fellow-Baptists at Huddersfield was evicted without warning from his lodgings, the cause, said Thomas, being 'Religious Bigotry'. Later, in February 1794, Dyson and Stutterd's suspected involvement with circulating the so-called 'Sheffield Papers', a printed list of the series of resolutions passed at a public meeting of 'the Friends of Peace & Reform' in Sheffield, nearly caused their imprisonment.[71] As with other rapidly industrialising towns such as Manchester and Birmingham, Sheffield had a reputation as a haven for pro-republican Dissent and political agitation.[72] It had its own Society for Constitutional Information (an offshoot of Wyvill's original Associational Movement), and its own radical press.[73] John Whitacre himself threatened to end their employment, and cross-examined them to gauge their degree of sympathy with Republican causes; he himself may have been a Dissenter, but he put aside his sympathies when called upon by the local gentry to denounce nonconformists, no doubt because his family had a standing in his local community which he felt obliged to maintain.[74] George Dyson, even more than Thomas Stutterd, expressed his anger at the government in his letters; 'what a Nation is there for uproar and madness but who makes it – the Despots'. The 'despots' were generally 'wicked men'; landlords, government, churchmen, and anyone in authority, and Dyson looked forward to a time when 'we shall be where the wicked cease from troubling & Despots cease to afflict us'.[75]

To read these letters written by Baptists during the 1790s, it is possible to gain a sense that an entire section of English society at this time were the victims of terrorism, on the grounds of a particular type of religious discrimination, given force by a fear of revolution that cut across class lines. In these years of political crisis, many nonconformists lived in fear of physical harm, that they might lose their livelihoods at any moment, members of society but only under sufferance. Little wonder the Huddersfield Baptists looked across the Atlantic upon hearing news of their growing congregations in Philadelphia; 'happy will be that man who has notic'd the impending Storm & flees to a land of Peace & Liberty, *America*'. Thomas Stutterd himself did not emigrate, and in the fragmentary latter part of his surviving correspondence, we find him still on the road in 1815, writing to his son Jabez, by now a grown man, thanking providence for having 'preserved me alive & in more comfortable circumstances than many', and grateful that 'one of the greatest evils I am exposed to is – the humourous invitations of friends to eat this & that'.[76]

Meanwhile, in Chichester, public concerts ended in 1813, and although Marsh continued his musical interests right up to his death in 1828, his withdrawal into private life reflected not only his advanced years, but also the decline in public sociability that was mirrored in provincial towns across the country. Promoting those with artistic talent was never going to cause a revolution, but his singular opinions in this regard had tested the limits of social mobility in a specific social context, at a moment when the public rules of polite society itself, which seemed so adamantine to Marsh's critics, were soon to become obsolete.

(IV)

The case studies presented here have offered two very different perspectives on ordinary life among late eighteenth-century English society, but they each have something in common in that they provide an antidote to the notion that 'singular' behaviour was limited to the more notorious figures from among the well-known rakes and hell-raisers of the period, who have received extensive study elsewhere. While some elements of English society were struggling to reconcile pluralistic religious beliefs, others were having what seemed to them equally pressing debates about what constituted good conduct and good taste. Whether in the realm of politics, religion or culture, the exercise of singularity, expressed in the realm of conscience, creed or aesthetic choice, did not *produce* of necessity a more atomised society, but tended towards the fragmentation of old solidarities, and the creation of new ones. Just as John Marsh sought out 'musical conversations' wherever he went, and found himself more in sympathy with a lower-class man of talent than a tone-deaf Lord, so Thomas Stutterd, in the face of so much hostility, found a network of kin and pseudo-kin in his fellow Baptists, who greeted him with hospitality wherever he went. These voluntary and spontaneous connections, underpinned by a common creed or interest, were what enabled these men to make sense of their lives, facilitating not only reciprocal hospitality and a promotion of mutual interests but a sense of meaning and purpose. They also produced hostility in a highly stratified society that continued to look unfavourably upon singularity.

Only recently have celebratory words such as 'diversity' been deployed to describe social difference, rather than forming the basis of critical value judgements; it took generations after the death of John Marsh and Thomas Stutterd before being *both* a 'musician' and 'shoemaker's son', or 'citizen' and 'Baptist' could be not only tolerated but considered both normal and desirable. Lest the Georgian period be considered the prototype of this modern precept, the life histories presented here are a reminder that the course of individual lives continued to be prescribed, especially in provincial society, by the pressures of social conformity and institutionalised discrimination.

Acknowledgements

Research for this chapter was made possible by the Huntington Library, San Marino, California, through their award of a Visiting Fellowship in Summer 2002. Mary Robertson of the Manuscripts Department of the Huntington Library helpfully drew my attention to the Stutterd papers, and her colleague Gayle Richardson provided much encouragement and advice. Paul Langford kindly recommended the original diaries of John Marsh. Scott Ashley, Anthony Fletcher and Elizabeth Foyster provided many thought-provoking comments, as did the contributors to this volume, and the Durham Early Modernists Group.

Notes

1. K. Wilson, *The Sense of the People. Politics, Culture and Imperialism in England, 1715–85* (Oxford, 1995); H. Barker, *Newspapers, Politics and Public Opinion in Late Eighteenth-Century England* (Oxford, 1998); J. Barry, 'The Press and the Politics of Culture in Bristol, 1660–1775', in J. Black and J. Gregory (eds), *Culture, Politics and Society in Britain, 1660–1800* (Manchester, 1991), pp. 49–81; R.J. Harris, *Politics and the Rise of the Press. Britain and France, 1620–1800* (London, 1996); *Ibid.*, *Politics and the Nation. Britain in the Mid-Eighteenth Century* (Oxford, 2002).

2. A seminal work on this subject was E.P. Thompson, *The Making of the English Working Class* (London, 1963); see also *Ibid.*, 'Eighteenth-Century English Society: Class Struggle Without Class?', *Social History*, 3 (1978); P.J. Corfield, 'Class by Name and Number in Eighteenth-Century Britain', *History*, 72, (1987); see also H. Perkin, *The Origins of Modern English Society* (London, 1969). The more recent focus upon the middle classes/middling sorts is exemplified by P. Earle, *The Making of the English Middle Class* (London, 1989) and D. Wahrman, *Imagining the Middle Class. The Political Representation of Class in Britain, c.1780–1840* (Cambridge, 1995).

3. J. Israel, *Radical Enlightenment: Philosophy and the Making of Modernity: 1650–1750* (Oxford, 2001); C. Muldrew, 'From a "light cloak" to an "iron cage": historical changes in the relation between community and individualism', in A. Shepard and P.J. Withington (eds), *Communities in Early Modern England* (Manchester, 2000), pp. 156–79; see also M. Mascuch, *The Origins of the Individualist Self: Autobiography and Self-Identity in England, 1591–1791* (Oxford, 1997). A. Macfarlane, *The Origins of English Individualism* (Oxford, 1978), and *Ibid.*, *On Individualism* (Lancaster, 1994).

4. M. Butler, *Romantics, Rebels and Reactionaries. English Literature and its Background, 1760–1830* (Oxford, 1981), p. 34.

5. Anon., *The Ambulator: or, the Stranger's Companion in a Tour Round London* (London, 1774), p. 36.

6. Baron George Anson, *A Voyage Round the World, in the Year MDCCXL*, 4 vols (6th edn, London, 1749), p. 140.

7. Anon., *Anecdotes, Bon Mots, Traits, Stratagems and Biographical Sketches of the Most Remarkable Highwaymen, Swindlers and Other Daring Adventurers* (London, 1797), p. 265.

8. R. Anderson, *The Life of Samuel Johnson, LLD* (London, 1795), p. 277 [my italics].

9. J. Almon, *Anecdotes of the Life of the Right Hon. William Pitt, Earl of Chatham*, vol. 3 (6th edn, London, 1797) [my italics].

10. These terms have been deployed retrospectively with the justification that they would have been meaningful in the era under discussion; since we lack extensive corroborating evidence, we shall never know whether and to what extent contemporaries described Marsh and Stutterd in these terms; examples are given hereafter of our subjects using this vocabulary.

11. HM54457. Since the diaries were compiled retrospectively from pocket books, references to dates vary in their precision; memories of childhood are often compressed to a single year, for example; elsewhere, the month is usually given, but not specific days, unless it was an event of especial importance to the author.

12. The Robins edition also unfortunately 'rationalises' certain quirks of an eighteenth-century hand for the modern reader, which are observed in quotations from the original diary in the present study. Manuscripts collection, Huntingdon Library, San Marino, California. References are indicated by the accession HM 54457/volume number/date/page (where given).

13. Robins, *John Marsh Journals*, p. xi.

14. HM54457, vol. 1 (1755), pp. 1–5.

15. *Ibid.*

16. HM54457, vol. 1 (1758), pp. 9–10.

17. HM54457, vol. 3 (August, 1770), p. 80.

18. HM54457, vol. 17 (August, 1796), pp. 169–70.

19. M. Girouard, *The English Town* (New Haven and London, 1990), pp. 127–44.

20. HM54457, vol. 3 (March, 1770), pp. 9–11.

21. The division was sometimes, but not always, along the lines of whether the town was a traditional market town or cathedral city, or whether it had an emergent entrepreneurial and proto-industrial character; Newcastle upon Tyne admitted tradesmen Derby excluded them. See Girouard, *English Town*, p. 134; H. Berry, 'Creating Polite Space: the Organisation and Social Function of the Newcastle Assembly Rooms', in H. Berry and J. Gregory (eds), *Creating and Consuming Culture in North-East England, 1660–1830* (Aldershot, 2004).

22. HM54457, vol. 3 (March, 1770), pp. 9–11.

23. HM54457, vol. 8 (June, 1783), pp. 109–10.

24. See HM54457, vol. 8 (May, 1783), p. 104, furniture purchased from 'Mr Gildings of Aldersgate St., London'; vol. 8 (June, 1783), p. 108; vol. 9 (October, 1784), p. 332.

25. HM54457, vol. 8 (July, 1783), p. 119. The Oxindens were a long-established family in this part of Kent, prominent during the Civil War; see A. M. Everitt, *The Local Community and the Great Rebellion* (London, 1969), pp. 6–7; see also *Ibid.*, *The Community of Kent and the Great Rebellion, 1640–1660* (London, 1966).

26. HM54457, vol. 8 (June–July, 1783), p. 120.

27. *Ibid.*, p. 123. The Derings were another prominent family in Kent; the orchards at Surrenden Dering were famed for the cultivation of over 150 fruit trees in the seventeenth century. In Everitt, *Local Community*, p. 7.

28. HM54457, vol. 8 (July, 1783), p. 125.

29. Susan Whyman highlights how this custom was regarded as old-fashioned even by the end of the seventeenth century. See S.E. Whyman, *Sociability and Power: the Cultural World of the Verneys, 1660–1720* (Oxford, 1999), p. 23.

30. HM54457, vol. 8 (July, 1783), p. 126.
31. H.R. French, 'Social Status, Localism and the "Middle Sort of People" in England, 1620–1750', *Past & Present*, 166 (2000), 66–99; see also *Ibid.*, 'The Search for the "Middle Sort of People" in England, 1600–1800', *Historical Journal*, 43 (2000), 277–93.
32. See V. A. C. Gatrell, *The Hanging Tree: Execution and the English People, 1770–1868* (Oxford, 1994) on contrasting social attitudes towards executions as public spectacles.
33. HM54457, vol. 8, (July, 1783), p. 128.
34. *Ibid.*
35. *Idem*, vol. 9 (May, 1784), pp. 33–9.
36. *Id.* (June, 1785), p. 160.
37. *Id.*, pp. 159–60.
38. J. Brewer, *Pleasures of the Imagination. English Culture in the Eighteenth Century* (London, 1998), p. 535.
39. HM54457, vol. 10 (December, 1785), pp. 42–3 [my italics].
40. *Ibid.*, vol. 9 (June, 1785), p. 165.
41. *Idem*, vol. 3 (April, 1772), p. 162.
42. *Id.*, vol. 17 (5 April, 1797), pp. 93–4. At the King's concert, the stewards usually kept order, but he recorded that one night 'I happen'd to sit immediately before 2 Ladies of *Quality*, who so annoy'd me by their perpetual Chattering all the time that I found it expedient to change my situation before the 2d. act ...'
43. Stutterd Papers, Manuscripts Collection, Huntington Library, San Marino, California. This collection was uncatalogued when the author studied it in July 2002.
44. An extensive literature on this stratum of society was inspired by Thompson's *Making of the English Working Class*, particularly as agents of radical politics, although there has been considerable debate as to whether nonconformist religion hindered the political progress of the more literate working men, such as weavers (as Thompson controversially argued), or encouraged it. See also M.R. Watts, *The Dissenters, vol. I, From the Reformation to the French Revolution* (London, 1978); D. Bythell, *The Handloom Weavers. A Study in the English Cotton Industry During the Industrial Revolution* (Cambridge, 1969); J. Rule, 'Employment and Authority: Masters and Men in Eighteenth century Manufacturing', in P. Griffiths, A. Fox and S. Hindle (eds), *The Experience of Authority in Early Modern England* (London, 1996), pp. 286–317.
45. The merchant-manufacturer 'W. & J. Whitacre' was still listed among the chief buyers at the Huddersfield wool market in Porson and White's *Directory of Leeds and the Clothing District* (1830). See W.B. Crump and G. Ghorbal, *History of the Huddersfield Woollen Industry* (Huddersfield, 1935), p. 110.
46. The first turnpike road to Huddersfield was opened in 1759, which gave access to Wakefield and Manchester; the road to Sheffield opened in 1777. Crump and Ghorbal, *Huddersfield*, p. 62. Innovations in cotton manufacture such as the fly-shuttle and spinning jenny were adopted in woollen manufacture, especially from the 1770s onwards. The adoption of Arkwright's 'scribbling' machine for carding cloth led to the number of mills on the Colne being doubled to over 100 between 1771 and 1800. See *Ibid.*, p. 70.
47. See for example HM/SP/Box 1, Jabez to Thomas Stutterd (8 February, 1786).

48. Weavers could be of high status: Richard Turner was the son of an attorney, apprenticed to Joseph Bentley, worsted weaver near Huddersfield in 1767. Jabez's difficulties arose from illness, and an inability to make ends meet: see E.J. Law, *Eighteenth-Century Huddersfield. The Day Book of John Turner, 1732–73* (Huddersfield, 1985), p. 8.

49. HM/SP/Box 1/vol. 4/f.56, John Whitacre to Thomas Stutterd (24 November, 1788).

50. HM/SP/Box 7/vol. 1/f.59, John Stutterd to Thomas Stutterd (1 March, 1783).

51. HM/SP/Box 5/vol. 3/f.1, George Dyson to Thomas Stutterd (30 March, 1796).

52. HM/SP/Box 5/vol. 2/f.60, Thomas to Mary Stutterd (23 September, 1795).

53. HM/SP/Box 3/vol. 2/f.68, Thomas to Mary Stutterd (12 October, 1792). On kerseymere, which derives from 'cashmere', see Crump and Ghorbal, *Huddersfield Wool Industry*, p. 73.

54. HM/SP/Box 1/vol. 1/f.72, Thomas to Mary Stutterd (31 December, 1787).

55. HM/SP/Box 1/vol. 1/f.64, John Stutterd to Thomas Stutterd (12 October, 1785).

56. HM/SP/Box 1/vol. 1/f.68, John Stutterd to Thomas Stutterd (9 June, 1786) [my italics].

57. HM/SP/Box 2/vol. 2/f.34, Thomas to Mary Stutterd (10 October, 1790).

58. HM/SP/Box 3/vol. 2/f.40, Thomas to Mary Stutterd (13 April, 1791).

59. HM/SP/Box 3/vo. 2/f.49, Thomas to Mary Stutterd (17 October, 1791). Rapin de Thoyras's *History of England* was translated from the French by Rev. N. Tindal and published in five volumes between 1732 and 1747.

60. HM/SP/Box 6/vol. 2/f.81, Thomas to Mary Stutterd (14 March, 1796).

61. HM/SP/Box 3/vol. 2/f.68, John to Thomas Stutterd (3 November, 1792).

62. HM/SP/Box 1/vol. 1/f.63, John to Thomas Stutterd (21 February, 1785).

63. HM/SP/Box 3/vol. 1/f.113, John to Thomas Stutterd (12 January, 1792).

64. HM/SP/Box 2/vol. 2/f.10, Thomas to Mary Stutterd (28 July, 1788).

65. HM/SP/Box 2/vol. 2/f.34, Thomas to Mary Stutterd (10 October, 1790).

66. *Ibid.*

67. HM/SP/Box 3/vol. 2/f.52, Thomas to Mary Stutterd (17 June, 1792). See L. Tyerman (ed.), *The Life and Times of the Rev. John Wesley MA*, 3 vols (1872).

68. See D. W. Lovegrove, *Established Church, Sectarian People: Itinerancy and the Transformation of English Dissent, 1780–1830* (London, 1988); D. Hempton, 'Religion in British Society, 1740–90', in J. Black (ed.), *British Politics and Society From Walpole to Pitt* (London, 1990).

69. HM54457, vol. 14 (April, 1790), p. 39.

70. *Ibid.*, vol. 15 (September, 1792), p. 28.

71. These papers followed on the heels of the first address of the Constitutional Society by six Sheffield Mechanics, published in 1791. See E. Royle and J. Walvin, *English Radicals and Reformers, 1760–1848* (Brighton, 1982), pp. 49–50.

72. See H.T. Dickinson, 'The Friends of America: British Sympathy with the American Revolution', in M.T. Davis (ed.), *Radicalism and Revolution in Britain, 1775–1848* (Basingstoke, 2000), pp. 20–1.

73. The *Sheffield Register*, for example, was the organ for the 'fierce independence and collective mentality' of the Sheffield cutlers; see Royle and Walvin, *English Radicals*, pp. 49–50.

74. Law, *Day Book of John Turner* (entry for 2 December, 1763). Whitacre's father, for example, was listed among the pall-bearers of Mr Samuel Fenton, attorney

of Greenhead, who was buried at Huddersfield in December, 1763; other pall-bearers included the vicar, and two physicians: Dr Thompson and Dr Sonister.

75. Dyson was a common name in the Huddersfield area: the Dyson family of Woodhouse were known to the lawyer John Turner in the 1750s (see e.g. Law, *Day Book of John Turner*, entries for 21 June, 1756, 7 September, 1757). Fittingly, he may have been an ancestor of the Huddersfield agitator Amos Dyson, who provoked the Dissenting polemic *Who are the Cowards and Deceivers? Or, Extracts From Correspondence Between J. Barker, A. Dyson and the Huddersfield Committee* (Newcastle upon Tyne, 1845).

76. HM/SP/Box 6/vol. 2/f.75, Thomas Stutterd to Jabez Stutterd (18 June, 1815).

7
Agency, Custom and the English Corporate System

Phil Withington

Urban historians have long regarded the cities and boroughs of early modern England as 'deeply rooted' in a 'complex of tradition' – a 'complex' that not only survived into the sixteenth and seventeenth centuries but 'witnessed a renewed emphasis'.[1] This idea of the traditional urban community has informed the assumption, still common to local historiography, that, until the onset of urbanisation in the last decades of the seventeenth century, towns were 'pre-modern' rather than 'early modern'.[2] More recently, it has been argued that urban 'tradition' was invented rather than immutable. Robert Tittler has noted that, in the course of the later sixteenth and seventeenth centuries, provincial townsmen constructed historical narratives that consolidated the autonomy of urban communities and the oligarchies that governed them.[3] Whether in their compilation of civic genealogies, transcription of civic record, or display of civic artefacts, the historical energies of civic elites were living proof of Keith Thomas's dictum that 'the most common reason for invoking the past was to legitimise the prevailing distribution of power'.[4] Jonathan Barry has discerned a later tradition of independent chronicling that differentiated (for example) inhabitants of Bristol from genteel 'foreigners', 'urbane' interlopers, and county antiquaries, the creation of civic memory contributing, in effect, to a sense of civic distinction.[5] Arguing more generally, Andy Wood has observed that a distinguishing feature of borough custom was that it was 'often a more overtly mutable construct' than that in manor and parish, while Adam Fox has stressed the politics that increasingly accompanied the transcription and possession of record within local communities.[6]

These accounts suggest that the 'complex of tradition' was nothing if not a product of agency and source of identity. Just as remembering was a deliberate and strategic act, so its material and symbolic outcomes were intrinsic to the way in which inhabitants of a locality saw their collective selves within local and national culture. There remains the tendency, however, to regard the use and impact of civic memory as part of a more general 'rise of oligarchy'. Just as civic elites were the primary agents of historical reinvention, so the identities so engendered reinforced their particular vision of the communities they governed. The writing of city histories is a case in point. As Peter Clark puts it, such texts were 'strategies' aimed at 'the shoring up and reassertion of the values of the civic community in a time of instability': 'motifs' for 'the rise of civic oligarchy in many English towns during the Tudor and early Stuart period'.[7] This approach is functional, regarding histories as 'devices' for 'creating a deferential citizenry, suitably impressed with the lineage of local government and the necessity of strong rule'.[8] It assumes that the wider reception of texts – and so the formation of identity – was passive and uncritical. And, to a large extent, it disregards alternative constructions and assertions of the past among freemen, burgesses and citizens. As a result, the complexities and contests of agency and identity are elided, the full gamut of ideological positions and agendas obscured.

This chapter addresses the politics of remembering and its implications for the identity and agency of not so much the individual person as the corporate bodies they constituted. The corporeality of community – and also the communal basis of public acts – was a crucial but often neglected feature of sixteenth- and seventeenth-century political culture, and also pivotal to the way contemporaries perceived themselves and legitimated public actors. The chapter suggests that an historicised framework for understanding both civic politics and the identities it spawned is not a sociological concept of 'oligarchy' so much as the Aristotelian notion of 'city commonwealth'. Propagated in both theory and practice in the second half of the sixteenth century, this structured two kinds of dispute in particular. One source of contention was constitutional – whether the 'public good' of cities and boroughs should be organised along 'aristocratic' or 'democratic' lines. Another was religious, citizens and burgesses increasingly seeking to control the 'common soul' of communities and the consciences of their fellow communicants. Civic 'traditions'– or what contemporaries regarded as 'customs' – were constitutive to this politics in a number of respects. In towns as elsewhere, the past was crucial to justifying, acting upon, and changing the present: the very legitimacy of the charters, orders, and rituals upon which civic governance rested was derived in large part from their 'customary' and 'ancient' status. Insofar as history was a living and formative presence, then agency was dependent on both the possession and interpretation of the materials of memory. As a result, the places, texts and rituals that embodied custom formed a contested set of resources that were used not only to legitimise authority but also critique, challenge and redefine it. The temporality of civic politics meant that remembering itself was political.

(I)

The ubiquity of 'custom' in sixteenth- and seventeenth-century England, and its importance for justifying and sanctioning collective or individual agency, is well known.[9] Constitutional and social historians have shown that custom was part of the repository of terms describing the precedents and prescriptions that formed the increasingly wide compass of English law, referring in particular to practices held to be 'time out of mind' or 'time immemorial': that is, extant before 1189. Customary law was a particular concern for courts of equity like Chancery and Exchequer. Their development from the middle of the sixteenth century provided an important arena for local customs to be claimed and contested as well as providing a mainspring for conceptions of England's 'ancient constitution'.[10] This increase in customary consciousness coincided with, and was perhaps informed by, the first consequences of European colonialism and humanism: explorations across space and time that uncovered 'Native' and 'Pagan' customs at once distant and unfamiliar. Viewed in these terms, customs were synonymous with the habits and rituals of any given culture – part of the nexus of 'Customs, Manners and Worships' that defined for Roger Williams the 'Rarities' of the Narragansett in seventeenth-century America, and through which peoples derived their identities.[11] His *Key into the language of America* divides these customs into 41 chapters ranging from 'family business' to 'news and discourse' to 'their religion', each describing patterns of behaviour at once resonant and dissonant with English beliefs and practices. In this way, custom served as an idiom through which the lifestyles and 'habits' of different peoples were described and explained anthropologically: by missionaries like Williams as well as travellers, merchants, soldiers, essayists and philosophers.[12] Their 'discoveries' were propagated to domestic audiences through print, theatre, and new commodities like tobacco that, for commentators like James VI and I, were inseparable from the 'barbarous' customs that governed their use among the 'wild, godless and slavish *Indians*'.[13] Moreover, in the shape of Ireland and other 'barbaric' margins temporal distances were shockingly reduced, providing a colonial 'laboratory' that was both cultural and constitutional.[14]

England underwent, in effect, custom-saturation: the realisation that, legally and anthropologically, people and the societies in which they lived conformed not to universal 'reason' so much as particular customs at once relative and distinct. The authors of this discursive shift were socially and intellectually diverse. They included inhabitants (and litigants) claiming the authority of local lore and knowledge; antiquarians and ethnologists who collected and observed customs; and lawyers paid to defend, attack, and invent them. Although articulated in various contexts and genres, the cumulative impact was an early-modern present that was self-evidently shaped by the near and distant (and the tangible and imagined) past. Whether as indigenous lore or proof-in-law, customs were historical products connecting the community which practised them organically to that past. They were attributes of place, in that they demarcated locations and their inhabitants as the inheritors of lore and law. And they were prescriptive, providing local, anthropological or legal templates for what and how things were, should be and would be done in future. The relativism that they embodied – as well as their palpable influence on behaviour and attitudes – posed, in turn, obvious problems for humanist and religious reformers. As Francis Bacon put it, 'there is no trusting to the force of nature nor to the bravery of words, except it be corroborate by custom'.[15] Anticipating the methodology of John Locke, Bacon illustrated the 'tyranny of custom' with anthropological and classical examples.[16] Custom's cultural power was evidenced by 'the Indians (I mean the sect of their wise men)' performing human sacrifices; by the brutality of Spartan rites of passage; by the importance that Irish rebels placed on the manner in which they were executed.[17] The Presbyterian preacher Edward Bowles likewise styled custom 'second nature'.[18] Just as custom meant that 'some places are so profane, that swearing is become the very dialect of the Town or Family where they dwell', so 'customs and constitutions' determined 'the dispositions of the people' (in this instance militating against a full unification between England and Scotland).[19]

Custom as an anthropological and legal 'fact' made for interesting tensions with the universalising demands of social and cultural reform, not least because exponents of the former were often proponents of the latter. Roger Williams' attempt to 'unlock some Rarities concerning the Natives themselves' had, for example, an ulterior end. As he explained, 'a man may, by this help, converse with *thousands* of *Natives* all over the Country'. '[By] such converse that it may please the *Father of Mercies* to spread *civility* (and in his own most holy season) *Christianity*; for *one Candle* will light *ten thousand* and it may please God to bless a *little leaven* to season the *mighty Lump* of those *Peoples* and *Territories*.'[20] It was knowledge of custom that provided the opportunity to change them. Bacon likewise concluded that, 'since custom is the principal magistrate of man's life, let men by all means endeavour to obtain good customs'. Echoing the insights of Richard Mulcaster, he emphasised education as the crucial mechanism of change. While 'the great multiplication of virtues upon human nature rests upon societies well ordained and disciplined', it was nevertheless the case that 'commonwealths and good governments do nourish virtue grown, but do not much mend the seeds'.[21] As significantly, insofar as reformers were also humanists who looked to classical antiquity for inspiration then the principles of virtue, civility and godliness with which they hoped to change society were as retrospective and universal as custom was historicised and particular. It followed that customs specific to place and time could nevertheless encapsulate more general and applicable principles of reformed behaviour: as Cathy Shrank has recently shown, England's Reformations were closely connected to humanist scholarship and state-craft.[22] As fervent a Calvinist as the Jacobean minister Stephen Denison could nevertheless acknowledge that 'Many of the heathens were virtuous, some excelled for justice, others for fortitude, others for temperance, others for prudence'.[23] Roger Williams repeatedly made a similar point in order to illustrate the corrupt customs of his countrymen. His ethnography showed that 'The sociableness of the nature of man appears in the wildest of them who love society; Families, cohabitation, and consociation of houses and towns together'. 'There is a savour of civility and courtesy even amongst these wild *Americans*, both amongst themselves and towards *strangers*':

> 'If Natures sons both wild and tame,
> Humane and Courteous be:
> How ill becomes it Sons of God
> To want Humanity?'[24]

The imperative of reform and the realities of custom were not, therefore, necessarily antithetical. Certainly Richard Mulcaster, perhaps the most influential humanist of the Elizabethan era, was extremely sympathetic to the power and persuasiveness of custom. Prescribing 'the right writing of our English tongue', he nevertheless noted 'I have been very careful never to depart from the *custom* of my country, because I desire either to please with liking, or to mislike without displeasing'. Pragmatism dictated accommodation on the part of the rational (and masculine) reformer. 'For where any ordinary *custom* doth seem of long time to have made her own choice, and that upon good shew, she will either like him that cleaves to her allowance, or not be displeased, where herself is not misliked.'[25] In contrast to other humanists seeking the wholesale refurbishment of the English alphabet, Mulcaster argued that 'if there be any hope to procure liking in such a thing as custom is to rule, it must needs come by following, and not by forcing.'[26] The history of reform showed that 'enforcing to the contrary, or altering too far is almost desperate, if not altogether, because it hath always missed, with loss of labour where it offered service'.[27] What worked for language also worked for law. Law, like language, was recognised as at once the repository of custom and the primary means for instituting reform; and the period's most influential lawyer, Edward Coke, was as committed to balancing common law's customary and reformatory potential as Mulcaster the linguist.

(II)

Royal charters of incorporation – granted at the sovereign's will through the office of the Lord Attorney – marked one intersection between these customary and reformatory sensibilities: Coke himself was personally responsible for the high profile incorporations of Windsor and Ludlow at the turn of the century.[28] Regarded as the culmination of customs, grants, precedents, and orders that urban inhabitants had accumulated, or claimed to have accumulated, over preceding centuries, charters of incorporation sanctioned the creation (or recognition) of a 'fictional person' that transcended the wills and interests of individual members. These 'body politics' had the capacity to act in their own right and on the behalf of their individual members. Governed and represented through an arrangement of civic offices that culminated with a common council, an incorporated community held properties and privileges in common, could act as a person through its common seal, and could sue (and be sued) in courts of law. In the majority of cases, common councils also claimed representation in parliament as well as the right to hold quarter sessions. The institutionalisation of agency that this represented was usually the result of years of petitioning on the part of townsmen: a contingent process that depended on the survival of written evidences like grants and charters as well as customs made binding through continual practice.[29] As such, they encapsulated the convergence – and possession – of time and place. When Henry Ireton defended the rights of 'freeman of a corporation' in the Putney Debates of 1647, he did so on the grounds that they constituted ' "a permanent" and "local" ... interest' in the kingdom.[30] As symbols of permanency, records were treasured and guarded possessions. St Andrew's 'Hutch' in Cambridge was kept in the parlour of the Guildhall and could be opened by one of four keys to the lock. These were held by the mayor; the borough treasurers; and two 'keepers of the key' elected separately by the aldermen and common council at the Feast of St Bartholomew. Failure to 'attend the mayor ... with the key in his keeping' when summoned resulted in a 5 *s.* fine. These measures were supplemented in 1631 when it was ordered 'a fair large book be provided ... wherein all the charters and evidences of this town shall be entered' and then placed in the Hutch. Thereafter, if 'it shall happen any such persons ... shall so take out any such charters evidences or writings', they must 'set down at the end of the book what writings they be and the day and year of the taking them out and subscribe their name'.[31]

Incorporated boroughs contributed to the more general pattern of economic, political, and cultural particularity that custom by definition structured. They also brought a more idealised sense of historical process to the present. Beyond their appeal to specific evidences, the kind of community they implied suggested a more universal process at work. Henry Manship suggested that '[Like] as in the beginning of the world', Great Yarmouth in Norfolk represented 'the gathering together and society of men begun not for one cause only ... but also for that they might in all things live the more commodiously together, and frame themselves a commonwealth'. Thereafter, there was nothing 'more worthy or better beseeming an excellent Prince, or well governed commonwealth, or more honourable or profitable a kingdom', than 'fair and well-built Towns and Cities'.[32] For certain commentators this process of urbanisation clearly preceded the Norman invasion. Just as John Speed placed England's myriad corporate resources in their Anglo-Saxon 'theatre', so Nathaniel Bacon argued that 'liberty of Township' was a 'liberty of market' initially derived from 'common right, and not as a corporation made by common charter; but as they are a multitude of people anciently gathered together and united'.[33] Likewise by specifying the kind of constitutions, powers, and customs that characterised a particular community, charters-of-incorporation were also tools of social and political reform both locally and nationally. In negotiating their privileges, burgesses at once linked their locales to metropolitan authority and opened a conduit for institutional and cultural changes that was articulated through rather than despite the language of custom. As Richard Butcher put it, 'the Reason, why the Princes and Policy of England have had a regards as it were fencing and hedging about the cities and ancient Boroughs of this land with Privileges and Immunities' was 'for the stronger Defence, Preservation, and Maintenance of the same'. Incorporation conjoined both 'The Conservation of the Customs of the Kingdom and the Common Right and Dignity of the Crown'.[34] By the early eighteenth century, Thomas Madox could generalise that 'In Ancient times little Difference was made ... between a populous Town that was gilded or incorporated and one that was not gilded or incorporated'. It was after the Conquest that 'the cities and towns of England were vested either in the Crown or else in the clergy or in the Baronage of Great Men'.[35] From that point, 'A Town not-corporate had succession only as an Aggregate Body or Community, or if you please as one generation succeeded another'. This he described as 'Natural Succession'. A 'Town-corporate', in contrast, 'had succession as an Aggregate Body or community too; [but] under a special Denomination, suppose of Mayor Bailiffs and Community ... And this was a complex kind of succession, to wit both Natural and Artificial'.[36]

For all his self-professed 'solidity of judgement', Madox failed to mention was that incorporation was a relatively recent process.[37] There were 44 incorporated cities and boroughs in England in 1540. By 1640 the figure had risen to 182–193 if Welsh boroughs are included, many more if the Irish Pale and plantations are also considered.[38] The scale of post-Reformation incorporation represented, in effect, the 'hedging and fencing' of what might be termed a corporate system of communities 'both Natural and Artificial': a process that had national as well as local implications.[39] As Sir Thomas Smith observed, citizens served *Republica Anglorum* 'in their cities and boroughs, or in corporate towns where they dwell'; and 'in the common assembly of the realm to make laws, which is called Parliament'.[40] The formation of a corporate system only made this truer over time. Between 1584 and 1641 the proportion of Commons' representation controlled by the boroughs rose from 79 per cent to 82 per cent. Over the same period, the proportion of borough representation in incorporated cities and boroughs – as opposed to unincorporated parliamentary boroughs without the requisite institutional resources – rose from 37 per cent to 63 per cent. As a result, the proportion of all parliamentary representation located within the corporate system rose from 35 per cent to 52 per cent.[41] This astonishing reorganisation of the parliamentary franchise was merely one aspect of a process that, in its simultaneous celebration and modulation of borough custom, was the urban equivalent of the humanist agenda to retain and reform the English vernacular. As Mulcaster put it, the introduction of 'strange' or 'incorporate' words was an inevitable feature of linguistic (and so cultural) embellishment. However, even as a word enhanced what he styled 'enfranchised' or 'natural English', it was required to 'wear our colours, since it will be one of us'.[42]

(III)

Historians have traditionally interpreted the growth of the 'corporate system' as the triumph of oligarchy: 'the domination of town government by a small and usually self-perpetuating body of the richest citizens', usually as a result of economic and social inequalities.[43] This process of communal differentiation was accompanied by significant encroachments into civic liberties by gentry and state.[44] More recent interpretations have refined and challenged the model. Tittler has distinguished between 'neutral' oligarchy – consisting of the relatively uncontroversial bureaucratisation and stratification of government that occurred in tandem with developments in state and society – and 'corrupt' oligarchy, whereby factions and parties monopolised and expropriated civic resources.[45] He has also shown that relations between burgesses and other interested parties, be they gentry, courtiers, or lawyers, were much more reciprocal (and empowering to citizens) than historians of patronage allowed – not least because they were mediated institutionally rather than reliant on personal largesse.[46] Ian Archer has likewise demonstrated that the logistics of governance made for a much more extensive culture of participation than the historiographical focus on benches of aldermen has allowed.[47] Slightly differently, Barry has pointed to a fairly resilient culture of 'bourgeois collectivism' within English towns. Despite various mutations over time – including greater social differentiation and the extension of government in the post-Reformation period – this collectivism demarcated the urban 'middling sort' as participants in a culture that was fundamentally associational and, on that basis, communally independent in both theory and practice.[48]

These models identify important aspects of civic culture as it developed in the sixteenth century: while there is no doubt that greater demands were made on the administrative capacities of local governors, so urban citizenship was clearly predicated on the idea of association. However, their reinterpretation of urban citizenship can be taken a stage further. So far as contemporaries were concerned, it was an Aristotelian notion of 'small' or 'city commonwealth' that formed the ideological framework for citizens, burgesses and freemen during the later sixteenth and early seventeenth centuries. 'Commonwealth' represented the means to a good life, whereby each freeman and his household could fulfil their moral and economic potential while serving, and benefiting from, the common or public good.[49] As Henry Manship put it, the burgesses of Great Yarmouth participated in:

> a certain community or Society, both of life and goods, which makes a civil body, formed and made of divers members, to live under one power, as it were under one Head and Spirit, and more profitably to live together in this mortal life, that they may the more easily attain unto life eternal for ever.[50]

Within this framework, 'oligarchy' was defined as a corrupt form of 'aristocracy': instead of 'the best' ruling for the benefit of all, as aristocracy prescribed, 'a few' ruled for the benefit of themselves. As such, oligarchy was part of a more general typology outlined by Sir Thomas Smith in which three established and beneficial forms of government were defined by their pejorative equivalents. In this way, the 'good and just' governments of *monarchy* (king), *aristocracy* ('governing of the best men'), and *democracy* ('commonwealth by the general name') were defined in relation to their 'evil and unjust' mutations. These included government by tyrant (*tyranny*), by the 'usurping of a few gentlemen, or a few of the richer or stronger sort' (*oligarchy*), or the 'usurping of the popular or rascal and viler sort because they be more in number' (*popular*).[51]

Aristotle identified many gradations of oligarchy and democracy, and the most successful and stable polities combined (in the unlikelihood of ideal-types working in practice) moderated elements of each, usually in combination with the active participation of what he called the 'middle class'. It was precisely this kind of mixed polity, or commonwealth, that Smith prescribed in his influential *De Republica Anglorum*.[52] However, he did so by simplifying Aristotle's complex and somewhat abstract typology into an applicable set of binaries of 'good' and 'evil' governmental forms. He and other Tudor humanists combined them with Ciceronian notions of 'civil conversation' that would facilitate constructive participation in government.[53] In so doing they developed the idea, central to English humanism from Erasmus and More onwards, that virtue and public service were possible within the English polity at the national and local level.[54] Viewed on these terms, the creation of the corporate system can be regarded as one aspect of a more general concern among Tudor statesmen to incorporate the 'better sort' of particular communities into public modes of counsel, consultation, and law at the local and national level. They aimed at the creation, in effect, of civic aristocracies, or at least civic polities with aristocratic potential. By this was meant a set of personal dispositions that were cultivated through customs and manners on a daily basis. Civic aristocracy was not the birthright of 'blood' and 'honour' so much as civil responsibility and civil sensibilities developed by commitment to, and participation in, those institutions structuring the commonwealth and public good. Just as the assumption that 'the best' or 'better sort' should govern and represent communities was a commonplace of later sixteenth and early seventeenth literature, so aristocratic conceits were transcribed onto the constitutional arrangements of not only England's cities and boroughs but also its manors, townships and parishes.[55] However, this in itself was not the promulgation of oligarchy so much as a Ciceronian belief in, and provision of, the rule of 'the best' and 'fittest' within the otherwise customary and differentiated localities of English society. It was, in turn, as local 'aristocrats' that citizens and burgesses were expected to partic-ipate in the larger structures of law, parliament, and the monarchical state, the 'better sort' of city commonwealths forming one element of what Mulcaster termed, following Aristotle, a national 'middling sort'.[56]

The promulgation of this vernacular civic humanism after 1540 was not unprecedented. Just as England's 'great' and 'ancient' cities provided a template for Aristotelian governance (Sir Thomas More wrote *Utopia* as a citizen of London, after all) so the 'commonwealth' ideology of the mid-sixteenth century popularised notions of public and common good.[57] Likewise, it was in the political and material ramifications of the Henrician and Edwardian Reformations that the genesis of the corporate system can be found. At a time when regular and legitimate forms of 'counsel' became a recurring demand of townsmen, and the retention or purchase of religious properties and institutions a pressing concern, incorporation was the most expensive, elaborate, but also effective means of preserving or extending communal resources.[58] The Shropshire borough of Ludlow was a case in point. Incorporated since 1461, its commonwealth was massively extended by the corporation's absorption of the wealthy Palmers' Guild in 1551.[59] The Guild held extensive lands in both town and county, maintained a grammar school, and performed charitable works, all of which were jeopardised by the Dissolution. Its preservation by Edwardian patent was, therefore, a political success for the burgesses that significantly enhanced their material and public wealth. In practice, disputes over the nature of office holding and the allocation of common land and resources intensified thereafter. By the

1590s there had developed opposing 'aristocratic' and 'democratic' camps or what the Recorder described as 'certain controversies between the Bailiffs, Twelve and Twenty Five councillors ... on the one party and the burgesses ... on the other party'.[60] Various attempts at resolution failed. A new charter of incorporation, successfully purchased in 1598 from Sir Edward Coke in order to counter a pending *quo warranto* against their government by the democrats, marked the aristocrats' bid to break once and for all opposition in the town.[61]

The politics of commonwealth that the conflict epitomised are examined elsewhere.[62] The point to be stressed here is that although Ludlow's 'better sort' of burgess secured a charter ostensibly reflecting the 'custom and using time out of mind', their control of the past and its implications for the present was hardly uncontested.[63] On the contrary, the Court of Exchequer provided democratic opposition with a perfect arena in which to rehearse quite different interpretations of the borough's constitutional development – so much so that the eventual victory of the aristocrats was drained of any customary, and so symbolic, authority. John Bradford, a weaver and burgess of middling wealth within the town, personified this democratic resistance. He explained that 'the new charter was procured ... to maintain [the aristocrats] former bad practices and insolent courses'; to prevent 'good government'; and to expropriate 'the lands belonging to this corporation'.[64] A close reading of the borough's documents showed that Ludlow was originally incorporated as a 'free borough' in the name of 'Bailiffs, Burgesses and Commonalty': the 'thirty seven burgesses chosen, called common council', were 'permitted to assist the Bailiff', but not govern.[65] Indeed, the aristocrat's recourse to 'prescription' was entirely fabricated.[66] The conception of custom that justified this opposition was not rooted in elusive notions of 'usage' and 'time immemorial', though a certain notion of civil sociability that transcended subsequent 'fencing and hedging' was clearly implied. In a subsequent court case relating to the allocation of church pews, Bradford outlined quite clearly his understanding of custom and its efficacy. The dispute concerned the right of churchwardens 'by virtue of their office' and 'according to their discretion, taking such reasonable and indifferent consideration thereof' to re-allocate pews that had become vacant. Bradford explained that as churchwarden he had 'often viewed the church book [and] seen and read in the same book that the custom and use hath been so many years past [that] all pews seats and kneeling places within the parish church of Ludlow' had been distributed accordingly'.[67] It was on similar grounds that one of the key demands of the democrats in

1593 was that 'our charter be read over in English one every third year'.[68]

It was, therefore, as reflective and knowledgeable citizens that Bradford and others described how, over time, manorial lordship in Ludlow had transmuted into burghal democracy without the insertion of conciliar governance. For all the aristocratic claims of custom, it was clear from extant charters that the Twelve and Twenty Five were to have 'no more power than the rest of the burgesses' over elections or lands 'nor to exclude the rest of the burgesses from their free elections'. Thereafter, there was no evidence of any general consent that the Twelve and Twenty Five 'should represent and supply the room of all the rest of the burgesses and commonalty of the said corporation'. There was no proof that burgesses had agreed that elections should not proceed 'in any large or ample manner as the whole body of the said town and corporation'. And 'the true meaning of the charter' was clearly not that the 'Twelve and Twenty Five' should select their own replacements. In fact, the institution of 'common council' was one of many recent innovations that the ruling faction was now seeking to legitimate with the 'new charter which they rather call A confirmation of government by usage from time out of mind'.[69]

This interpretation of borough history convinced neither the Court of Exchequer nor the Privy Council, the Barons eventually ruling that the new charter indeed 'ratified and confirmed ... the said long course' of government in Ludlow.[70] The ruling reflected the aristocratic preferences of the late Elizabethan regime; the pre-eminence of common law over equity; and also the skill with which the self-styled patricians of Ludlow characterised their opponents as 'seditious' and 'populist'. This characterisation was only confirmed when the democrats forcibly seized the common hall and the records and offices it held.[71] The accusations of the burgesses were nevertheless persuasive enough to place the governance of Ludlow under close metropolitan supervision.[72] At the same time, an informal campaign of insult, libel and gossip against the personal capacities of 'so called common councillors' could only emphasise the disjunction between civic custom and personal disposition that the charter had wrought, severely damaging the 'good reputation and credit of this reputation' in the process.[73] Indeed, the fact that, over the course of the sixteenth and seventeenth centuries, Ludlow underwent more re-incorporations than any other city commonwealth aside from Newcastle-upon-Tyne hardly suggests the remorseless 'rise of oligarchy' of historiographical orthodoxy. On the contrary, it points to an intense civic politics in which the imperatives of commonwealth – and its historical antecedents – were routinely and authoritatively asserted and defended.

(IV)

In turn-of-the-century Ludlow contrasting conceptions of commonwealth were sustained by entirely different readings of the same historical documents. While the majority of burgesses discerned in their records a democratic and broadly participatory past, the governing elites argued for the evolution of an enclosed and aristocratic citizenship that distinguished councillors as 'better' than their neighbours. It should be reiterated that democracy and aristocracy in this instance were Aristotelian in nature and specific to the jurisdictions and resources of the particular borough. While John Bradford abhorred the personal qualities and structural organisation of the current body politic, he was quite as committed to preventing incursions by interlopers who could not claim the permanency requisite of urban freedom. As such, both aristocracy and democracy were specific to place and explicitly exclusionary: they characterised relations among a particular body of freemen, the boundaries of which were vigorously defended, and which were not necessarily coterminous with the town as a whole. Inclusion in turn denoted enfranchisement – either through the formal ritual of becoming free of guild and corporation or an active inhabitancy that involved *de facto* participation in local governance. In Ludlow, the borough jurisdiction coincided with that of the parish and the guilds were fully integrated into the civic polity: excluded from this commonwealth was the 'urbane' population of lawyers, gentry and officials attached to the Council of the Marches. As the King's Messenger Rowland Higgins discovered in 1630, his wealth and status was not enough to place him among 'the better rank and sort of the parish of Ludlow (who had interest therein)'.[74]

In seventeenth-century Cambridge, in contrast, the commonwealth of 'free burgesses' had no control over the urban economy; had little to do with parish government; and exercised no magisterial powers. In a town dominated by the university and colleges – commonwealths in their own right, and with much more effective links with metropolitan authority – the civic interest was effectively limited to power of fairs and markets, borough common lands and parliamentary representation. City commonwealth in Cambridge was a compromised and somewhat marginal urban presence.[75] For all (or perhaps because) of its structural weaknesses, the 'body of burgesses' was 'thoroughly democratic'. As

F. W. Maitland explained, 'Despite the conciliar organs that it has evolved, despite the twelve aldermen and twenty four common councillors, all the important affairs of the corporation are brought before a general assembly in which … all the burgesses have votes'. Unlike in Ludlow, 'there never took place that transfer of power to a select body'.[76] If the survival of 'common days' was one mainstay of civic democracy, electoral procedures were another, burgesses retaining those rituals of ballot and lottery that for Aristotle were 'democratic' in the purest sense of the term.[77]

The annual elections for mayor, bailiffs (overseers of the market) and other executive offices were a case in point. Attended by all the free burgesses, the ritual began with each of the 24 common councillors bringing 'his name written in a like piece of paper' to a table in front of the mayor and 12 aldermen. Two aldermen selected by the mayor 'enclosed in several balls of wax of one colour and quality' the 'names so written' and placed them in a box. While another alderman chose one of the balls 'for the bench', the burgesses 'being neither Alderman nor of the Twenty-Four' appointed a fellow burgess to choose another. These were delivered to the mayor 'to be opened, And these persons whose names in the said two balls are written' were to 'go together into some place within the house' in order to empanel 12 burgesses – 3 from each of the borough's 4 wards. These 12 burgesses then chose a further 6 burgesses to make a panel of 18. It was this panel that chose the officers for the year. Each decision-making stage of the process was timed 'by an hour glass' and failure to make choice within the hour resulted in a significant fine. The mayor was empowered with the casting vote if there was an 'equality of voices'. And electors took two oaths intended to ensure the ritual remained fully democratic: they promised to 'have not laboured to bring any man to office for this year', and swore that the criteria for choosing burgesses 'for the government of this Town' was that they were 'meet and sufficient'.[78] The election of burgesses to parliament was conducted along the same principles, though a panel of 8 rather than 18 chose the 2 representatives.[79]

The election had all the semblance of continuity and permanency: the survival of democracy in an era of oligarchy. Likewise the 'oath of any free burgess' called on freemen to 'swear that the liberties privileges customs ordinances orders goods and all the rights of the Town of Cambridge from henceforth as much as in you lie you shall keep and maintain'.[80] However, their antecedents were more complex than this rhetoric suggests. Both rituals were transcribed in a book of orders compiled between 1608 and 1611. This was the outcome of a survey of 'all the former orders of this town, to the end that such thereof as are against the law, or idle, or superfluous or by alteration of time should be found fit to be changed might be suppressed and annihilated'.[81] Authority for the survey in turn emanated from the charter of incorporation of 1605, which empowered the burgesses to make and enforce laws 'for the greater public good, the commonweal and the good ruling of the borough'.[82] This allowed the selection and transcription of 'the ancient orders' of the borough 'into one book' according to the consent of the common council, the advice of common lawyers, and 'their best wisdom and discretion'.[83] Although the 1605 charter did not specify conciliar enclosure in the manner of Ludlow, the process of customary and legal refurbishment certainly did. For example, preceding the orders for elections and oaths was another purging the aldermanic bench on the grounds that its current membership (which exceeded the number of 12) was 'unlawful and contrary to the ancient customs and ordinances of this town'. This was followed by another order reconstituting 'the Twenty-Four commonly called the common counsel' as an autonomous and self-selecting body. Not only were the common counsellors listed by name., when, in future, a place 'shall happen to be void', they were to 'supply of the places such persons ... as in their discretions shall be then thought meet'.[84]

Just as oligarchy in Ludlow should not obscure its democratic resistance, so democracy in Cambridge was neither a medieval throwback nor antithetical to reform. On the contrary, as a means of constituting a seventeenth-century city commonwealth it was entirely legitimate so long as 'populism' did not ensure. Moreover, it was within the parameters of civic democracy that further reforms were implemented. Over the next ten years customs and orders were surveyed and appropriated on a regular basis. This affected a variety of rituals that ranged from debating and electoral procedures in the council chamber, the manner of borough feasts, and the apparel of burgesses, to the regulation of fairs and markets, the maintenance of borough common lands, and control of the common chest. The main agent of reform was fish merchant Thomas French, the mayor who instigated the book of orders in 1608. His primacy was confirmed in 1616 when he was empowered with sole responsibility for negotiating a new charter of incorporation for the 'amending and bettering' the material and constitutional resources of the borough.[85] While clearly committed to civic democracy, French also assumed that the customs that constituted it encouraged personal dispositions requisite of civic and civil society. A preamble to a civic order agreed at the height of his influence was a case in point. In February 1615 it was noted that 'there is nothing more acceptable unto

God nor pleasing unto man [for] the brethren to live together in unity'. It 'being likewise taught by examples in all civil governed common- wealths that where people in uniformity live according to good orders thus towns and cities flourish and increase', so 'controversy and disobedience' ruined even 'great monarchies'. Finally, 'those which refuse to be subject to authority are unworthy to enjoy the benefits of societies, And for that, that if everyone may live according to his own will without order or restraint there would be no peaceable government but desolation and confusion'.[86] This articulation of the commonwealth ideal – that the 'will' of individuals was subordinate to civil society and its institutions – was directed not at 'the plebs' (as the 'aristocrats' in Ludlow described their 'democratic' opponents) so much as wealthier burgesses now refusing to comply with the borough's sumptuary customs. It chastised, in effect, those civic gentry who felt themselves 'better' than their brethren.

The downfall of French stemmed in large part from his inability to reincorporate Cambridge as a city of 'mayor, aldermen, and citizens'. Opposed by the university, his failure was also symptomatic of resist- ance among certain of the burgesses: resistance that was likewise artic- ulated through the control and use of record. In 1615 it was recorded that 'in this [common day] book there hath been divers misdemeanours committed and done by crossing out of some orders adding unto other orders diminishing from some orders and adding ... disgraceful words unto some others'. Alderman John Wicksted, a client of Lord Ellesmere (the borough's High Steward), reluctantly confessed to the crime once he was 'personally and peremptorily accused'. The object of his illicit amendments – Thomas French – was authorised by the common coun- cil to instigate 'further talk and conference ... between them'. It seems the scribal changes were designed to imply financial improprieties during French's mayoralty: this at a time when the fish merchant was about to head the campaign to incorporate Cambridge as a city. As punishment, Wicksted acknowledged that 'false and untrue/he is a knave that writ false'. He also promised to provide the town not only with 'a new book well bound with good paper but also be at the charge of the writing into the said new book all the orders grants and inscrip- tions in the common day book now written'.[87] However, it was Wicksted who had the subsequent (if not the last) laugh, sitting on a committee of six in 1631 empowered to succeed where French had failed and renew the charter.[88] The charter was duly purchased with the support of Thomas Lord Coventry, who had in the meantime become the borough's High Steward. As inconclusive as the 1605 document, it nevertheless reflected a new phase of reformatory pressure that was articulated not through the legal and indigenous appropriation of custom so much as the imposition of edicts and decrees from the Privy Council. As Coventry warned in 1633, failure to comply with his recent batch of 'admonishments' would make him 'much repent my pains herein, as in other things'.[89] These edicts were aristocratic rather than democratic in nature. His central concern, like that of his allies among the burgesses, was the sort of person serving on the common council. As he put it, 'I admonish and require you' to ensure that 'decayed and unfit' burgesses 'be removed from their places and others of the ablest of the Town for quality and estate to be placed in their room'. Although he had previously communicated with the burgesses on this matter, 'I am informed nothing has yet been done ... albeit there are many able men in the Town fit to be of the Twenty-Four'.[90]

This attempt to gentrify the borough – to institute 'aristocracy' by other means – can hardly be said to have 'caused' the civil war. However, it was an important context for the civic politicking at the end of the decade that saw Oliver Cromwell return to parliament after a wait of 12 years. Cromwell was made free of the borough with the help of 'puritan' burgesses – the son of Thomas French, also Thomas, prominent among them.[91] He was then elected to both the Short and Long Parliaments with 'the greatest part of the Burgesses of the Town being present'. This was despite the rule of residency, passed by French's father in 1609, which required representatives to be permanent householders. More importantly, it was in the face of prior claims of clientage made by Sir John Finch, Privy Councillor and High Steward.[92] In the meantime, the common-council that he had repeatedly sought to reform now overturned an important legacy of Coventry's interventions. At the mayoral elections of 1641, the ritual of selection ground to a halt when the common councillors chosen to select the officers refused to take their second oath unless a letter from Coventry, and the 'order' it had resulted in, 'be abrogate and made void'. This letter had imposed a rule of seniority on elections. Rather than relying on the discretion of electors, they were to choose the oldest alderman 'and so to descend in course of succession'. It was now pointed out that this contradicted their oath that mayors be 'meet and sufficient'. After 'some debate and altercation' the common councillors won the day and proceeded to elect by discretion.[93] The following year Cromwell's ally, Robert Twells, was likewise propelled to the mayoralty, the burgesses 'conceiving his fitness for the place now in these dangerous times to be most valuable for the Town and good for the common wealth'.[94] A year later Wicksted gave up his place of alderman 'by writing'. His resignation coincided with the refusal of Alderman Samuel Spalding to accept the mayoralty on the grounds that 'according to the ancient customs of this town [the mayor] ought to have been chosen according to their turns'.[95] Spalding had sat with Wicksted on the 1631 committee to purchase a charter. He was also a central figure in civic politics at the Restoration, replacing none other than the ejected Thomas French as mayor in 1662 by 'the King's Majesties Commissioners' and hounding French for 'several writings' that he retained after his expulsion.[96] In 1643, however, he expressed his 'absolute resolution not to hold the office if he could anyway avoid it'. That his outburst survives at all is somewhat fortuitous, as the common council subsequently ordered that 'the entries touching Mr Spalding's election be altered, and to be entered "for Important Reasons he refused to hold the office of mayor" leaving out his conceived Reasons for undue election'.[97] Their interference with civic record was symptomatic of the fact, long known in Cambridge, that it was through the control and appropriation of custom that legitimate actions depended, and the agency of the larger body determined.

(V)

When, in the early summer of 1641, Oliver Cromwell and John Lowry wrote to the 'Mayor, Aldermen of Cambridge with the rest of that Body present there', they did so 'in the practice of the representative' seeking the sanction of 'the Body represented'. In this instance, they required 'conformity' for the parliamentary 'Protestation' recently passed by 'the members of that Body'. Having received their copy, it was recorded in the Common-Day book that the Protestation was 'read and afterwards subscribed by the Mayor, Aldermen and others present in the hall of the said common day'.[98] The exchange was a quintessential act of urban citizenship, burgesses and their representatives working through the appropriate channels of corporate town and parliament to offer 'counsel' to their monarch. Its context was the formation, over the previous 150 years, of a corporate system of city commonwealths designed in part for precisely the purpose of mediated consultation: a process that transformed customary and ancient forms of government even as it appropriated them. Beyond its essential Aristotelianism, the form, content, and agency that this corporeality took was, in turn, the product of any number of personal acts and contests between particular members: democrats and aristocrats, oligarchs and populists, saints and reprobates, parliamentarians and royalists. The contingency that this implies in turn makes for no easy conflation between citizenship and other political allegiances: the corporate system is no reinvention of the 'Whiggish' wheel. On the contrary, it was in the immediate politics of custom and place that identities were forged and decisions made. Cromwell himself was, of course, fully inured in this politics of commonwealth: an opponent of one civic aristocracy, in Huntingdon in the later 1620s, it was hardly surprising that he should appeal to the democrats (and puritans) of neighbouring Cambridge in 1640.[99] That is not to claim that the precepts of citizenship defined him or were even his primary source of identity. Contemporary writers knew as well as social historians that the idiosyncrasies of the person and vagaries of custom were too complex for that. It is to reclaim a context for thought and action that historians have, by and large, ignored: a context in which collective as much as individual bodies were regarded as sentient and active persons.

Notes

1. W.T. MacCaffery, *Exeter, 1540–1640. The Growth of an English County Town* (Cambridge MA, 1958), pp. 5, 281; J.T. Evans, *Seventeenth-century Norwich. Politics, religion, and government, 1620–1690* (Oxford, 1979), pp.1–2.
2. C. Phythian Adams, 'Introduction: an Agenda for English Local History', in Ibid. (ed.), *Societies, Cultures, and Kinship, 1580–1850* (London, 1996), pp. 1, 8.
3. R. Tittler, *The Reformation and the Towns in England. Politics and Political Culture, c.1540–1640* (Oxford, 1998), ch. 13.
4. K. Thomas, 'The Perception of the Past in Early Modern England', Creighton Lecture, London University (1983), pp. 2–4.
5. J. Barry, 'Provincial Town Culture, 1640–1780: Urbane or Civic?', in J.H. Pittock and A. Wear (eds), *Interpretation and Cultural History* (Basingstoke, 1991), pp. 210, 223.
6. A. Wood, 'The Place of Custom in Plebeian Political Culture: England, 1550–1800', *Social History*, 22, 1 (1997), p. 47; A. Fox, 'Custom. Memory, and the Authority of Writing', in P. Griffiths, A. Fox and S. Hindle (eds), *The Experience of Authority in Early Modern England* (Basingstoke, 1996), pp. 89–116.
7. P. Clark, 'Visions of the Urban Community: Antiquarians and the English City before 1800', in D. Fraser and A. Sutcliffe (eds), *The Pursuit of Urban History* (London, 1983), pp. 113, 111.
8. Tittler, *Reformation and the Town*, p. 293.
9. For useful overviews see Wood, 'The Place of custom', pp. 46–9; K. Wrightson, 'The Politics of the Parish', in Griffiths *et al.*, *Experience of Authority*, pp. 22–5.
10. Wood, 'The Place of Custom', p.47; J.G.A. Pocock, *The Ancient Constitution and the Feudal Law. A Study of English Historical Thought in the Seventeenth Century* (Cambridge, 1987), pp. 42–3, 46–7.

11. R. Williams, *A Key into the Language of America or, An Help to the Language of the Natives of that Part of America, called New-England* (1643).

12. See Joan-Pau Rubies, *Travel and ethnology in the Renaissance. South India Through European eyes, 1250–1625* (Cambridge, 2000).

13. James I, King of England *A Counter-blaste to Tobacco* (1604), B2.

14. J. Ohlmeyer, ' "Civilizinge of those rude partes": Colonialisation Within Britain and Ireland, 1580s–1640s', in N. Canny (ed.), *The Origins of Empire* (Oxford, 2001), p. 146.

15. F. Bacon, 'On Custom', in B. Vickers (ed.), *Francis Bacon. A Critical Edition of the Major Works* (Oxford, 1996), p. 418.

16. J. Locke, 'Second Tract on Government', in M. Goldie (ed.), *Locke. Political Essays* (Cambridge, 1997), p. 59.

17. Bacon, 'On Custom', p. 419.

18. E. Bowles, *The Duty and Danger of Swearing* (York, 1656), p. 12.

19. *Ibid.*; E. Bowles, *Manifest Truths, or an Inversion of Truth Manifest* (1646), A2.

20. Williams, *Key in to the Language*, p. 3.

21. Bacon, 'On Custom', pp. 419–20.

22. C.Shrank, *Writing the Nation in Reformation England* (Oxford, 2004).

23. S.Denison, *An Exposition upon the First Chapter of the Second Epistle of Peter* (1622), p. 47. For an exploration of Denison's ideas see P. Lake, *The Boxmaker's revenge. 'Orthodoxy, 'Heterodoxy' and the Politics of the Parish in early Stuart London* (Stanford, 2001), chs 2–3.

24. Williams, *Key in to the language*, pp. 47, 9–10.

25. R. Mulcaster, *The First Part of the Elementarie* (1582), pp. 226–7.

26. *Ibid.* For alternative models see C. Shrank, 'Rhetorical Constructions of a National Community: the Role of the King's English in Mid-Tudor writing', in A. Shepard and P.J. Withington (eds), *Communities in Early Modern England. Networks, Place, Rhetoric* (Manchester, 2000), pp. 180–98.

27. Mulcaster, *Elementarie*, p. 227.

28. R.R. Tighe and J.E. Davis (eds), *Annals of Windsor: Being a History of the Castle and Town* (London, 1858), pp.647, 54–7. For Ludlow, see below and P. Withington, *The Politics of Commonwealth. Citizens and Freemen in Early Modern England* (Cambridge, 2005), ch.3.

29. For the politics of the process see C.F. Patterson, *Urban Patronage in Early Modern England. Corporate Boroughs, the Landed Elite, and the Crown, 1580–1640* (Stanford, 1999), pp. 164–80.

30. A. Sharp (ed.), *The English Levellers* (Cambridge, 1998), p. 108.

31. Cambridge County Record Office (CCRO), City Box II, 9, f. 11, 202.

32. H. Manship, *The History of Great Yarmouth* ed. C.J. Palmer (Great Yarmouth, 1854), pp. 23–4. See also R. Tittler, *Townspeople and Nation. English Urban Experiences 1540–1640* (Stanford, 2001), ch.5.

33. J. Speed, *The Theatre of the Empire of Great Britain* (1611), Preface; N. Bacon, *The Continuation of an Historical Discourse of the Government of England* (1651), p. 82.

34. R. Butcher, *The Survey and Antiquity of the Town of Stamford in the County of Lincoln* (1717), pp. 19–20.

35. T. Madox, *'Firma Burgi', or an Historical Essay Concerning the Cities, Towns and Boroughs of England* (1726), pp. 4, 37.

36. Madox, *Firma Burgi*, p. 50.

37. *Ibid.*, Preface.
38. The figures are based on Tittler, *Reformation and the Towns*, pp. 345–50.
39. P. Slack, *From Reformation to Improvement. Public Welfare in Early Modern England* (Oxford, 1999), p. 26.
40. Sir Thomas Smith, *De Republica Anglorum* (1583), p. 29.
41. These figures are taken from Withington, *Politics of Commonwealth*, ch.2.
42. Mulcaster, *Elementarie*, pp. 226, 154.
43. The summary is from J. Barry, 'Introduction', in *Ibid.* (ed.), *The Tudor and Stuart Town. A Reader in English Urban History* (Harlow, 1990), p. 24.
44. J.E. Neale, *The Elizabethan House of Commons* (London, 1949), ch.7.
45. Tittler, *Reformation and the Towns*, p. 183.
46. *Ibid.*, p. 175.
47. I.A. Archer, 'Politics and Government 1540–1700', in P. Clark (ed.), *The Cambridge Urban History of Britain, vol. II, 1540–1840* (Cambridge, 2000), pp. 241–6.
48. J. Barry, 'Bourgeois Collectivism? Urban Association and the Middling Sort', in J. Barry and C. Brooks (eds), *The Middling Sort of People. Culture, Society and Politics in England, 1550–1800* (Basingstoke, 1994), pp. 84–112.
49. S. Everson (ed.), *Aristotle. The Politics and the Constitution of Athens* (Cambridge, 1996), pp. xxiv–xxxii.
50. Manship, *History*, p. 23.
51. Smith, *De Republica Anglorum*, p. 3.
52. *Ibid.*, p. 6.
53. J. Richards, *Rhetoric and Courtliness in Early Modern Literature* (Cambridge, 2003), pp. 83–6.
54. M. Todd, *Christian Humanism and the Puritan Social Order* (Cambridge, 1987), pp. 184, 189.
55. The best account of the sociology of this process remains K. Wrightson, *English Society 1580–1680* (London, 1982), pp. 225–6.
56. R. Mulcaster, *Positions Wherein Those Primitive Circumstances be Examined, Which are Necessarie for the Training up of Children* (1581), p. 188. For the process of self-recognition at a national level see K. Wrightson, ' "Sorts of people" in Tudor and Stuart England', in Barry and Brooks, *Middling Sort of People*, p. 48.
57. Slack, *Reformation to Improvement*, pp. 12–14; K. Wrightson, *Earthly Necessities. Economic lives in Early Modern Britain* (New Haven, 2000), pp. 149–53; E.H. Shagan, *Popular Politics and the English Reformation* (Cambridge, 2003), pp. 274–80.
58. R.W. Hoyle, *The Pilgrimage of Grace and the Politics of the 1530s* (Oxford, 2001), 19–20, 97, 425–8, 433–9; Tittler, *Reformation and the Towns*, ch.5.
59. Shropshire County Record Office (SCRO), Q63, 'Copies of Charters and Grants to the Town of Ludlow' (ed.) W. Felton, p. 52; M. Faraday, *Ludlow 1085–1660. A Social, Economic, and Political history* (Chichester, 1991), p. 91.
60. SCRO, LB2/1/16, f. 40.
61. P. Williams, 'Government and Politics in Ludlow, 1590–1642', *Transactions of the Shropshire Archaeological Society*, 56, (1957–8), p. 287; Faraday, *Ludlow*, pp. 35–7.
62. Withington, *Politics of Commonwealth*, ch.3.
63. SCRO, LB7/755. Other examples of customary government include LB7/736; LB7/741a; LB7/744.

64. National Archives (NA), E134/39 and 40 Elizabeth/Mich. 37, items 97 and 98.
65. SCRO, LB7/737.
66. SCRO, LB7/741b.
67. Hereford County Record Office (HCRO), HD4/2/17, 1611, Joyce Larkin c. William Sherwood.
68. SCRO, LB2/1/6, f. 38.
69. SCRO, LB7/768; LB7/741a.
70. SCRO, LB7/743.
71. *Ibid.*
72. SCRO, LB1/4.
73. SCRO, LB2/1/16, f. 42.
74. HCRO, HD4/2/17, 1639, Guardians of Ludlow c. Rowland Higgins.
75. The place of city commonwealth in Cambridge is considered in Withington, *Politics of Commonwealth*, ch.4.
76. F.W. Maitland and M. Bateson (eds), *The Charters of the Borough of Cambridge* (Cambridge, 1901), p. xi.
77. Aristotle, *Politics*, p. 105.
78. CCRO, City Box II, 9, 'Orders 1608–1611', ff. 8v, 5v.
79. *Ibid.*, f. 10v.
80. CCRO, City Shelf C, Book 7, f. 2.
81. CCRO, City Box II, 9, f. 1 and reverse end, f. 1.
82. Maitland and Bateson, *Charters*, p. 117.
83. CCRO, City Box II, 9, ff. 7v, 10.
84. CCRO, City Box II, 9, f.7v.
85. CCRO, City Shelf C, Book 7, f. 68v.
86. CCRO, City Shelf C, Book 7, f. 58.
87. CCRO, City Shelf C, Book 7, ff. 25v, 27, 33, 33v.
88. CCRO, City Shelf C, Book 7, f. 198.
89. CCRO, City Shelf C, Book 7, f. 218.
90. *Ibid.*
91. J.S. Morrill, 'The Making of Oliver Cromwell', in J.S.A. Adamson and J.S. Morrill (eds), *Oliver Cromwell and the English Revolution* (Harlow, 1990), pp. 19–48.
92. CCRO, City Shelf C, Book 7, ff.313, 329.
93. CCRO, City Shelf C, Book 7, ff. 341, 210, 342.
94. CCRO, City Shelf C, Book 7, f. 357.
95. CCRO, City Shelf C, Book 7, f. 462v.
96. CCRO, City Shelf C, Book 8, ff. 153, 153v, 158.
97. CCRO, City Shelf C, Book 7, f. 362v, 368.
98. CCRO, City Shelf C, Book 7, f. 332–333.
99. NA SP16 176, 34.

Bibliography

(I) Printed primary sources

Almon J., *Anecdotes of the Life of the Right Hon. William Pitt, Earl of Chatham*, vol. 3 (6th edn, London, 1797).

Anderson R., *The Life of Samuel Johnson, LLD* (London, 1795).

Anon., *The Ambulator: Or, the Stranger's Companion in a Tour Round London* (London, 1774).

Anon., *Anecdotes, Bon Mots, Traits, Stratagems and Biographical Sketches of the Most Remarkable Highwaymen, Swindlers and Other Daring Adventurers* (London, 1797).

Anon., *The Batchelor's Directory: Being a Treatise of the Excellence of Marriage* (1694).

Anon., *The Compleat Justice*, 7th edn (1661).

James I, King of England, *A Counter-blaste to Tobacco* (1604).

Anon., *An Ease for Overseers of the Poore: Abstracted from the Statutes* (Cambridge, 1601).

Anon., *The Maidens Best Adorning: Or, A Directory for the Female-Sex: Being, A Fathers Advice to his Daughter* (1687).

Anon., *The Maids Complaint against the Batchelors* (1675).

Anon., *Marriage Asserted: In Answer to a Book Entituled Conjugium Conjurgium: Or, Some Serious Considerations on Marriage* (1674).

Anon., *Marriage Promoted. In a Discourse of its Ancient and Modern Practice* (1690).

Anon., *The New Parliament of Women* (1683).

Anon., *The New Westminster Wedding, or the Rampant Vicar. Being a Full Relation of the Late Marriage of J-P-, Clerk. to E. Hook, Spinster* (1693).

Anon., *The Tickler Tickled: Or, The Observator upon the Late Trials of Sir George Wakeman & c. Observed: By Margery Mason, Spinster* (1679).

Anon., *Who are the Cowards and Deceivers? Or, Extracts From Correspondence Between J. Barker, A. Dyson and the Huddersfield Committee* (Newcastle upon Tyne, 1845).

Anon., *The Women's Complaint against Tobacco* (1675).

Anson, Baron George, *A Voyage Round the World, in the Year MDCCXL*, 4 vols (6th edn, London, 1749).

Arch J., *From Ploughtail to Parliament. An Autobiography* (London, 1986).

Armitage G.J. (ed.), 'Allegations for Marriage Licences issued by the Dean and Chapter of Westminster, 1558–1699; also for those issued by the Vicar-General of the Archbishop of Canterbury, 1660–1679', *Harleian Society*, 23 (1886).

Armitage G.J. (ed.), 'Allegations for Marriage Licences issued from the Faculty Office of the Archbishop of Canterbury at London, 1654–1869', *Harleian Society*, 24 (1886).

Armitage G.J. (ed.), 'Allegations for Marriage Licences issued by the Bishop of London, 1520–1620', *Harleian Society*, 25 (1887).

Arthington H., *Provision for the Poore, Now in Penurie* (London, 1597).

Astell M., *A Serious Proposal to the Ladies Parts I & II* (ed.) P. Springborg (London, 1997).

Atkinson J.C. (ed.), 'North Riding Quarter Sessions Records', *North Riding Record Society*, 1–9 (1884–92).

Bacon F., *The Essays or Counsells, Civill and Morall. Newly Enlarged* (1625).

Bacon N., *The Continuation of an Historical Discourse of the Government of England* (1651).

Barber F., *Directions for Love and Marriage. In Two Books, Translated by a Person of Quality* (1677).

Bates-Harbin E.H. (ed.), 'Quarter Sessions Records of the County of Somerset', *Somerset Record Society*, 23–4 (Taunton, 1907).

Behn A., *The Ten Pleasures of Marriage and the Second Part, The Confession of the New Married Couple*, ed. J. Harvey (London, 1922).

Behn A., *The Rover and Other Plays*, ed. J. Spencer (Oxford, 1995).

Blaxton J., *The English Usurer; or Usury Condemned by the most Learned Divines of the Church of England* (1634).

Blount T., *Glossographia* (1656).

Blount T., *Nomo-Lexicon: A Law-Dictionary* (1670).

Bowles E., *Manifest Truths, or an Inversion of Truth Manifest* (1646).

Bowles E., *The Duty and Danger of Swearing* (York, 1656).

Burnet G., *A Defence of Polygamy and Divorce* (1680).

Butcher R., *The Survey and Antiquity of the Town of Stamford in the County of Lincoln* (1717).

Campegij Ioannis, *Tractatus Universi Iuris*, 4 vols (Venice, 1584).

Candler A., *Poetical Attempts* (Ipswich, 1803).

Cavendish M., Duchess of Newcastle, *CCXI Sociable Letters* (1664).

Cavendish M., *The Convent of Pleasure* (1668).

Cavendish M., Duchess of Newcastle, *Plays, Never before Printed* (1668).

Chandler P. (ed.), *Hearth Tax Returns for Dudley and Stourbridge, 1664–1666–1674* (1992).

Chapman G., Jonson B. and Marston J., *Eastward Ho (1605)* (ed.) R.W. Van Fossen (Manchester, 1979).

Chaucer G., *The Tales of Canterbury*, ed. R.A. Pratt (Boston, 1974).

Clare J., *The Parish*, (Harmondsworth, 1985).

Cockburn J.S. (ed.), 'Western Circuit Assize Orders, 1629–1648: A Calendar', *Camden Society*, 4th ser., 17 (1976).

Coke E., *The Second Part of the Institutes of the Lawes of England* (1642). Journals of the House of Commons, II, 1693–97 (London, 1803).

Conset H., *The Practice of the Spiritual or Ecclesiastical Courts* (London, 1685).

Cooper T., *The Art of Giving* (1615).

Cutlack S.A., 'The Gnosall Records, 1679 to 1837: Poor Law Administration', *Collections for A History of Staffordshire, Part I* (1936).

Dalton M., *The Country Justice* (London, 1618).

Davies D., *The Case of Labourers in Husbandry* (London, 1795).

Day W.G. (ed.), *The Pepys Ballads*, II & IV (Woodbridge, 1987).

Defoe D., *Robinson Crusoe* (1719).

Denison S., *An Exposition upon the First Chapter of the Second Epistle of Peter* (1622).

Dobson A. (ed.), *The Diary of John Evelyn*, III (London, 1906).

Dunning R., *A Plain and Easie Method Shewing How the Office of Overseer of the Poor May be Managed* (London, 1685).

Dunton J., *The Challenge Sent by a Young Lady to Sir Thomas- &c. or, The Female War* (1697).

Ebsworth J.W. (ed.), *The Roxburghe Ballads Illustrating the Last Years of the Stuarts*, VII (Hertford, 1893).

Eden W., *The State of the Poor*, 3 vols (London, 1797).

Emmison F.G. (ed.), *Early Essex Town Meetings: Braintree, 1619–1636, Finchingfield, 1626–1634* (Chichester, 1970).

Equiano O., *The Interesting Narrative of the Life of Olaudah Equiano* (Harmondsworth, 1995).

Everson S. (ed.), *Aristotle. The Politics and the Constitution of Athens* (Cambridge, 1996).

Goldie M. (ed.), *John Locke, Political Writings* (Cambridge, 1997).

Gouge W., *Of Domesticall Duties* (1622).

Gough R., *The History of Myddle*, ed. D. Hey (Harmondsworth, 1981), p. 11.

Greaves R.W. (ed.), 'The First Ledger Book of High Wycombe', *Buckingham Record Society*, 11 (1947).

Greene D.G. (ed.), 'The Meditations of Lady Elizabeth Delaval Written Between 1662 and 1671', *Surtees Society*, 190 (1978).

Harland J. (ed.), 'A Volume of Court Leet Records of the Manor of Manchester in the Sixteenth Century', *Chetham Society*, o.s. 63 (1864).

Harriott J., *Struggles through Life* (London, 1816).

Harrison W., *The Description of England*, ed. G. Edelen (New York, 1968; reprint 1994).

Hervey F. (ed.), *Suffolk in the XVIIth Century: The Breviary of Suffolk by Robert Reyce* (London, 1902).

Hodges T., *A Treatise of Marriage. With a Defence of the 32th Article of Religion of the Church of England* (1679).

Horsfall Turner J. (ed.), *The Rev. Oliver Heywood B.A., 1630–1702: His Autobiography, Diaries, Anecdote and Event Books* (Bingley, 1883).

Howell James D.E. (ed.), 'Norfolk Quarter Sessions Order Book, 1650–57', *Norfolk Record Society*, 26 (1955).

Hudson W. and Tingey J.C. (eds), *The Records of the City of Norwich*, II (Norwich and London, 1910).

Hutton W., *The Life of William Hutton* (1816).

Hyde P. and Harrington D. (eds), *Hearth Tax Returns for Faversham Hundred, 1662–1671* (Faversham, 1999).

Kidder R., *Charity Directed: Or, The Way to Give Alms to the Greatest Advantage* (1676).

Kussmaul A. (ed.), 'The Autobiography of Joseph Mayett of Quainton 1783–1839' *Buckinghamshire Record Society*, 23 (1986).

Law E.J., *Eighteenth-Century Huddersfield. The Day Book of John Turner, 1732–1773* (Huddersfield, 1985).

Le Hardy W. (ed.), *Hertford County Records*, 9 vols (Hertford, 1905–39)

Lister J. (ed.), 'West Riding Sessions Records, 1597–1642', *Yorkshire Archaeological Society Record Series*, 3, 54 (1888–1915).

Locke J., *The Reasonableness of Christianity as Delivered in the Scriptures* (1695).

Longstaffe W.H.D. (ed.), 'Memoirs of the Life of Mr. Ambrose Barnes, Late Merchant and Sometime Alderman of Newcastle upon Tyne', *Surtees Society*, 50 (1866).

Madox T., *'Firma Burgi', or an Historical Essay Concerning the Cities, Towns and Boroughs of England* (1726).

Maitland F.W. and Bateson M. (eds), *The Charters of the Borough of Cambridge* (Cambridge, 1901).

Manley T., *Nomothetes: The Interpreter* (1672).

Manship H., *The History of Great Yarmouth,* ed. C.J. Palmer (Great Yarmouth, 1854).

Marshall J.D. (ed.), *The Autobiography of William Stout of Lancaster 1665–1752* (Manchester, 1967).

Marx K., *The Eighteenth Brumaire of Louis Bonaparte* (1852).

Marx K., *Collected Works,* 4 (1975).

Minsheu J., *Ductor in Linguas; The Guide Into Tongues* (1617).

Mulcaster R., *Positions Wherein Those Primitive Circumstances be Examined, Which are Necessarie for the Training up of Children* (1581).

Mulcaster R., *The First part of the Elementarie* (1582).

Palsgrave J., *Les Clarcissement de la langueu francoyse* (1530).

Parkinson R. (ed.), 'The Life of Adam Martindale', *Chetham Society,* 4 (1845).

Partridge E., *A Dictionary of Slang and Unconventional English* (ed.) P. Beale, 8th edn (London, 1984).

Penney N. (ed.), *The Household Account Book of Sarah Fell of Swarthmoor Hall* (Cambridge, 1920).

Pound J.F. (ed.), 'The Norwich Census of the Poor 1570', *Norfolk Record Society,* 40 (1971).

Ratcliff S.C., Johnson H.C. and Williams N.J. (eds), *Warwick County Records,* 9 vols (Warwick, 1935–64).

Redwood B.C. (ed.), 'Quarter Sessions Order Book, 1642–1649', *Sussex Record Society,* 54 (1954).

Reynel C., *The True English Interest* (1674).

Reyner E., *Considerations Concerning Marriage* (1657).

Robinson E. (ed.), *John Clare's Autobiographical Writings* (Oxford, 1986).

Rogers J., *A Treatise of Love* (London, 1632).

Rosenheim J.M. (ed.), 'The Notebook of Robert Doughty, 1662–1665', *Norfolk Record Society,* 54 (1989).

Rowlands S., *The Bride* (1617).

Russell P.D.D. (ed.), *Hearth Tax Returns for the Isle of Wight 1664–1674* (Isle of Wight, 1981).

Salzman L.F. (ed.), 'The Town Book of Lewes 1542–1701', *Sussex Record Society,* 48 (1945–46).

Saxby M., *Memoirs of a Female Vagrant Written by Herself* (London, 1806).

The Complete Works of William Shakespeare (Ware, 1996), p. 280.

Sharp A. (ed.), *The English Levellers* (Cambridge, 1998).

Shiels W.J. (ed.), 'Archbishop Grindal's Visitation, 1575, Comperta et Detecta Book', *Borthwick Texts and Calendars: Records of the Northern Province,* 4 (1977).

Shorrocks D. (ed.), 'Bishop Still's Visitation 1594, and The "Smale Booke" of the Clerk of the Peace for Somerset, 1593–5', *Somerset Record Society,* 84 (1998).

Slack P. (ed.), 'Poverty in Early Stuart Salisbury', *Wiltshire Record Society,* 31 (1975).

Smith, Sir Thomas, *De Republica Anglorum* (1583).

Smith V. (ed.), 'The Town Book of Lewes 1702–1837', *Sussex Record Society,* 69 (1972–73).

Sokoll T. (ed.), *Essex Pauper Letters 1731–1837* (Oxford, 2001).

Speed J., *The Theatre of the Empire of Great Britain* (1611).

Stevenson J. and Davidson P. (eds), *Early Modern Women Poets: An Anthology* (Oxford, 2001).

Storey M. (ed.), *John Clare: Selected Letters* (Oxford, 1990).

Tawney R.H. and Power E. (eds), *Tudor Economic Documents, I* (London, 1924).

Thale M. (ed.), *The Autobiography of Francis Place* (Cambridge, 1972).

Thirsk J. and Cooper J.P. (eds), *Seventeenth Century Economic Documents* (Oxford, 1972).

Thornton A., 'The Autobiography of Mrs Alice Thornton of East Newton, Co. York', *Surtees Society*, 62 (1875).

Tilley M.P., *A Dictionary of the Proverbs in England in the Sixteenth and Seventeenth Centuries* (Michigan, 1950).

Tullie G., *An Answer to a Discourse concerning the Celibacy of the Clergy* (Oxford, 1688).

Tyndale W., *The Obedience of a Christian Man*, ed. D. Daniell (London, 2000).

Vaisey D. (ed.), *The Diary of Thomas Turner* (Oxford, 1985).

Various, *The Morning-Exercise at Cripplegate: or Several Cases of Conscience Practically Resolved, by sundry Ministers, September 1661* (1661).

Vickers B. (ed.), *Francis Bacon. A Critical Edition of the Major Works* (Oxford, 1996).

Vives J.L., *The Office and Duetie of an Husband* (1555).

Waters R.E.C. (ed.), *A Statutory List of the Inhabitants of Melbourne, Derbyshire, in 1695* (London, n.d).

Weales G. (ed.), *The Complete Plays of William Wycherley* (New York, 1967).

Wharton H., *A Treatise of the Celibacy of the Clergy, Wherein its Rise and Progress are Historically Considered* (1688).

Wheatley H.B. (ed.), *Stow's Survey of London* (London, 1912).

Williams R., *A Key into the Language of America or, An Help to the Language of the Natives of that Part of America, called New-England* (1643).

Woodhead A., *A Discourse Concerning the Celibacy of the Clergy* (Oxford, 1688).

Wyatt P. (ed.), 'The Uffculme Wills and Inventories 16th to 18th Centuries', *Devon and Cornwall Record Society*, n.s. 40 (Exeter, 1997).

(II) Unpublished theses

Auffenberg T.L., 'Organised English Benevolence: Charity Briefs, 1625–1705' (Vanderbilt University Unpubl. PhD Thesis, 1973).

Barker-Read M., 'The Treatment of the Aged Poor in Five Selected West Kent Parishes From Settlement to Speenhamland, 1662–1797' (Open University Unpubl. PhD Thesis, 1988).

Froide A.M., 'Single Women, Work, and Community in Southampton 1550–1750' (Duke University Unpubl. PhD Thesis, 1996).

Hill J., 'Poverty and Poor Relief in Shropshire, 1550–1685' (Liverpool University Unpubl. MA Thesis, 1973).

Muldrew C., 'Credit, Market Relations, and Debt Litigation in Late Seventeenth Century England,with Particular Reference to King's Lynn' (Cambridge University Unpubl. PhD Thesis, 1990).

Ottaway S., 'The "Decline of Life": Aspects of Ageing in Eighteenth-Century England' (Brown University Unpubl. PhD Thesis, 1998).

Spicksley J.M., 'The Early Modern Demographic Dynamic: Celibates and Celibacy in Seventeenth Century England' (University of Hull Unpubl. PhD Thesis, 2001).

(III) Printed secondary sources

Articles

Amussen S., 'Gender, Family and the Social Order, 1560–1725', in A.J. Fletcher and J. Stevenson (eds), *Order and Disorder in Early Modern England* (Cambridge, 1985).

Andrew D., 'To the Charitable and Humane: Appeals for Assistance in the Eighteenth-Century London Press', in H. Cunningham and J. Innes (eds), *Charity, Philanthropy and Reform* (London and New York, 1998).

Archer I.A., 'Politics and Government 1540–1700' in P. Clark (ed.), *The Cambridge Urban History of Britain, vol. II, 1540–1840* (Cambridge, 2000).

Baker J.H., 'Male and Married Spinsters', *American Journal of Legal History*, 21 (1977).

Barkley Brown E., 'Polyrhythms and Improvization: Lessons for Women's History', *History Workshop Journal*, 31 (1991).

Barry J., 'The Press and the Politics of Culture in Bristol, 1660–1775', in J. Black and J. Gregory (eds), *Culture, Politics and Society in Britain, 1660–1800* (Manchester, 1991).

Barry J., 'Provincial Town Culture, 1640–1780: urbane or civic?', in J.H. Pittock and A. Wear (eds), *Interpretation and Cultural History* (Basingstoke, 1991).

Barry J., 'Identité Urbaine et Classes Moyennes Dans L'Angleterre Moderne', *Annales ESC*, 48, 4 (1993).

Barry J., 'Bourgeois Collectivism? Urban Association and the Middling Sort', in J. Barry and C. Brooks (eds), *The Middling Sort of People. Culture, Society and Politics in England, 1550–1800* (Basingstoke, 1994).

Beier A.L., ' "Utter Strangers to Industry, Morality and Religion": John Locke on the Poor', *Eighteenth-Century Life*, 12 (1988).

Ben-Amos I.K., 'Gifts and Favors: Informal Support in Early Modern England', *Journal of Modern History*, 72 (2000).

Berlin M., 'Reordering Rituals: Ceremony and the Parish, 1520–1640', in P. Griffiths and M. Jenner (eds), *Londinopolis: Essays in the Cultural and Social History of Early Modern London* (Manchester, 2000).

Berry H., 'Creating Polite Space: the Organisation and Social Function of the Newcastle Assembly Rooms', in H. Berry and J. Gregory (eds), *Creating and Consuming Culture in North-East England, 1660–1830* (Aldershot, 2004).

Boulton J., 'Neighbourhood Migration in Early Modern London', in P. Clark and D. Souden (eds), *Migration and Society in Early Modern England* (London, 1987).

Bourdieu P., 'Structures, Habitus, Power: Basis for a Theory of Symbolic Power', in N.B. Dirks *et al.* (eds), *Culture/Power/History A Reader in Contemporary Social Theory* (New Jersey, 1994).

Braddick M. and Walter J., 'Introduction: Grids of Power: Order, Hierarchy and Subordination in Early Modern Society', in M.J. Braddick and J. Walter (eds), *Negotiating Power in Early Modern Society: Order, Hierarchy and Subordination in Britain and Ireland* (Cambridge, 2001).

Bray A., 'To be a Man in Early Modern Society: The Curious Case of Michael Wigglesworth', *History Workshop Journal*, 41 (1996).

Broad J., 'The Smallholder and Cottager After Disafforestation: A Legacy of Poverty?', in J. Broad and R. Hoyle (eds), *Bernwood: The Life and Afterlife of a Forest* (Preston, 1997).

Brooks C., 'Apprenticeship, Social Mobility and the Middling Sort, 1550–1800', in J. Barry and C. Brooks (eds), *The Middling Sort of People: Culture, Society and Politics in England, 1550–1800* (London, 1994).

Byrne A., 'Singular Identities: Managing Stigma, Resisting Voices', *Women's Studies Review*, 7 (2000).

Canning K., 'Feminist History after the Linguistic Turn: Historicizing Discourse and Experience', *Signs*, 19, 2 (1994).

Capp B., 'The Double Standard Revisited: Plebeian Women and Male Sexual Reputation in Early Modern England', *Past & Present*, 162 (1999).

Carter M., 'Town or Urban Society? St. Ives in Huntingdonshire, 1630–1740', in C. Phythian-Adams (ed.), *Societies, Cultures and Kinship, 1580–1850: Cultural Provinces and English Local History* (Leicester, 1993).

Carter P., 'Poor Relief Strategies: Women, Children and Enclosure in Hanwell, Middlesex, 1780–1816', *The Local Historian*, 25 (1995).

Cavallo S., 'The Motivations of Benefactors: An Overview of Approaches to the Study of Charity', in J. Barry and C. Jones (eds), *Medicine and Charity Before the Welfare State* (London, 1991).

Clancy M., 'Documenting the Self: Abelard and the Individual in History', *Historical Research*, 76 (2003).

Clark P., 'Migration in England During the Late Seventeenth and Early Eighteenth Centuries', *Past & Present*, 83 (1979).

Clark P., 'Visions of the Urban Community: Antiquarians and the English City Before 1800', in D. Fraser and A. Sutcliffe (eds), *The Pursuit of Urban History* (London, 1983).

Corfield P.J., 'Class by Name and Number in Eighteenth-Century Britain', *History*, 72 (1987).

Crawford P., 'The Challenges to Patriarchalism: How did the Revolution affect Women?' in J. Morrill (ed.), *Revolution and Restoration. England in the 1650s* (London, 1992).

Crawford P., 'Women and Property: Women as Property', *Parergon*, 19, 1 (2002).

Cressy D., 'Describing the Social Order of Elizabethan and Stuart England', *Literature and History*, 3 (1976).

Davies C.S.L., 'Slavery and Protector Somerset: The Vagrancy Act of 1547', *Economic History Review*, 2nd ser., 19 (1966).

Davis N.Z., ' "Women's History" in Transition: the European Case', *Feminist Studies*, 3 (1976).

Dickinson H.T., 'The Friends of America: British Sympathy with the American Revolution', in M.T. Davis (ed.), *Radicalism and Revolution in Britain, 1775–1848* (Basingstoke, 2000).

Dobson M.J., 'The Last Hiccup of the Old Demographic Regime: Population Stagnation and Decline in Late Seventeenth and Early Eighteenth-Century South-East England', *Continuity and Change*, 4 (1989).

Donagan B., 'The Web of Honour: Soldiers, Christians, and Gentlemen in the English Civil War', *Historical Journal*, 44, 2 (2001).

Edwards V., 'The Case of the Married Spinster: An Alternative Explanation', *American Journal of Legal History*, 21 (1977).

Eley G. and Nield K., 'Farewell to the Working Class?', *International Labor and Working-Class History*, 57 (2000).

Emmison F.G., 'Poor Relief Accounts of Two Rural Parishes in Bedfordshire, 1563–1598', *Economic History Review*, 3 (1931–32).

Emmison F.G., 'The Care of the Poor in Elizabethan Essex: Recently Discovered Records', *Essex Review*, 61 (1953).

Finn M.C., *The Character of Credit: Personal Debt in English Culture, 1740–1914* (Cambridge, 2003).

Fletcher A.J., 'Honour, Reputation and Local Officeholding in Elizabethan and Stuart England', in A.J. Fletcher and J. Stevenson (eds), *Order and Disorder in Early Modern England* (Cambridge, 1985).

Fox A., 'Custom, Memory, and the Authority of Writing', in P. Griffiths, A. Fox and S. Hindle (eds), *The Experience of Authority in Early Modern England* (Basingstoke, 1996).

Fraser A., 'John Clare's Gypsies', *Northamptonshire Past and Present*, 4 (1970–71).

French H.R., 'Social Status, Localism and the "Middle Sort of People" in England, 1620–1750', *Past & Present*, 166 (2000).

French H.R., 'The Search for the "Middle Sort of People" in England, 1600–1800', *Historical Journal*, 43 (2000).

French H.R., ' "Ingenious & Learned Gentlemen" – Social Perceptions and Self-Fashioning Among Parish Elites in Essex, 1680–1740', *Social History*, 25 (2000).

Gibson-Graham J.K., Resnick S.A. and Wolff R.D., 'Class in a Poststructuralist Frame', in J.K. Gibson-Graham, S.A. Resnick and R.D. Wolff (eds), *Class and Its Others* (Minneapolis, 2000).

Gowing L., 'Ordering the Body: Illegitimacy and Female Authority in Seventeenth-century England', in M.J. Braddick and J. Walter (eds), *Negotiating Power in Early Modern Society: Order, Hierarchy and Subordination in Britain and Ireland* (Cambridge, 2001).

Griffiths P., 'Masterless Young People in Norwich, 1560–1645', in P. Griffiths, A. Fox and S. Hindle (eds), *The Experience of Authority in Early Modern England* (Basingstoke, 1996).

Harte N.B., 'State Control of Dress and Social Change in Pre-Industrial England', in D.C. Coleman and A.H. John (eds), *Trade, Government and Economy in Pre-Industrial England Essays presented to F.J. Fisher* (London, 1976).

Hastrup K., 'The Semantics of Biology: Virginity', in S. Ardener (ed.), *Defining Females: The Nature of Woman in Society* (London, 1978).

Hay D., 'Property, Authority and the Criminal Law', in D. Hay, P. Linebaugh, J.G. Rule, E.P. Thompson and C. Winslow (eds), *Albion's Fatal Tree. Crime and Society in Eighteenth-Century England* (London, 1975).

Hempton D., 'Religion in British Society, 1740–90', in J. Black (ed.), *British Politics and Society From Walpole to Pitt* (London, 1990).

Hindle S., 'Hierarchy and Community: The Swallowfield Articles of 1596', *Historical Journal*, 42 (1999), p. 850.

Hindle S., 'The Political Culture of the Middling Sort in English Rural Communities, c.1550–1700', in T. Harris (ed.), *The Politics of the Excluded, c.1500–1850* (London, 2001).

Hindle S., 'Dearth, Fasting and Alms: The Campaign for General Hospitality in Late Elizabethan England', *Past & Present*, 172 (2001).

Hindle S., 'Dependency, Shame and Belonging: Badging the Deserving Poor, c.1550–1750', *Cultural and Social History*, 1, 1 (January 2004).

Hogg M. and McGarty C., 'Self-categorisation and Social Identity', in D. Abrams and M. Hogg (eds), *Social Identity Theory; Constructive and Critical Advances* (London, 1990).

Hogg M.A., Terry D.J. and White K.M., 'A Tale of Two Theories: A Critical Comparison of Identity Theory with Social Identity Theory', *Social Psychology Quarterly*, 58, 4 (1995).

Holmes G.S., 'Gregory King and the Social Structure of Pre-Industrial England', *Transactions of the Royal Historical Society*, 5th ser., 27 (1977).

Holton R., 'Has Class Analysis a Future? Max Weber and the Challenge of Liberalism to *Gemeinschaftlich* Accounts of Class', in D.J. Lee and B.S. Turner (eds), *Conflicts about Class: Debating Inequality in Late Industrialism* (Harlow, 1996).

Hufton O., 'Women Without Men: Widows and Spinsters in Britain and France in the Eighteenth Century', *Journal of Family History*, 9 (1984).

Hughes A., 'Gender and Politics in Leveller Literature', in S.D. Amussen and M.A. Kishlansky (eds), *Political Culture and Cultural Politics in Early Modern England: Essays Presented to David Underdown* (Manchester, 1995).

Ingram M., 'Law, Litigants and the Construction of "honour": Slander Suits in Early Modern England', in P. Coss (ed.), *The Moral World of the Law* (Cambridge, 2000).

Innes J., 'Prisons for the Poor: English Bridewells, 1555–1800', in F. Snyder and D. Hay (eds), *Labour, Law and Crime: An Historical Perspective* (London, 1987).

Innes J. and Styles J., 'The Crime Wave: Recent Writing on Crime and Criminal Justice in Eighteenth-century England', in A. Wilson (ed.), *Rethinking Social History. English Society 1570–1920 and its Interpretation* (Manchester, 1993).

Johnson R., 'Thompson, Genovese and Socialist Humanism', *History Workshop Journal*, 6 (1978).

Jones I.F., 'Aspects of Poor Law Administration, Seventeenth to Nineteenth Centuries, From Trull Overseers' Accounts', *Somerset Archaeological and Natural History Society Proceedings*, 95 (1951).

King P., 'Decision-makers and Decision-making in the English Criminal Law 1750–1800', *Historical Journal*, 27 (1984).

King P., 'Edward Thompson's Contribution to Eighteenth-Century Studies. The Patrician-Plebeian Model Re-examined', *Social History*, 21 (1996).

King P., 'Pauper Inventories and the Material Lives of the Poor in the Eighteenth and Early Nineteenth Centuries', in T. Hitchcock, P. King and P. Sharpe (eds) *Chronicling Poverty. The Voices and Strategies of the English Poor, 1640–1840* (Basingstoke, 1997).

King P. 'Summary Justice and Social Relations in Eighteenth-century England', *Past & Present*, 183 (2004).

King P., 'The Poor, the Law and The Poor Law. The Summary courts and Pauper Strategies in Eighteenth and Early Nineteenth Century England', in S. King and R. Smith (eds), *Poverty and Relief in England 1500–1800* (Woodbridge, forthcoming).

King S., 'Reconstructing Lives: The Poor, the Poor Law and Welfare in Calverley 1650–1820', *Social History*, 22 (1997).

King S., 'Reclothing the English Poor, 1750–1840', *Textile History. Special Issue on the Dress of the Poor*, 33, 1 (2002).

King W.J., 'Punishment for Bastardy in Early Seventeenth-Century England', *Albion*, 10 (1978).

Langbein J.H., '*Albion's* Fatal Flaws', *Past & Present*, 98 (1983).

Lanser S.S., 'Singular Politics: The Rise of the British Nation and the Production of the Old Maid', in J.M. Bennett and A.M. Froide (eds), *Singlewomen in the European Past 1250–1800* (Philadelphia, 1999).

Linebaugh P., '(Marxist) Social History and (Conservative) Legal History. A Reply to Professor Langbein', *New York University Law Review*, 60 (1985).

Mendelson S., 'The Civility of Women in Seventeenth-Century England', in P. Burke, B. Harrison and P. Slack (eds), *Civil Histories: Essays Presented to Sir Keith Thomas* (OUP, 2000).

Mitson A., 'The Significance of Kinship Networks in the Seventeenth Century: South-West Nottinghamshire', in C. Phythian-Adams (ed.), *Societies, Cultures and Kinship, 1580–1850: Cultural Provinces and English Local History* (Leicester, 1993).

Money J., 'Teaching in the Market-Place, or "Caesar adsum jam forte: Pompey Aderat": The Retailing of Knowledge in Provincial England During the Eighteenth Century', in J. Brewer and R. Porter (eds), *Consumption and the World of Goods* (London, 1993).

Morrill J.S., 'The Making of Oliver Cromwell', in J.S.A. Adamson and J.S. Morrill (eds) *Oliver Cromwell and the English Revolution* (Harlow, 1990).

Muldrew C., 'Interpreting the Market: The Ethics of Credit and Community Relations in Early Modern England', *Social History*, 18 (1993).

Muldrew C., 'From a "light cloak" to an "iron cage": Historical Changes in the Relation Between Community and Individualism', in A. Shepard and P.J. Withington (eds), *Communities in Early Modern England* (Manchester, 2000).

Muldrew C., ' "Hard food for Midas": Cash and its Social Value in Early Modern England', *Past & Present*, 170 (2001).

Newman-Brown W., 'The Receipt of Poor Relief and Family Situation: Aldenham, Hertfordshire 1630–90', in R.M. Smith (ed.), *Land, Kinship and Life-Cycle* (Cambridge, 1984).

Offer A., 'Between the Gift and the Market: The Economy of Regard', *Economic History Review*, 50 (1997).

Ohlmeyer J., ' "Civilizinge of Those Rude Partes": Colonialisation Within Britain and Ireland, 1580s–1640s', in N. Canny (ed.), *The Origins of Empire* (Oxford, 2001).

Orr B., 'Whores' Rhetoric and the Maps of Love: Constructing the Feminine in Restoration Erotica', in C. Brant and D. Purkiss (eds), *Women, Texts and Histories 1570–1760* (London, 1992).

Pahl R., 'Is the Emperor Naked? Some Questions on the Adequacy of Sociological Theory', in D.J. Lee and B.S. Turner (eds), *Conflicts about Class: Debating Inequality in Late Industrialism* (Harlow, 1996).

Phelps Brown E.H. and Hopkins S.V., 'Seven Centuries of the Prices of Consumables, Compared with Builders' Wage-rates', in E.M. Carus-Wilson (ed.), *Essays in Economic History*, II (London, 1962).

Pound J., 'An Elizabethan Census of the Poor: The Treatment of Vagrancy in Norwich, 1570–1580', *University of Birmingham Historical Journal*, 8 (1962).

Quinn S., 'Money, Finance and Capital Markets', in R. Floud and P. Johnson (eds), *The Cambridge Economic History of Modern Britain, Volume I: Industrialisation 1700–1860* (Cambridge, 2004).

Reid D., 'Reflections on Labor History and Language', in L.R. Berlanstein (ed.), *Rethinking Labor History: Essays on Discourse and Class Analysis* (Urbana and Chicago, 1993).

Rule J., 'Employment and Authority: Masters and Men in Eighteenth-century Manufacturing', in P. Griffiths, A. Fox and S. Hindle (eds), *The Experience of Authority in Early Modern England* (London, 1996).

Rushton N.S., 'Monastic Charitable Provision in Tudor England: Quantifying and Qualifying Poor Relief in the Early Sixteenth Century', *Continuity and Change*, 16 (2001).

Sawday J., 'Self and Selfhood in the Seventeenth Century', in R. Porter (ed.), *Rewriting the Self Histories from the Renaissance to the Present* (London, 1997).

Scott J.W., 'Women's History', in P. Burke (ed.), *New Perspectives on Historical Writing* (Cambridge, 1991).

Sharpe P., 'Poor Children as Apprentices in Colyton, 1598–1830', *Continuity and Change*, 6 (1991).

Shepard A., 'Legal Learning and the Cambridge University Courts, c.1560–1640', *Journal of Legal History*, 19 (1998).

Shepard A., 'Manhood, Credit and Patriarchy in Early Modern England, c. 1580–1640', *Past & Present*, 167 (2000).

Shrank C., 'Rhetorical Constructions of a National Community: the Role of the King's English in Mid-Tudor Writing', in A. Shepard and P.J. Withington (eds), *Communities in Early Modern England. Networks, Place, Rhetoric* (Manchester, 2000).

Slack P., 'Poverty and Politics in Salisbury, 1597–1666', in P. Clark and P. Slack (eds), *Crisis and Order in English Towns, 1500–1700: Essays in Urban History* (London, 1972).

Smith H., 'English "Feminist" Writings and Judith Drake's An Essay in Defence of the Female Sex (1696)', *Historical Journal*, 44 (2001).

Smith R.M., 'Some Issues Concerning Families and their Property in Rural England 1250–1800', in R.M. Smith (ed.), *Land, Kinship and Lifecycle* (Cambridge, 1984).

Sokoll T., 'Negotiating a Living: Essex Pauper Letters from London, 1800–1834', *International Review of Social History*, 45 (2000).

Sokoll T., 'Early Attempts at Accounting the Unaccountable: Davies' and Eden's Budgets of Agricultural Labouring Families in Late-eighteenth Century England', in T. Pierenkemper (ed.), *Zur Okonomik des Privaten Haushalts* (Frankfurt, 1991).

Sokoll T., 'Old Age in Poverty: The Record of Essex Pauper Letters, 1780–1834', in T. Hitchcock, P. King and P. Sharpe (eds), *Chronicling Poverty: The Voices and Strategies of the English Poor, 1640–1840* (London and New York, 1997).

Souden D., 'Migrants and the Population Structure of Later Seventeenth-Century Provincial Cities and Market Towns', in P. Clark (ed.), *The Transformation of English Provincial Towns* (London, 1984).

Spufford M., 'Puritanism and Social Control?', in A.J. Fletcher and J. Stevenson (eds), *Order and Disorder in Early Modern England* (Cambridge, 1985).

Stapleton B., 'Inherited Poverty and Lifecycle Poverty: Odiham, Hampshire, 1650–1850', *Social History*, 18 (1993).

Stone L., 'Social Mobility in England', *Past & Present*, 33 (1966).

Styles J., 'Involuntary Consumers? Servants and their Clothes in Eighteenth-Century England', *Textile History. Special Issue on the Dress of the Poor*, 33, 1 (2002).

Styles J., 'Custom or Consumption? Plebeian Fashion in Eighteenth-century England', in M. Berg and E. Eger (eds), *Luxury in the Eighteenth-century. Debates, Desires and Delectable goods* (London, 2003).

Tajfel H. and Forgas J.P., 'Social Categorization: Cognitions, Values and Groups', in J.P. Forgas (ed.), *Social Cognition: Perspectives on Everyday Understanding* (London, 1981).

Taylor J.S., 'Voices in the Crowd: The Kirkby Lonsdale Township Letters, 1809–36', in T. Hitchcock. P. King and P. Sharpe (eds), *Chronicling Poverty: The Voices and Strategies of the English Poor, 1640–1840* (London and New York, 1997).

Thomas K., 'The Double Standard', *Journal of the History of Ideas*, 20 (1959).

Thompson E.P., 'The Crime of Anonymity', in D. Hay, V.A.C. Gatrell and P. Linebaugh (eds), *Albion's Fatal Tree* (London, 1975).

Thomas K., 'Age and Authority in Early Modern England', *Proceedings of the British Academy*, 62 (1976).

Thompson E.P., 'Eighteenth-Century English Society: Class Struggle Without Class?', *Social History*, 3 (1978).

Underwood M., 'The Structure and Operation of the Oxford Chancellor's Court, from the Sixteenth to the Early Eighteenth Century', *Journal of the Society of Archivists*, 6 (1978).

van Leeuwen M.H.D., 'Logic of Charity: Poor Relief in Preindustrial Europe', *Journal of Interdisciplinary History*, 24 (1994).

Wales T., 'Poverty, Poor Relief and the Lifecycle: Some Evidence from Seventeenth-century Norfolk', in R.M. Smith (ed.), *Land, Kinship and Lifecycle* (Cambridge, 1984).

Walker G., 'Expanding the Boundaries of Female Honour in Early Modern England', *Transactions of the Royal Historical Society*, 6th ser., 6 (1996).

Walter J., 'Public Transcripts, Popular Agency and the Politics of Subsistence in Early Modern England', in M.J. Braddick and J. Walter (eds), *Negotiating Power in Early Modern Society: Order, Hierarchy and Subordination in Britain and Ireland* (Cambridge, 2001).

Walter J. and Wrightson K., 'Dearth and the Social Order in Early Modern England', *Past & Present*, 71 (1976).

Weiner C.Z., 'Is a Spinster an Unmarried Woman?', *American Journal of Legal History*, 20 (1976).

Williams P., 'Government and politics in Ludlow, 1590–1642', *Transactions of the Shropshire Archaeological Society*, 56 (1957–58).

Wood A., 'The Place of Custom in Plebeian Political Culture: England, 1550–1800', *Social History*, 22, 1 (1997).

Wright S., ' "Churmaids, Huswyfes and Hucksters": The Employment of Women in Tudor and Stuart Salisbury', in L. Charles and L. Duffin (eds), *Women and Work in Pre-Industrial England* (London, 1985).

Wrightson K., 'The Social Order of Early Modern England: Three Approaches', in L. Bonfield, R.M. Smith and K. Wrightson (eds), *The World We Have Gained. Histories of Population and Social Structure* (Oxford, 1986).

Wrightson K., 'Estates, Degrees, and Sorts: Changing Perceptions of Society in Tudor and Stuart England', in P. Corfield (ed.), *Language, History and Class* (London, 1991).

Wrightson K., ' "Sorts of people" in Tudor and Stuart England', in J. Barry and C. Brooks (eds), *The Middling Sort of People. Culture, Society and Politics in England, 1550–1800* (Basingstoke, 1994).

Wrightson K., 'The Politics of the Parish in Early Modern England', in P. Griffiths, A. Fox and S. Hindle (eds), *The Experience of Authority in Early Modern England* (London, 1996).

Books

Adair R., *Courtship, Illegitimacy and Marriage in Early Modern England* (Manchester, 1996).

Alexander J.C. and Seidman S., *Culture and Society Contemporary Debates* (Cambridge, 1990).

Ambler R., *Churches, Chapels and the Parish Communities of Lincolnshire 1660–1900* (Lincoln, 2000).

Amussen S.D., *An Ordered Society: Gender and Class in Early Modern England* (Oxford, 1988).

Anderson P., *Arguments Within English Marxism* (London, 1980).

Aughterson K. (ed.), *Renaissance Woman: A Sourcebook Constructions of Femininity in England* (1995).

Barber C., *Early Modern English* (London, 1976).

Barker H., *Newspapers, Politics and Public Opinion in Late Eighteenth-century England* (Oxford, 1998).

Barry J. (ed.), *The Tudor and Stuart Town. A Reader in English Urban History* (Harlow, 1990).

Barry J. and Brooks C. (eds), *The Middling Sort of People Culture, Society and Politics in England, 1550–1800* (Basingstoke, 1994).

Beier A.L., *Masterless Men: The Vagrancy Problem in England, 1580–1640* (London, 1985).

Braddick M.J. and Walter J. (eds), *Negotiating Power in Early Modern Society. Order, Hierarchy and Subordination in Britain and Ireland* (Cambridge, 2001).

Bradley H., *Fractured Identities. Changing Patterns of Inequality* (Cambridge, 1996).

Breitenberg M., *Anxious Masculinity in Early Modern England* (Cambridge, 1996).

Brenner R., *Merchants and Revolution* (Cambridge, 1994).

Brewer J., *Pleasures of the Imagination. English Culture in the Eighteenth Century* (London, 1998).

Brewer J. and Styles J. (eds), *An Ungovernable People: the English and Their Law in the Seventeenth and Eighteenth Centuries* (London, 1980).

Brooks C.W., *Pettyfoggers and Vipers of the Commonwealth The 'Lower Branch' of the Legal Profession in Early Modern England* (Cambridge, 1986).

Burgess G., *The Politics of the Ancient Constitution An Introduction to English Political Thought, 1603–1642* (Basingstoke, 1992).

Burnett J. (ed.) *Useful Toil. Autobiographies of Working People from the 1820s to the 1920s* (Harmondsworth, 1977).

Burnett J., Vincent D. and Mayall D. (eds), *The Autobiography of the Working Class. An Annotated Critical Bibliography. Volume I. 1790–1900* (New York, 1984).

Butler M., *Romantics, Rebels and Reactionaries. English Literature and its Background, 1760–1830* (Oxford, 1981).

Bythell D., *The Handloom Weavers. A Study in the English Cotton Industry During the Industrial Revolution* (Cambridge, 1969).

Capp B., *When Gossips Meet: Women, Family, and Neighbourhood in Early Modern England* (Oxford, 2003).

Carroll B. (ed.), *Liberating Women's History* (Chicago, 1976).

Carter P., *Men and the Emergence of Polite Society, Britain 1660–1800* (Harlow, 1999).

Cox J.C., *Bench-Ends in English Churches* (Oxford, 1916).

Craig J., *Reformation, Politics and Polemics: The Growth of Protestantism in East Anglian Market Towns, 1500–1610* (Aldershot, 2001).

Cressy D., *Birth, Marriage and Death Ritual, Religion and the Life Cycle in Tudor and Stuart England* (Oxford, 1997).

Cressy D., *Travesties and Transgressions in Tudor and Stuart England* (Oxford, 2000).

Crompton R., Devine F. and Savage M. (eds.), *Renewing Class Analysis* (Oxford, 2000).

Crump W.B. and Ghorbal G., *History of the Huddersfield Woollen Industry* (Huddersfield, 1935).

Dyer C., *Standards of Living in the Later Middle Ages: Social Change in England, c.1200–1520* (Cambridge, 1989).

Earle P., *The Making of the English Middle Class* (London, 1989).

Eccles A., *Obstetrics and Gynaecology in Tudor and Stuart England* (London, 1982).

Erickson A.L., *Women and Property in Early Modern England* (London, 1993).

Evans J.T., *Seventeenth-century Norwich. Politics, Religion, and Government, 1620–1690* (Oxford, 1979).

Everitt A.M., *The Community of Kent and the Great Rebellion, 1640–1660* (London, 1966).

Everitt A.M., *The Local Community and the Great Rebellion* (London, 1969).

Ewen C.L., *Witchcraft and Demonianism: A Concise Account Derived from Sworn Depositions And Confessions Obtained in the Courts of England and Wales* (London, 1933).

Faraday M., *Ludlow 1085–1660. A Social, Economic, and Political History* (Chichester, 1991).

Fletcher A.J., *Reform in the Provinces: The Government of Stuart England* (New Haven, 1986).

Fox A., *Oral and Literate Culture in England 1500–1700* (Oxford, 2000).

Foyster E.A., *Manhood in Early Modern England: Honour, Sex and Marriage* (Harlow, 1999).

Gatrell V.A.C., *The Hanging Tree: Execution and the English People, 1770–1868* (Oxford, 1994).

Girouard M., *The English Town* (New Haven and London, 1990).

Goldberg P.J.P. (ed.), *Woman is a Worthy Wight: Women in English Society c.1200–1500* (Stroud, 1992).

Goldthorpe J.H., with Llewellyn C. and Payne C., *Social Mobility and Class Structure in Modern Britain* (Oxford, 1987).

Görlach M., *Introduction to Early Modern English* (Cambridge, 1991).

Gowing L., *Domestic Dangers: Women, Words, and Sex in Early Modern London* (Oxford, 1996).

Greenblatt S., *Renaissance Self-Fashioning From More to Shakespeare* (Chicago, 1980).

Greer G., Medoff J., Sansone M. and Hastings S. (eds), *Kissing the Rod. An Anthology of Seventeenth Century Women's Verse* (London, 1988).

Griffiths P., *Youth and Authority Formative Experiences in England, 1560–1640* (Oxford, 1996).

Hampson E.M., *The Treatment of Poverty in Cambridgeshire, 1597–1834* (Cambridge, 1934).

Hanson E., *Discovering the Subject in Renaissance England* (Cambridge, 1998).

Harris R.J., *Politics and the Rise of the Press. Britain and France, 1620–1800* (London, 1996).

Harris R.J., *Politics and the Nation. Britain in the Mid-Eighteenth Century* (Oxford, 2002).

Hartman M. and Banner L. (eds), *Clio's Consciousness Raised: New Perspectives on the History of Women* (New York, 1974).

Hewitt J.P., *Self and Society: A Symbolic Interactionist Social Psychology*, 8th edn (Boston, 2000).

Hey D., *An English Rural Community: Myddle Under the Tudors and Stuarts* (Leicester, 1974).

Hill C., *Society and Puritanism in Pre-Revolutionary England* (Harmondsworth, 1964).

Hill C., *The World Turned Upside Down: Radical Ideas During the English Revolution* (Harmondsworth, 1972).

Hill C., *Change and Continuity in Seventeenth-century England* (London, 1974).

Hindle S., *On the Parish?: The Micro-Politics of Poor Relief in Rural England, c.1550–1750* (Oxford, 2004).

Hitchcock T., *English Sexualities, 1700–1800* (London, 1997).

Hitchcock T., King P. and Sharpe P. (eds), *Chronicling Poverty. The Voices and Strategies of the English Poor, 1640–1840* (Basingstoke, 1997).

Horne T.A., *Property Rights and Poverty: Political Argument in Britain, 1605–1834* (Chapel Hill, 1990).

Hoyle R.W., *The Pilgrimage of Grace and the Politics of the 1530s* (Oxford, 2001).

Hudson P., *The Genesis of Industrial Capital, a Study of the West Riding Wool Textile Industry c.1750–1850* (Cambridge, 1986).

Hull S., *Chaste, Silent and Obedient English Books for Women 1475–1640* (San Marino, 1982).

Hunt M., *The Middling Sort: Commerce, Gender and the Family in England, 1680–1780* (California, 1996).

Ingram M., *Church Courts, Sex and Marriage in England, 1570–1640* (Cambridge, 1987).

Israel J., *Radical Enlightenment: Philosophy and the Making of Modernity: 1650–1750* (Oxford, 2001).

Jenkins R., *Social Identity* (London, 1996).

Johnson P., *Saving and Spending; The Working Class Economy in Britain 1870–1939* (Oxford, 1985).

Jones J., *Family Life in Shakespeare's England: Stratford-upon-Avon 1570–1630* (Stroud, 1996).

Kelly J., *Women, History and Theory. The Essays of Joan Kelly* (Chicago and London, 1984).

Kerr B., *Bound to the Soil: A Social History of Dorset, 1750–1918* (London, 1968).

King P., *Crime, Justice and Discretion in England 1740–1820* (Oxford, 2000).

King S., *Poverty and Welfare in England 1700–1850* (Manchester, 2000).

Lake P., *The Boxmaker's Revenge. 'Orthodoxy', 'heterodoxy' and the Politics of the Parish in Early Stuart London* (Stanford, 2001).

Landry D., *The Muses of Resistance: Laboring-class Women's Poetry in Britain 1739–1796* (Cambridge, 1990).

Langford P., *A Polite and Commercial People: England 1727–1783* (Oxford, 1992).

Laslett P., *Family Life and Illicit Love in Earlier Generations* (Cambridge, 1977).

Laslett P., *The World We Have Lost Further Explored* (London, 1983).

Lemire B., *Fashion's Favourite: The Cotton Trade and the Consumer in Britain 1660–1800* (Oxford, 1991).

Lemire B., *Dress, Culture and Commerce. The English Clothing Trade before the Factory, 1660–1800* (London, 1997).

Lerner G., *Why History Matters. Life and Thought* (New York and Oxford, 1997).

Lovegrove D.W., *Established Church, Sectarian People: Itinerancy and the Transformation of English Dissent, 1780–1830* (London, 1988).

MacCaffery W.T., *Exeter, 1540–1640. The Growth of an English County Town* (Cambridge MA, 1958).

Macfarlane A., *Witchcraft in Tudor and Stuart England: A Regional and Comparative Study* (London, 1970).

Macfarlane A., *The Origins of English Individualism the Family, Property and Social Transition* (Oxford, 1978).

Macfarlane A., *On Individualism* (Lancaster, 1994).

Machann C., *The Genre of Autobiography in Victorian Literature* (Ann Arbor, 1994).

Mascuch M., *The Origins of the Individualist Self: Autobiography and Self-Identity in England, 1591–1791* (Cambridge, 1997).

Mauss M., *The Gift: Forms and Functions of Exchange in Archaic Societies* (London, 1969).

McKendrick N., Brewer J. and Plumb J., *The Birth of a Consumer Society. The Commercialisation of Eighteenth-century England* (London, 1982).

Mead G.H., *Mind, Self and Society: From the Standpoint of a Social Behaviourist* (ed.) C.W. Morris (Chicago, 1934).

Mendelson S.H., *The Mental World of Stuart Women Three Studies* (Sussex, 1987).

Mendelson S. and Crawford P., *Women in Early Modern England* (Oxford, 1998).

Muldrew C., *The Economy of Obligation: The Culture of Credit and Social Relations in Early Modern England* (London, 1998).

Myers N., *Reconstructing the Black Past; Blacks in Britain 1780–1830* (London, 1996).

Neale J.E., *The Elizabethan House of Commons* (London, 1949).

Neale R.S., *Class in English Society 1680–1850* (Oxford, 1981).

Oakley A. and Mitchell J. (eds), *The Rights and Wrongs of Women* (London, 1976).

Pakulski J. and Waters M., *The Death of Class* (London, 1996).

Palmer R. (ed.), *The Rambling Soldier* (Gloucester, 1985).

Patterson C.F., *Urban Patronage in Early Modern England. Corporate Boroughs, the Landed Elite, and the Crown, 1580–1640* (Stanford, 1999).

Perkin H., *The Origins of Modern English Society* (London, 1969).

Phythian Adams C. (ed.), *Societies, Cultures, and Kinship, 1580–1850* (London, 1996).

Pocock J.G.A., *The Ancient Constitution and the Feudal Law. A Study of English Historical Thought in the Seventeenth Century* (Cambridge, 1987).

Porter J., *The Vertical Mosaic, An Analysis of Social Class and Power in Canada* (Toronto, 1965).

Pressnell L.S., *County Banking in the Industrial Revolution* (Oxford, 1956).

Rappaport N., *Diverse World Views in an English Village* (Edinburgh, 1993).

Richards J., *Rhetoric and Courtliness in Early Modern Literature* (Cambridge, 2003).

Roper L., *Oedipus and the Devil. Witchcraft, Sexuality and Religion in Early Modern Europe* (London and New York, 1994).

Rowbotham S., *Hidden from History* (London, 1973).

Royle E. and Walvin J., *English Radicals and Reformers, 1760–1848* (Brighton, 1982).

Rubies, J-P., *Travel and Ethnology in the Renaissance. South India Through European Eyes, 1250–1625* (Cambridge, 2000).

Sahlins M., *Stone-Age Economics* (London, 1974).

Schen C.S., *Charity and Lay Piety in Reformation London, 1500–1620* (Aldershot, 2002).

Scheuermann M., *In Praise of Poverty. Hannah More Counters Thomas Paine and the Radical Threat* (Lexington, KY, 2002).

Scott J.C., *Domination and the Arts of Resistance: Hidden Transcripts* (New Haven, 1990).

Scott J.W., *Gender and the Politics of History* (New York and Oxford, 1988).

Scott J.W. (ed.), *Feminism and History* (Oxford, 1996).

Shagan E.H., *Popular Politics and the English Reformation* (Cambridge, 2003).

Shapin S., *A Social History of Truth: Civility and Science in Seventeenth-century England* (Chicago, 1994).

Sharpe P., *Population and Society in an East Devon Parish: Reproducing Colyton, 1540–1840* (Exeter, 2002).

Sharpe J.A., 'Defamation and Sexual Slander in Early Modern England: The Church Courts at York', *Borthwick Papers*, 58 (1980).

Shepard A., *Meanings of Manhood in Early Modern England* (Oxford, 2003).

Shoemaker R., *Prosecution and Punishment: Petty Crime and the Law in London and Rural Middlesex, c. 1660–1725* (Cambridge, 1991).

Shotter J. and Gergen K. (eds), *Texts of Identity* (London, 1989).

Shrank C., *Writing the Nation in Reformation England* Oxford, 2004).

Skevington S. and Baker D. (eds), *The Social Identity of Women* (London, 1989).

Slack P., *The Impact of Plague* (Oxford, 1985).

Slack P., *Poverty and Policy in Tudor and Stuart England* (London and New York, 1988).

Slack P., *From Reformation to Improvement: Public Welfare in Early Modern England* (Oxford, 1998).

Smail J., *The Origins of Middle Class Culture: Halifax, Yorkshire, 1660–1780* (1994).

Smith H., *The Ecclesiastical History of Essex Under the Long Parliament and Commonwealth* (Colchester, 1933).

Spufford M., *Contrasting Communities, English Villagers in the Sixteenth and Seventeenth Centuries* (Cambridge, 1974).

Spufford M., *Small Books and Pleasant Histories Popular Fiction and its Readership in Seventeenth-century England* (Cambridge, 1981).

Staves S., *Players' Sceptres Fictions of Authority in the Restoration* (London, 1979).

Stedman Jones G., *Languages of Class: Studies in English Working Class History 1832–1982* (Cambridge, 1983).

Stevenson L.C., *Praise and Paradox: Merchants and Craftsmen in Elizabethan Popular Literature* (Cambridge, 1984).

Stone L., *The Crisis of the Aristocracy, 1558–1641* (Oxford, 1965).

Stretton T., *Women Waging Law in Elizabethan England* (Cambridge, 1998).

Tew J., *Social Theory, Power and Practice* (Basingstoke, 2002).

Thomas K., *Religion and the Decline of Magic: Studies in Popular Beliefs in Sixteenth and Seventeenth Century England* (London, 1971).

Thomas K., 'The Perception of the Past in Early Modern England', Creighton Lecture, London University (1983).

Thompson E.P., *The Making of the English Working Class* (London, 1963).

Thompson E.P., *Whigs and Hunters: The Origins of the Black Act* (Harmondsworth, 1975).

Thompson E.P., *Customs in Common* (Harmondsworth, 1993).

Thompson R., *Unfit for Modest Ears: A Study of Pornographic, Obscene and Bawdy Works Written or Published in England in the Second Half of the Seventeenth Century* (London, 1979).

Tighe R.R. and Davis J.E. (eds), *Annals of Windsor: Being a History of the Castle and Town* (London, 1858).

Tittler R., *The Reformation and the Towns in England. Politics and Political Culture, c.1540–1640* (Oxford, 1998).

Tittler R., *Townspeople and Nation. English Urban Experiences 1540–1640* (Stanford, 2001).

Todd J., *The Sign of Angellica: Women, Writing and Fiction, 1660–1800* (London, 1989).

Todd M., *Christian Humanism and the Puritan Social Order* (Cambridge, 1987).

Tomkins A. and King S. (eds), *The Poor in England, 1700–1850. An Economy of Makeshifts* (Manchester, 2003).

Tyerman L. (ed.), *The Life and Times of the Rev. John Wesley MA*, 3 vols (1872).

Underdown D., *Fire From Heaven: Life in an English Town in the Seventeenth Century* (London, 1992).

Wahrman D., *Imagining the Middle Class. The Political Representation of Class in Britain, c.1780–1840* (Cambridge, 1995).

Walsham A., *Providence in Early Modern England* (Oxford, 1999).

Watts M.R., *The Dissenters, vol. I, From the Reformation to the French Revolution* (London, 1978).

Wells R., *Wretched Faces: Famine in Wartime England, 1763–1803* (Gloucester, 1988).

Wheale N., *Writing and Society: Literacy, Print and Politics in Britain 1590–1660* (London, 1999).

Whyman S.E., *Sociability and Power in Late-Stuart England The Cultural World of the Verneys 1660–1720* (Oxford, 1999).

Whyte I.D., *Migration and Society in Britain 1550–1830* (London, 2000).

Wilson K., *The Sense of the People. Politics, Culture and Imperialism in England, 1715–1785* (Oxford, 1995).

Withington P., *The Politics of Commonwealth. Citizens and Freemen in Early Modern England* (Cambridge, 2005).

Wood A., *The Politics of Social Conflict: The Peak Country, 1520–1770* (Cambridge, 1999).

Wrightson K., *English Society 1580–1680* (London, 1982).

Wrightson K., *Earthly Necessities. Economic Lives in Early Modern Britain* (New Haven, 2000).

Wrightson K. and Levine D., *Poverty and Piety in an English Village: Terling, 1525–1700* (2nd edn, Oxford, 1995).

Wrigley E.A. and Schofield R.S., *The Population History of England 1541–1871. A Reconstruction* (Cambridge, 1989).

Zeldin T., *France 1848–1945; Anxiety and Hypocrisy* (Oxford, 1977).

Index

Lightning Source UK Ltd.
Milton Keynes UK
UKOW05f0624050617
302667UK00032B/745/P